# BANK MERGERS IN A DEREGULATED ENVIRONMENT

## Promise and Peril

Bernard Shull
Gerald A. Hanweck

# Q

QUORUM BOOKS
Westport, Connecticut • London

**Library of Congress Cataloging-in-Publication Data**

Shull, Bernard, 1931–
    Bank mergers in a deregulated environment: promise and peril / Bernard Shull, Gerald
A. Hanweck.
      p.   cm.
    Includes bibliographical references and index.
    ISBN 1–56720–379–5 (alk. paper)
    1. Bank mergers—United States.   2. Bank mergers—Europe, Western.   3. Banks and
banking—Deregulation—United States.   4. Banks and banking—Deregulation—Europe,
Western.   I. Hanweck, Gerald A.   II. Title.
HG1722.S585   2001
332.1′6—dc21          00–042557

British Library Cataloguing in Publication Data is available.

Library of Congress Catalog Card Number: 00–042557
ISBN: 1–56720–379–5

First published in 2001

Quorum Books, 88 Post Road West, Westport, CT 06881
An imprint of Greenwood Publishing Group, Inc.
www.quorumbooks.com

Printed in the United States of America

The paper used in this book complies with the
Permanent Paper Standard issued by the National
Information Standards Organization (Z39.48–1984).

10   9   8   7   6   5   4   3   2   1

To Janice, steadfast and undaunted,
and to Joe, Celia, and Silas, unforgotten

Bernard Shull

To Barbara for her patience, Jerry Jr. for his insight,
and Julia and Gregory for their tolerance

Gerald A. Hanweck

# Contents

# Tables and Figures

## FIGURES

# Preface

The idea for this book developed out of a conference on antitrust and banking, sponsored by the Office of the Comptroller of the Currency in November 1995, which one of the authors organized and in which both participated. The conference brought together bankers, bank regulators, private attorneys, and academic economists who focused on the massive bank merger movement that had been enabled by the liberalization of long-existing restrictions on interstate expansion, and by revisions in merger policy standards that facilitated the combination of very large banking organizations. At the time it had become clear that the wave of bank mergers and acquisitions that was initiated in the 1980s and had continued through the 1990s was likely to sustain itself into the next century, in part due to implementation of the Riegle–Neal Interstate Banking Act, which had opened the door to interstate branching.

In the past, both authors had been active in the bank competition policy process on a day-to-day basis at the Federal Reserve Board and the Office of the Comptroller of the Currency; and, periodically, outside the federal banking agencies in connection with specific mergers and litigation. The conference gave us an opportunity to view recent institutional and policy developments in perspective—to look back at how competition policy in banking had developed, and to look forward toward likely outcomes of current developments and their ultimate consequences.

We began with the understanding that the merger movement was a product of banking deregulation that had wiped away the anticompetitive restraints imposed as a failure-preventing measure during the 1930s, and that deregulation promised more intense competition and greater efficiency. We also began with the standard economic presumption that function follows form; that is, that industry behavior and performance would be altered in profound ways by the massive structural reorganization that was occurring.

Precisely how behavior and performance would be altered was not, however, clear. Among other things, an element of uncertainty was added to conventional analysis by the unique nature of banking regulation, the continuing involvement of government in banking, as well as the changing character of banking markets affected by new financial instruments, entry of nonbanking firms, and the emergence of electronic technologies.

Uncertainty notwithstanding, the changes taking place and those in prospect inevitably brought into question the efficacy of current bank competition policy. The policy had developed in the 1950s and 1960s to address competitive issues that then existed. The financial environment in which it developed included severe regulatory restrictions on branch office locations and deposit rates of interest, high concentration in local markets, and price and market-sharing agreements that had been permitted and encouraged by both law and regulation. To some extent, the policy had been altered with the prospect of increasing competition in the early years of deregulation. But it had not been subsequently adjusted to the wave of mergers that had followed. It seemed to us likely that any policy so established would need, at the least, to be modified if it were to deal successfully with the problems that radical change invariably produces.

An understanding of the consequences of the wave of mergers that had been unleashed by deregulation required an economic analysis of the structural changes that were developing. A more thorough understanding also required an appreciation for the unique character of banking policy that incorporated not just concerns about competition, but concerns about bank safety and soundness; the latter concerns have produced a variety of methods for reducing systemic risk, and have always affected competition in banking. Safety and soundness concerns have been sustained over centuries and, based on the logic underlying experience, seemed likely to continue into the indefinite future. More than simply a compilation of entertaining or distressing stories, historical review suggested some enduring relationships among banks, bank customers, and government that illuminated our economic analysis.

We found discordant ideas vigorously debated at the 1995 conference. A number of participants strongly voiced the opinion that antitrust enforcement in banking was irrelevant, or at least in the process of becoming so, but for vastly different reasons. On one side, some argued that the current focus of merger policy, on local competition in the sale of banking services, was out of touch with the new reality of regional and national competition that had been produced by technological advance and legislative change. Others argued that enforcement was deficient by virtue of its liberality in permitting bank mergers that were without economic or social benefit, and that raised substantial risks.

Here we have attempted a careful reassessment of current policy in the face of changing market conditions. In doing so, we have incorporated both historical review and economic analysis. We have concluded that the promise of deregulation confronts a peril in its native son, the merger movement, and that competition policy has, indeed, lost relevance. We have made proposals for changes in policy, based on our analysis, to sustain and augment the achievement of deregulation.

Today it is apparent that in addition to mergers among commercial banks, which have dramatically reduced the number of independent banking firms and spawned immensely large banking organization, we can now expect widespread combinations of banking, insurance and securities firms, as permitted by the Gramm–Leach–Bliley Financial Modernization Act of 1999. These combinations will produce still larger financial institutions, with an entrée to commercial activities through merchant banking. The prospect now is not simply for banking reorganization, but for reorganization of the financial system in the direction of universal banking, with its political and social as well as economic consequences. These ongoing developments reinforce the need for immediate attention to a policy that is facilitating changes that are perilous.

We wish to acknowledge a number of people who, in one way or another, and sometimes unknowingly, have provided substantial assistance in the formulation of this work and its completion. These include Stephen A. Rhoades of the Federal Reserve Board and Lawrence J. White of New York University, who provided helpful comments on several of our papers that contained essential analysis; Eugene A. Ludwig, former comptroller of the currency, who supported and participated in the 1995 conference; and Philip Bartholomew, Office of the Comptroller of the Currency, who suggested and helped launch the conference. We also wish to acknowledge the generous assistance of colleagues in the Financial Structure Section of the Federal Reserve Board in providing data and ideas, and colleagues who participated in seminars at the Comptroller's Office and at meetings of the Western Economic Association, who listened with critical ears to various parts of what became this book.

# CHAPTER 1

# Introduction

There has always been a political tension in the United States between the perceived public need to regulate commercial banks and the deep-seated institutional presumption that competition among private firms is the optimum regulator. The periodic instability of banking and the widespread impact of instability on other sectors of the economy has provided ample, though not the only, reason for direct government intervention. Nevertheless, the heralded benefits of competition have periodically persuaded Congress, and even those public agencies responsible for assuring the safety and soundness of banks, that interference with the operations of free markets should be kept to a minimum.

Sixty-five years ago, in the depths of the Great Depression with thousands of banks failing, the case for regulation, including extensive restrictions on competition, overwhelmed the free market presumption. It was not for another thirty years, in the wake of post–World War II economic growth and with the Depression a fading memory, that procompetitive public policy, including a general application of the antitrust laws to banking, reemerged. And it was not until the early 1980s, with the anticompetitive measures of the Depression unraveling in inflationary-induced market circumventions, that formal "deregulation" initiated the process of eliminating not only the restrictions of the Depression, such as maximum rates of interest on deposits and constraints on securities dealing, but also restrictions on branch banking that had originated in the nineteenth century.

Over the last fifteen years, the liberation of banking from anticompetitive government controls, and particularly new powers to branch almost anywhere throughout the United States, has initiated a merger wave of unprecedented proportions. At the same time, "financial modernization" legislation, which became effective in March 2000 (Gramm–Leach–Bliley Act), has been designed to facilitate additional combinations of banking, insurance, and securities firms by permitting banks, principally organized as "financial holding companies," to engage in a broad range of investment banking, insurance, merchant banking, and related commercial activities.

For the most part due to the ongoing consolidation in the banking industry, the number of banking organizations has fallen dramatically. Historically unprecedented megamergers, including acquisitions, have created banking organizations with more than half a trillion dollars in assets overnight, such as the combination of Bank of America with Nations Bank in mid-1998. Such mergers have rapidly increased national concentration of banking assets in the ten largest banking companies.

These and related changes have enormous implications for bank performance, the welfare of bank customers, and the stability of the financial system. While mergers can be beneficial, they can also be damaging. This merger movement, like others before it, raises issues of great significance.

The aim of this book is to evaluate the ongoing bank merger movement, and current bank competition policy that aims to sustain and promote banking competition. In the process, we develop proposals for modifying policy that would strengthen the beneficial effects of the banking reorganization underway. We address these aims through a review of current developments, economic analysis, and on the basis of a historical perspective that makes both the current reorganization and the need to modify policy understandable. The chapters that follow trace the historical development, complex objectives, and current implementation of competition policy in the United States, and evaluate the changes that have altered policy from constraining large bank mergers to facilitating them; and a merger movement that, for good and bad, is now in the process of irreversibly changing banking structure and the performance of banks. Chapter 2 provides a brief review of public policies in the early days of modern banking. Chapter 3 continues this story from the promonopoly policies that accompanied the establishment of the first banks in the United States in the late eighteenth century to the initiation of procompetitive policy after World War II. Chapter 4 traces the evolution of current policy, initiated in the early 1960s, to the present. Chapter 5 is an inquiry into the motivations underlying the current merger movement. Chapter 6 provides an analysis of the structural and performance changes now facilitated by policy standards. It projects likely future outcomes and evaluates their economic implications.

We reach the conclusion that banking deregulation, largely responsible for the current merger movement, will not achieve its high expectations for improved consumer welfare unless current competition policy is modified. Proposals for changes in policy, consistent with the historically unique character of the banking industry, are developed in Chapter 7. A summary and conclusions are provided in Chapter 8.

The remainder of this chapter is devoted to background information and preliminary ideas on the issues developed throughout the remainder of the book.

## BANKS IN THE 1980s: A NEAR DEATH EXPERIENCE?

The current merger movement has accelerated during a period of high bank profits and few failures. During the decade of the 1980s, however, things were different. The savings and loan (S&L) industry succumbed to inflation, high interest rates, depressed real estate markets, inept and fraudulent management, and misguided regulatory forbearance that fostered excessive risk taking. Thousands of S&Ls became insolvent and it required major banking legislation, the Financial Institutions Reform, Recovery and Enforcement Act of 1989 (FIRREA) that established the Resolution Trust Corporation (RTC), to clean up the mess. By the time FIRREA was passed, commercial banking confronted a similar threat.[1]

In the mid-1980s, small farm banks in the Midwest suffered through an agricultural depression. Through the remainder of the decade, substantial amounts of foreign and real estate loans went bad at some of the largest banks, and they approached, if they did not reach, insolvency. Simultaneously, large and traditionally profitable bank customers found they could borrow as or more cheaply in the commercial paper market than from commercial banks; and large banks found that they were losing their best customers to direct financing in the financial markets.

Financial assets in the commercial banking sector increased far more slowly between 1981 and 1990 than the assets of many other important financial institutions. The proportion of the total held by commercial banks fell from almost 36 percent in 1981 to about 29 percent in 1990, and to a little over 23 percent in 1998 (Table 1.1).

At the same time, the profit rates in banking dropped to extraordinarily low levels. The return on assets and equity for all insured banks reached a low of 0.08 and 1.29, respectively, in 1987, and remained relatively depressed through 1991 (Table 1.2). Only 11 banks had failed in 1981; over 200 failed in 1989 (Table 1.3). These failure rates, at levels unseen since the Great Depression, depleted the Federal Deposit Insurance Corporation's (FDIC) Insurance Fund.

In 1991, Congress reorganized bank supervision by passing the Federal Deposit Insurance Corporation Improvement Act (FDICIA), a comprehensive reform bill, providing, among other things, for a new, refinanced Bank Insurance Fund (BIF), and a separate Savings Association Insurance Fund

### Table 1.1
### Financial Assets of Selected Financial Institutions (Selected Years, 1981–1998)

| FINANCIAL INSTITUTIONS | 1981 | 1985 | YEAR 1990 | 1995 | 1998* | Change 1981-90 | 1990-98 |
|---|---|---|---|---|---|---|---|
| | $billions | $billions | $billions | $billions | $billions | (%) | (%) |
| Commercial Banking | $1,618.6 | $2,376.3 | $3,338.6 | $4,492.8 | $5,481.2 | 106.3 | 164.2 |
| Savings Institutions | 826.8 | 1,275.3 | 1,357.7 | 1,031.7 | 1,055.3 | 64.2 | 77.7 |
| Credit Unions | 70.9 | 134.5 | 217.0 | 310.7 | 379.3 | 206.1 | 174.8 |
| Life Insurance Companies | 507.5 | 796.1 | 1,367.4 | 2,057.9 | 2,644.4 | 169.4 | 193.4 |
| Other Insurance Companies | 194.4 | 298.6 | 533.5 | 740.3 | 866.2 | 174.4 | 162.4 |
| Private Pension Funds | 530.2 | 1,232.1 | 1,610.9 | 2,656.7 | 3,644.9 | 203.8 | 226.3 |
| State & Local Retirement Funds | 222.8 | 398.7 | 820.4 | 1,517.9 | 2,056.0 | 268.2 | 254.3 |
| Finance Companies | 230.9 | 365.3 | 611.5 | 672.3 | 781.5 | 164.8 | 127.8 |
| Mortgage Companies | 16.4 | 24.7 | 49.2 | 33.0 | 58.9 | 200.0 | 119.7 |
| Money Market Mutual Funds | 186.3 | 242.4 | 493.3 | 745.3 | 1,249.7 | 164.8 | 253.3 |
| Other Mutual Funds | 59.8 | 245.9 | 608.4 | 1,852.8 | 3,117.3 | 917.4 | 512.4 |
| Security Brokers & Dealers | 59.8 | 156.0 | 262.1 | 568.1 | 871.8 | 338.3 | 332.6 |
| Real Estate Investment Trusts | 3.2 | 8.2 | 13.2 | 25.1 | 55.3 | 312.5 | 418.9 |
| Issuers of Asset-backed Securities | 0.0 | 39.4 | 285.4 | 716.7 | 1,297.1 | ---- | 454.5 |
| Totals | $4,527.6 | $7,593.5 | $11,568.6 | $17,421.3 | $23,588.9 | 155.5 | 203.9 |

*Source*: Board of Governors of the Federal Reserve System, *Flow of Funds Accounts* (various issues).

*1998 data are as of the third quarter outstandings of the Flow of Funds Accounts.

(SAIF). The latter was not fully refinanced until 1998, with an arrangement for repaying the bonds that had been issued by the RTC to finance the resolution of insolvent S&Ls.

Many observers looked at the balance sheets and income statements of commercial banks and concluded that banking was a declining industry whose traditionally dominant position had been irreparably compromised. Some believed that it was on its way to extinction. As matters turned out, the assets recorded on the balance sheets of banks proved to be a deficient measure of their output.[2]

Evaluation of better measures, including off–balance sheet activities and the activities of bank holding company affiliates, demonstrated that the death of the commercial banking organization had been exaggerated. Banks had, among other things, adapted to the loss of large business borrowers by expanding their fee-generating activities, including the provision of credit guarantees for commercial paper, loan commitments, mortgage origination, interest

Table 1.2
Profits, Capital, and Loan Losses (All Insured Commercial
Banks, 1986–1999)

| YEAR | Return On: | | Ratio of Capital Account-to-Assets | Ratio of Loan Loss Prov.-to-Assets (%) |
| | Assets | Equity | | |
| --- | --- | --- | --- | --- |
| 1986 | .62 | 9.83 | 6.19 | .81 |
| 1987 | .08 | 1.29 | 6.02 | 1.30 |
| 1988 | .71 | 11.61 | 6.28 | .65 |
| 1989 | .47 | 7.33 | 6.21 | .98 |
| 1990 | .47 | 7.29 | 6.45 | .97 |
| 1991 | .51 | 7.71 | 6.75 | 1.03 |
| 1992 | .91 | 12.66 | 7.51 | .78 |
| 1993 | 1.20 | 15.34 | 8.00 | .47 |
| 1994 | 1.15 | 14.61 | 7.78 | .28 |
| 1995 | 1.17 | 14.66 | 8.11 | .30 |
| 1996 | 1.19 | 14.46 | 8.20 | .36 |
| 1997 | 1.23 | 14.70 | 8.33 | .40 |
| 1998 | 1.19 | 13.93 | 8.49 | .32 |
| 1999 | 1.31 | 15.34 | 8.37 | na |

*Source*: Federal Deposit Insurance Corporation, *Annual Reports and Quarterly Banking Profile* (various issues).

*Data are at annual rates as of December 31, 1999 reports.

rate and currency swaps, and securitization. The bottom line was that, despite the difficulties of the 1980s and early 1990s, the news of commercial banking's decline was not supported by the evidence.

As can be seen in Tables 1.2 and 1.3, after 1991 profits rose to record levels, bank capital increased substantially, and loan loss provisions, reflecting expected write-offs, dropped to low levels. The number of bank failures declined to insignificance. By October 1993, an expansionary monetary policy had forced short-term interest rates to low levels that had not existed since the 1960s; long-term rates remained relatively high. The result was one of the steepest yield curves of the century, and it persisted for several years. It gave banks an opportunity to borrow at low short-term rates, and to lend at up-

Table 1.3
Number of Mergers, Charters, and Failures (Insured Commercial Banks, 1980–1998)

| Year | Mergers | Large Bank Mergers | New Charters** | Failures |
|------|---------|--------------------|----------------|----------|
| 1980 | 190 | 0 | 206 | 8 |
| 1981 | 359 | 1 | 199 | 11 |
| 1982 | 420 | 2 | 316 | 27 |
| 1983 | 428 | 5 | 366 | 44 |
| 1984 | 441 | 6 | 400 | 80 |
| 1985 | 475 | 9 | 318 | 112 |
| 1986 | 473 | 9 | 248 | 131 |
| 1987 | 649 | 18 | 212 | 182 |
| 1988 | 468 | 14 | 228 | 193 |
| 1989 | 350 | 3 | 201 | 203 |
| 1990 | 366 | 6 | 175 | 159 |
| 1991 | 345 | 16 | 107 | 105 |
| 1992 | 401 | 22 | 73 | 94 |
| 1993 | 436 | 17 | 59 | 42 |
| 1994 | 446 | 15 | 48 | 11 |
| 1995 | 345 | 14 | 110 | 6 |
| 1996 | 297 | 21 | 148 | 5 |
| 1997 | 255 | 24 | 207 | 1 |
| 1998 | 444 | 30 | 193 | 3 |
| 1999* | 417 | na | 231 | 7 |
| Totals | 8,005 | 232 | 3,814 | 1,417 |

*Source*: This table is adapted from data in Stephen Rhoades, "Bank Mergers and Industrywide Structure, 1980–94," Staff study no. 169, Board of Governors of the Federal Reserve System, 1996. Updated information has been provided by Stephen Rhoades. Data for 1999 are from Federal Deposit Insurance Corporation, *Quarterly Banking Profile, Fourth Quarter 1999* (Washington, D.C.: FDIC, 1999).

*Data as of September 30, 1999. **Data on new charters include charters provided to establish holding companies organizing new banks and others that do not constitute new entry into banking.

*Note*: Large bank mergers are defined as those in which each organization had $1 billion or more in assets. Concentration data are consolidated for banking organizations.

wards of 300 basis points higher in risk-free long-term treasury securities. These developments substantially improved bank profitability without increasing the credit risks incurred as banks invested heavily in Treasury and government agency securities while limiting direct lending.

This reversal of fortunes might have been expected. It is consistent with a historical experience. Banks have repeatedly recovered from what seemed desperate circumstances: in the several decades before the Civil War; in the late nineteenth century; and, of course, in the 1930s. For one reason or another, banks have proved enormously adaptable to changes in market demand and profit opportunities. And, in recent years, they have had substantial support from monetary policy.

## THE MERGER MOVEMENT AND STRUCTURAL CHANGE

In the 1960s, the American banking system was composed of over 13,000 commercial banking organizations and thousands of special purpose savings institutions and credit unions; the vast majority were small local and regional firms. The proportion of deposits held by the largest banking organizations in metropolitan areas throughout the United States, which approximated local markets for retail banking customers, was high, reaching levels that could generally be accepted as noncompetitive. In rural areas, one- and two-bank towns were ubiquitous.

Since then, mergers and failures have cut the number of commercial banking organizations in the United States roughly in half. The bulk of the decline dates from the early 1980s. There were a little over 12,200 banking organizations in 1980 and a little over 5,930 in 1998.[3] The number of savings associations (thrifts), now close substitutes for commercial banks, have also declined precipitously, from about 3,418 in 1980 to 1,713 in 1998.

Between 1980 and 1998 there were about 7,400 mergers of independent commercial banking organizations, and 1,417 failures (Table 1.3). Mergers involving "large" banking organizations with over $1 billion in assets each, have increased dramatically.

Among the most striking large bank mergers have been the combinations of the Chase Manhattan and Manufacturers Hanover with Chemical Banking Corporation, Security Pacific and Continental Bank with BankAmerica Corporation, C&S/Sovran with NCNB Corporation, Barnett with Nations Bank, Core State with First Union, and NationsBank with Bank of America. The new giants, now ranging from $300 billion to $800 billion in assets, continue to grow through consolidation.

For the nation as a whole, concentration in the largest organizations has been increasing. In local areas, both metropolitan and rural, concentration has not changed very much on average. In many areas, however, it has been high for years, and remains so.

Projections suggest that a decade from now, the banking industry is likely to include far fewer banking organizations, of which a handful will be very large, with national and international scope; the remainder will be local and regional institutions. The large organizations are likely to be true conglomerates, combining the ownership of commercial and industrial firms with banking and other financial operations. These few are likely to control a much higher proportion of banking assets in the United States than what they now hold.

## COMPETITION AND MERGER POLICY IN BANKING

There have always been special competition policies for banking, distinct from whatever other policies applied to business in general. As indicated, competition among banks was restricted in the earliest days of banking in the

United States; and before that in many European countries on whose institutions early U.S. banks were modeled. Government intervention to restrict competition was not whimsical; as discussed in the chapters that follow, it served vital political needs.

Distinct from other private sector business, banking continues to be subject to a unique combination of law, regulation, and rules aimed at achieving complex public purposes, including not simply the welfare of its customers, but economic and financial stability, and the welfare of communities in which bank offices are located.

Multipurpose public objectives were met by laws controlling the issuance of new bank charters, the location of banking offices, and requiring other types of regulation and supervision. When the Sherman and Clayton antitrust laws were passed, in 1890 and 1914 respectively, banking was largely immunized. Industry self-regulation, including agreements on interest rates on deposits and loans, through clearinghouse and county banking associations, was ignored by Congress and state legislatures, and generally accepted as necessary, if not desirable. In the Depression of the 1930s, self-regulation was reinforced by public regulation that, probably with greater effect, suppressed banking competition.

It was not until after World War II that Congress began to unravel the public suppression of competition in banking. A new bank merger policy that directed the federal banking agencies (Office of the Comptroller of the Currency [OCC], the Federal Reserve [Fed], and the FDIC) to evaluate mergers for their competitive impact evolved quickly, through court decision as well as congressional action, into the application of antitrust law standards to banking. It provided for "prior approval" in which the Antitrust Division of the Justice Department could block bank mergers approved by the federal agencies.

The constraints of the Clayton Act, the Sherman Act, and their adaptation to banking through the Bank Merger and Holding Company Acts, reflect a deep understanding of merger as a two-edged sword. The opportunity to merge is clearly a necessary condition for free capital markets, and must be presumed to have socially beneficial or, at least, nonharmful effects. Among other things, mergers can facilitate the exit of relatively inefficient firms and increase efficiency at acquiring firms. Moreover, by easing the entry of the efficient into new markets, they may intensify competition. But, in Clayton Act terms, mergers may also "substantially lessen competition or tend to create a monopoly." They can eliminate effective competitors, result in cartel-like agreements, and produce inefficiency.

Merger policy in general, and for banking in particular, aims to separate the "good" from the "bad." There is every reason to believe that this purpose was substantially met when bank merger policy was first implemented. But the policy was designed by Congress and the courts in a banking environment far different from the one that exists today. Branching was severely restricted, and so were new charters; Regulation Q still limited the rates banks could pay on time and savings deposits; savings institutions and credit unions, to say nothing of other financial service providers, were still only peripheral threats in commercial banking markets. Even though policy was designed to constrain large bank mergers, it did so within the framework of restricted branching, where local market structure, not national structure, was at stake. It did not contemplate the kinds of mergers, among widely separated institutions, now possible. The megamergers of the last decade were beyond comprehension.

Moreover, current policy was designed in an era when bank failure rates were extraordinarily low as a result of the fail-safe systems imposed by law and regulation in the Great Depression. In addition to the establishment of federal deposit insurance and the development of stabilizing fiscal and monetary policies, seemingly risky activities had been constrained by the Glass–Steagall Act and, as noted, competition among banks effectively stymied. The subtext of the policies was that all banks were too important to fail. To this end, the new policies were a complete success. From the 1940s to the 1970s, only a handful of banks failed each year, usually as a result of insider abuse or fraud.

Deregulation has effected a major shift in policy orientation. It supports the desirability of competition and the usefulness of failure to eliminate inefficiency and ineptitude. Today, Congress and the federal banking agencies only perceive the failure of the largest banking organizations as creating the kind of problem that requires public intervention because it might constitute the threat of a systemic event; only the largest banking organizations are "too-big-to-fail."

As a practical matter, the federal banking agencies and the Justice Department have adjusted merger policy to new, more competitive conditions established through deregulation. The adjustment has included the view that few, if any, mergers are likely to have a substantial anticompetitive effect; the only ones denied on competitive grounds have been small banks in rural areas. Under current policy standards, there is a question as to whether any barrier to future mergers of even the largest banking organizations will exist.

Whatever one's expectation about the merits of these structural developments, it is important to consider systematically what, if any, problems are developing. It is argued in the following section that the merger movement itself is creating a "postderegulation" environment that again requires adjustment in bank merger policy; and that a reevaluation of policy is not only timely, but overdue.

## THE UNCERTAIN FUTURE: PROMISE AND PERIL

Today, new and larger banks are entering new market areas and new financial and commercial activities. Opportunities for both banks and their customers are expanding rapidly. Structural reorganization in banking has enormous promise for benefit. But it remains to be seen whether the promise will be fulfilled.

It is not surprising that the liberalization of branching laws would result in large numbers of mergers. Many bankers, regulators, and economists view the structural change as a long overdue rationalization that will improve efficiency and promote bank diversification and stability. In contrast, rapid developments in information technology and management produce an incentive for mergers to achieve larger size and reduce the risks of a necessarily large investment to take advantage of these technologies. There are fewer savings institutions and credit unions now than there were in 1980, but those that remain have become more like commercial banks, offering a wider variety of consumer and small business services. In 1998, credit unions became an even closer substitute by winning the right, through new legislation, to expand beyond the limitations of their traditional "common bonds." Bank customers can now also find substitutes for some traditional banking services at nonbanking financial companies, such as money market mutual funds and mortgage brokers. Finally, the elimination of restrictions on branch banking has lowered barriers to entry by outside banks that, in and of itself, imposes competitive pressure on local institutions.

Some look to a longer-run future where the markets in which consumers and small businesses purchase banking services, traditionally local and highly concentrated, become regional and national in scope, with the smaller group of remaining banks large enough to provide significant competition for all customers.

Nevertheless, there remains cause for concern about increasing concentration in an industry vital to consumers and small businesses that, despite dramatic changes in information technology, appears to have remained limited to local markets for many of their financial services. The largest banks in local metropolitan areas are now likely to be in a position to dominate markets in a way that was not previously possible. There is the specter of a small group of "megabanks" with immense economic and political power, higher "prices" for locally-limited customers and a deterioration in credit terms for smaller business borrowers.

The issues of "big" versus "small," and "efficiency" versus "opportunity" have periodically occurred in banking over the past 200 years. They have repeatedly been addressed by major banking legislation whose mandates have invariably been eroded over time by market developments. In the current transitional state, driven by a merger movement, questions of efficiency, the role of small banks and opportunities for small business, and the efficacy of competition and competition policy for banking inevitably arise again. Whatever one's expectation about the future of the banking system, it is important to consider systematically what, if any, problems are posed before the process is completed, and to evaluate existing competition policy so that it might be modified to strengthen the beneficial effects of structural change.

Will the intense competition that the new world of banking promises prevail? Will higher concentration nevertheless lead to competitive prices for banking services? Will, in the end, government let banks compete regardless of the effects of competition on "safety and soundness?" In prosperous times, when bank profits are high, it is easy to answer these questions in the affirmative. When and if problems reoccur, in a new structural setting, the answers will not be so unequivocal. Small bank failures are one thing. The government of the United States has never had to deal with a potential failure of a huge conglomerate organization, like the Credit Lyonnais of France, the big banks of Germany, or the *kieratsus* of Japan.[4]

The answers are not written in stone. Much depends on how public policy, antitrust, and bank regulatory policy adapt to deal with bank mergers during this transformation.

## NOTES

1. For a detailed treatment of the banking problems of the 1980s, see Federal Deposit Insurance Corporation (1997).

2. This issue was the subject of a number of papers in Federal Reserve Bank of Chicago 1993.

3. More detail on changes in banking industry structure is provided in Chapter 4. See also Rhoades 1995, Savage 1993, and FDIC 1998.

4. Some may argue that Continental Illinois, which failed in 1984, was large enough to have given U.S. regulators a sense of the problem. However, Continental was not a financial conglomerate, such as those mentioned above. It was neither geographically nor globally a bank of major importance; it was only a large bank. For a discussion of this failure see FDIC 1997.

## REFERENCES

Federal Deposit Insurance Corporation (FDIC). 1997. *History of the Eighties*. Washington, D.C.: FDIC.

FDIC. 1998. *Quarterly Banking Profile, Third Quarter 1998*. Washington, D.C.: FDIC.

Federal Reserve Bank of Chicago. 1993. *Proceedings of a Conference on Bank Structure and Competition*. Chicago: Federal Reserve Bank of Chicago.

Rhoades, Stephen. 1996. "Bank Mergers and Industrywide Structure, 1980–94." Staff study, no. 169. Board of Governors of the Federal Reserve System.

Savage, Donald. 1993. "Interstate Banking: A Status Report." 79 *Federal Reserve Bulletin*, 1075–1089.

# CHAPTER 2

# Banking and Government
# in the Early Days of Banking

> Even in Andrew Jackson's day, it was recognized that banking problems
> have deep roots and a lively future.
>
> L. C. Henderson[1]

When the first commercial banks were chartered in the United States in the late eighteenth century, modern banking in the Western world was already centuries old. Questions about how banks should function, what kind of assets and liabilities they should have, what role the government should play in their organization, ownership and/or regulation, and how much competition there should be had already been asked and answered repeatedly, and in a variety of ways.

A number of leaders in the American colonies knew a good deal about European banking experience. With the Continental Congress in desperate financial straits during the Revolutionary War, Alexander Hamilton wrote to Robert Morris about organizing a bank:

Most nations have found it necessary to institute banks. . . . Venice, Genoa, Hamburgh, Holland and England are examples of their utility. Great Britain is indebted for the immense efforts she has been able to make in so many illustrious and successful wars essentially to that vast fabric of credit raised on [the] foundation [of the Bank of England]. 'Tis by this alone she now menaces our independence.[2]

Thereafter, the Bank of North America, the first American commercial bank, materialized, as had the legendary Bank of Venice before it, to meet "the necessities of the Republic."[3] The "necessities," at the time, were an inability of Congress to pay George Washington's troops. The Bank of North America, and the banks that Congress and state legislatures chartered thereafter were, in fact, modeled on the Bank of England, "a private establishment employed as a public agent."[4]

There were, as Hamilton observed, other models in Venice, Genoa, Hamburgh, and Holland. Differences aside, they all had an important element in common—a close affiliation between banks and government. As shown in this chapter, this close affiliation has existed from the earliest days of banking in Western Europe. It had important implications for banking policy and competition.

The nature of the relationship and its underlying conditions throw light on discussions of the last several decades as to how banks have been special. The historical review of this chapter, in combination with experience in the United States examined in Chapter 3, illuminates the distinctive achievement of the procompetitive banking policy established in the United States in the early 1960s, as well as continuing impediments to a policy that would treat banks like any other private business.

## A BRIEF HISTORY OF BANKING IN WESTERN EUROPE

The several related functions from which banking coalesced, including the valuing and exchanging of different monies, the extension of credit, the safekeeping of wealth, and the provision of a payments system, can be traced back thousands of years to the earliest civilizations of the Middle East, India, and China.[5] In Rome, banks accepted deposits, provided loans and transferred funds on the basis of oral contracts made in the presence of witnesses.[6] In the tenth century, Jewish court bankers in Baghdad, under the auspices of the Abbasid Caliphate, accepted deposits, transmitted funds over long distances through letters of credit, and made loans to the Caliph on the security of anticipated tax revenues.[7]

After centuries of commercial quiescence in Europe, modern deposit banking emerged in the twelfth century along with the resurgence of business activity. Trade increased the influx of diverse and differentially debased coins into the city-states of the Mediterranean, and created a need for specialists in exchange who gradually developed a deposit business and, out of that, a banking business.[8] Such specialists constituted a new class of "money changers" (*campsores*, *cambiatores*, or *bancherii*).

Notarial minute books in Genoa in the twelfth and thirteenth centuries have left a record of banking transactions involving trade and credit. Other documents reveal that by 1200, it was customary for Genoese merchants to have bank accounts and to use them in order to make payments by transfer.[9] Depositors were permitted overdrafts, and interbank arrangements permitted the transfer of funds by debtors even if the creditor had his account with another banker. Most bankers did not own their bank, but rented it from merchants who did not elect to operate as bankers.[10] Elsewhere in Italy other Mediterranean cities, Sienna, Lucca, Florence, Venice, and Barcelona among others, banking similarly developed. In the thirteenth and fourteenth centuries merchants became identified as bankers also, expanding their financial as well as their commercial activities internationally.[11]

The location of banking offices was originally affected by a long-existing legal requirement that contracts and orders be oral, rather than written. In an era when few could read and write, the written word was not trusted. Oral transactions made it necessary that business be done in person and, therefore, that banks be accessible to their customers. While the "home office" of a bank might literally be the banker's home, business was often transacted at temporary stalls in public places, behind a table or bench (*bancum*).[12]

In these early days, there was nothing in law to keep merchants from becoming bankers, or to limit the activities in which bankers engaged. In Lucca, for example, money changers invested in real estate, livestock, and mining, as well as mercantile enterprise.[13] In England, Italian merchant bankers traded in wool, lead, wine, and horses.[14]

In the expanding commercial environment, coin proved an inferior means of payment. With funds on deposit from many customers, banks could arrange for the secure transfer of funds on their books to satisfy debts; that is, in "bank money" rather than coin. The new payments system began as local transfers of funds, but as early as the twelfth century, fairs at Champagne, Flanders, and elsewhere provided opportunities for merchant bankers to establish correspondents in commercial centers, arrange for money conversions, and undertake interregional transfers and clearance.[15]

Bankers learned early from experience that, with a sufficient number of independent depositors, deposit fluctuations would normally be moderate and/or predictable, and permit the necessary liquidity with fractional reserves. Fractional reserves allowed them to inject new credit and "money" into the financial system.[16] From the depositors point of view, general acceptance of bank-generated debt required the belief that coin would be available when lawfully demanded; and, ultimately, legal assurance that holders in due course would be able to enforce an unconditional right to payment.

At the beginning of the sixteenth century, giro banks dominated the payments systems of Europe. The financial instruments of modern banking, the bill of exchange and the promissory note, were available, but not as negotiable instruments. In the Moslem world, where the commercial revolution came earlier, a negotiable bill of exchange was in use as early as the eighth century. It could "pass from hand to hand by . . . indorsement; . . . the payee had a right of recourse against the drawer in the event of nonpayment by the acceptor." Lombard lawyers, in Northern Italy in the eighth and ninth centuries, seem also to have developed documents that overcame ancient legal impediments to negotiability. But their efforts had been lost when banking emerged in the Mediterranean city-states in the late middle ages.[17]

By the middle of the seventeenth century, however, the bill of exchange had again become a negotiable instrument; and, thereafter, the promissory note. In the eighteenth century, bankers in Europe were dealing in negotiable financial instruments, coin, and bullion, accepting deposits, transferring them in satisfaction of debt, extending credit by discounting notes, permitting overdrafts, and issuing promissory notes payable to the bearer on demand.

The following is a list of important events in the development of early banking. Some have been previously referred to, and others are discussed in the next several sections.

**Prior to 2500 B.C.**

|  |  |
|---|---|
|  | Ancient Sumer: |
|  | Silver as medium of exchange |
|  | Deposit and credit transactions |
| Sixth Century B.C. | Coinage by Lydians |
| 300–400 B.C. | Coinage by Alexander |

**Middle Ages and Renaissance**

| | |
|---|---|
| Eighth Century | Credit transactions in Islam |
| Tenth Century | Letters of credit; tax anticipation loans in Islam |
| Eleventh Century | Money changers in Spain (Aragon) |
| Twelfth Century | Early banking documents indicate money changers in Italian cities (1154–64) and regulation in Genoa |
| Thirteenth Century | Merchant bankers in Genoa |
| | Failure of Leccacorvo bank (1259) |
| | Evidence of demand and time deposits, fractional reserves, transfers on banks' books, and overdrafts in Italian cities |
| | Regulation and bank failure in Barcelona, Valencia, Tortosa. |
| Fourteenth Century | Report of paper money in China by Marco Polo |
| | Failure of Ricciardi of Lucca on default of Edward I |
| | Failure of Bardi & Peruzzi of Florence on default of Edward III (1340s) |
| | First municipal bank in Barcelona (Taula de Canvi) |
| | Introduction of bill of exchange by Italian merchant bankers |
| | Establishment of Medici banking company in Florence (1397) |

| Fifteenth Century | City council of Barcelona makes private banking illegal (1438); forbids acceptance of deposits (1499) |
| | Banking crises and bank failure in Italian cities (1470–1520) |
| | Jacob Fugger's company established (1487) and becomes principal money lender to Habsburg emperor Maximilan (1490) |
| Sixteenth Century | Establishment of public bank in Venice (Banco della Piazza di Rialto, 1587) |
| Seventeenth Century | Establishment of Bank of Amsterdam (1609) |
| | Establishment of second public bank in Venice (Banco del Giro, 1619) |
| | Establishment of Bank of Hamburgh (1619) |
| | Seizure of merchant's money in royal treasury by Charles I of England (1640) |
| | Development of "goldsmith's promissory notes" (mid-seventeenth century) |
| | Default by Charles II of England (1672) |
| | Establishment of Bank of England (1694) |
| Eighteenth Century | Collapse of John Law's Mississippi Company (1720) |
| | South Sea Company fails causing financial panic in England ("South Sea Bubble," 1720) |
| | Failure of the Bank of Amsterdam (1790s) |

## SOVEREIGN LOANS, PUBLIC FINANCE, AND BANK FAILURE

"Moneyers" is the term given to the craftsmen, organized in guilds, that operated the mints of Europe during the Middle Ages. In the later years of the Roman Empire, they became entrusted with what was considered a public service and a reflection of sovereignty. They were forbidden to abandon their craft; their children, as well as their property were attached to the guilds. The guilds were made collectively responsible for the payment of taxes owned by members, for forgeries by individual workers, and the prompt delivery of coin quotas. They were also exempted from military and ordinary labor services. They apparently found their privileges a sufficient compensation for the restrictions imposed. There is evidence that by the fifth century they were rich and well organized.[18]

After the fall of Rome, the minting of coin in Europe became a private business. However, from the seventh through the ninth centuries, rulers reasserted control over the mints, having coins stamped as to weight and purity, and appropriating seigniorage.[19] The interest of kings and emperors in monetary affairs has always been clear. "It is only since they began to use money," John Hicks remarked, "that they have been short of money."[20]

Banking provided a remarkable new means of funding and payment; it was a natural attraction to sovereigns. The first part of this section focuses on the public finance aspects of early banking. The second part discusses the instability of banking, and the problems posed by periodic bank failure.

### Sovereign Loans and Public Finance

*Pecunia nervus belli* (money is the sinews of war), became a truism during centuries of warfare.[21] In European feudal societies, kings did not differentiate between their sovereignty and their property, and physical control over persons was hardly distinguishable from control over land. They imposed extraordinary levies during wars. Vassals paid according to their means—military service by barons, food and material by estates, and money by cities and religious orders. In consolidating power, in a developing money economy, kings took control of the army, and personal obligations in terms of commodities and services were transformed into money obligations.[22] Mercenary troops were used by the Italian city-states during the Renaissance, and others before them.[23]

Repeated armed conflict in Europe, from the thirteenth century on, expanded the demand for bank credit. The sovereign lending of Italian merchant bankers to rulers at war has been extensively documented—the Ricciardi of Lucca to Edward I of England, and Florentine bankers to Edward III. In Venice, from the thirteenth century on, it was common for private bankers to send cash to pay troops, furnish letters of credit to ambassadors, draw bills of exchange for the payment of a subsidy or tribute, and to meet the expenses of galley commanders.[24] In 1403, an act was passed tying the volume of international lending by banks to their government loans; bankers were forbidden to ship or send away by land either merchandise or money beyond the amount of one-and-a-half times the loans which had been made to the government. Both voluntary and forced loans, for which the "investor–tax payer" received government bonds, compelled merchants to withdraw bank funds.[25] In the sixteenth and seventeenth centuries, bank money continued to finance government expenditures.[26]

From ancient times, war finance produced innovations that made permanent changes in fiscal and monetary arrangements. A recent two-volume compilation of papers, edited by Larry Neal, entitled *War Finance,* was dedicated to the subject.[27] For banking, war finance was important enough to be embodied in a myth of origin. In the nineteenth century, the public Bank of Venice (Banco del Giro) was widely believed to be the first modern bank in the Western world, the product of a forced loan imposed by Duke Vitale, Mitchel II in 1171 on the merchants of Venice during a war. Rather than issuing bonds, a Chamber was established to record the amounts borrowed and to manage the fund. Interest payments entered in the record could be transferred by one creditor to another. Payments for merchandise and bills of exchange were

required by law to be made in *banco* (notes of the bank); debtors were required to keep money in the bank so that creditors could receive payment by
transfer from one account to another. The convenience of using "bank money"
attracted merchants to make deposits and obtain bank credits and, according
to the story, the Chamber became the Bank of Venice.[28]

In the 1870s, records were uncovered by academic researchers that showed
the story to be apocryphal.[29] The bank that became known as the Bank of
Venice did originate in a government debt, but it had been established in
1619, not 1171. The myth accurately identified the importance of war finance,
but displaced the origin of the bank by about half-a-millennium.[30]

It is now widely accepted that myths are not simply fanciful stories, but
deliver significant messages. Duke Vitale, Mitchel II's Chamber was plausibly consistent with experience in memorializing the connection between the
financial needs of governments and the development of modern banking.

### Bank Failure

The contribution of modern banking to economic development, as well as
public finance, was well understood. But benefits did not come without costs.
Banks repeatedly failed.[31] Well-known institutions that achieved fame and
fortune for themselves and their communities collapsed with disasterous effects; the Bonsignori in Sienna in 1298, the Ricciardi of Lucca, and the Bardi
and Peruzzi of Florence around 1345.

From the thirteenth century on, bank failure was common. By the sixteenth
century, Venice had extensive experience with bank failure.[32] Tommaso
Contarini, in a speech to the Venetian Senate in 1584, calculated that the
number of banks known to have existed in Venice since its founding was 103,
of which 96 had failed and 7 succeeded. Some have questioned his numbers,
but the survival rate he indicates was probably not exaggerated.[33] Despite the
high failure rate, he concluded that it would have been impossible to sustain
the commerce of the city without banking, and probably the city itself.[34]

The economic historian Raymond de Roover found that the fifteenth century was a particularly troubled period for banks.

Possibly, repeated bank failures shook the confidence of the merchant class and aroused
the hostility of the public authorities. In the Low Countries, especially, the dukes of
Burgundy adopted a policy which became increasingly inimical toward the money-
changers; and the monetary ordinances repeatedly forbade them to accept deposits
and to make payments by transfer.[35]

Sovereign credit was one of the reasons for failure. Defaults by rulers to
whom banks had made loans proved to be one of the more important reasons
for bank failure. The Ricciardi, who had financed Edward I's castle building
in England, lending him £400,000 between 1272 and 1310, failed when they

could not collect the debt. The Bardi and Peruzzi who helped finance Edward III in the Hundred Years War are now remembered as being among the earliest of many lenders that were ruined by a ruler's default.[36]

Loans to royalty were less secure than loans to prosperous merchants and free towns because they often could not be secured by enforceable pledges of assets or revenues. Towns could pledge the wealth of their burghers to perpetuity, and had to make good their commitments to preserve sovereignty. Merchant credit was secured by physical assets. Princes, on other hand, could not bind their subjects to pay debts, nor usually their successors. Alfred Marshall, the well-known nineteenth-century English economist, explained that "people generally, and traders in money in particular, had learnt by experience that a prince who found it inconvenient to discharge a debt, which he had incurred, simply set it aside; or as the saying goes, 'threw his sword into the scale' to make up the balance.'"[37] According to Raymond de Roover, "excessive advances to the government—nearly always in order to finance a war—repeatedly caused suspension of specie payment and the subsequent depreciation of bank money."[38]

Early banking developments in England were also closely tied to sovereign delinquency. Contemporary accounts indicate that after Charles I appropriated funds deposited for safekeeping in the Royal Mint in 1640, merchants decided it was safer to hold them with others, among whom were London goldsmiths.[39] Goldsmiths were makers and sellers of gold and silver wares, and cutters and vendors of precious stones. In the thirteenth century, they had been given the function of ascertaining that coins made by the Royal Mint were of the lawful weight, diameter and composition ("Trial of the Pyx"). They were equipped to hold gold and silver securely.[40] When some goldsmiths found themselves with money for which they had no immediate use, they began to make loans at interest by discounting the notes of borrowers. Finding the business profitable, they solicited deposits and paid interest. Discovering that the deposit receipts they provided were circulating as currency, they recognized that a fractional reserve in coin would be adequate. They became known for discounting bills and issuing promissory notes, payable to bearer on demand, that circulated as currency. The goldsmiths' guild, with a Royal charter dating to 1327, was entitled "The Wardens and Commonalty of the Mystery of Goldsmiths of the City of London." A seventeenth-century pamphleteer announced that the "mystery" of the new goldsmiths was banking.[41]

With the Restoration (1660), goldsmiths became lenders to Charles II, though they apparently had not forgotten his father's expropriation. The interest they charged appears to have included a substantial risk premium; "taking barefaced of him ten pound for the hundred, and by private contracts, . . . above twenty, and sometimes thirty in the hundred, to the great dishonor of the government."[42]

In January 1672, Charles II stopped making payments on his debt. "This was a national calamity," according to a prominent economic historian, "the more so as during the . . . thirty-two years, thus concluded, the custom of depositing money with the modern bankers had become so universal that, when several goldsmiths were compelled to suspend payment, not only merchants, but widows and orphans were found to be amongst the victims."[43] The goldsmiths, thereafter, decided that "the less they had to do with the Government the better it was for them."[44] The Crown was forced to look for other ways to provide for its financial requirements. Ultimately, as discussed below, it found the Bank of England.

Sovereign lending aside, deposit banking proved fragile for now familiar reasons. Without the possibility of investing in liquid assets, fractional reserves (even though high) exposed banks to runs which proved disastrous. Banks typically invested some of their resources directly in their own and other business ventures which often proved risky, and resulted in failure.[45] Speculative excesses, volatility in financial markets, and unstable prices contributed to periodic crises.[46]

The combination of speculative excesses with mismanagement was a recipe for disaster that resulted in the collapse of both the British South Sea Company and the Royal Bank of France in 1720; and which, thereafter, was permanently enshrined in financial literature as the South Sea and Mississippi bubbles. The South Sea Company had been chartered by the British Parliament to trade in the South Atlantic. It was also engaged in a variety of financial transactions, including the funding of a portion of the government debt.[47] It crashed in the wake of a speculative boom in its stock, and managerial fraud. The French Royal Bank traced its origin to the Bank of Law & Company organized by John Law under a charter from the king of France. It extended large amounts of credit to the *Compagnie d'Occident*, a trading company given rights by the French government to trade in the Louisiana territory, and with whom it merged in 1718. It issued an enormous volume of bank notes, based on real property, before the speculative bubble burst.[48]

## THE SEARCH FOR STABILITY

Economic and financial disruption, resulting from banking failures, currency problems, and "bubbles," focused the attention of public authorities. Defaults often caused suspensions and depreciation of bank money.[49] Authorities searched for banking stability through more regulation, and then in the repression of competition through the establishment of public banks and privately-organized monopolies. Public endorsement did not make banks immune to default and insolvency. Both the South Sea Company and the French Royal Bank made this clear; but "official agencies" were more likely to survive.[50]

The first part of this section describes the type of regulation that appeared early in the history of Western banking. The following two sections describe the establishment and functioning of two different types of banks with public functions: the Bank of Amsterdam and the Bank of England. Each institutional arrangement illuminates the unique competitive issues raised by banking.

### Regulation

Banking laws, regulations and public oversight developed with banking itself as a corollary to the business that required public trust to function effectively. In the twelfth century, money changers in Lucca were required to swear that they would commit "no theft, no trick nor falsification."[51] In Genoa, the government required money changers to keep their cash and records available for inspection, and to obtain guarantors responsible, up to a limit, for their debts.[52] Monthly testing of scales was instituted in Venice as early as 1266, and in 1270 bankers were required to provide security in the form of government bonds.[53] In Barcelona in 1284, the books of the money changers were held to be competent evidence of payment by credit transfer if their authenticity had been sworn to before the vicar. More detailed oversight was instituted in the first years of the fourteenth century.[54]

Venice was renowned for its regulation.[55] In 1374, the Senate prohibited bankers from dealing in copper, tin, iron, lead, saffron, and honey, to keep banks from undertaking risky activities, and/or to prevent them from monopolizing the specified commodities. An act in 1450 restricted bank credit to both foreigners and citizens for the purpose of purchasing silver, except in the amount of funds the borrower already had in the bank, plausibly to limit lending for speculative purposes, and/or to prevent a corner on silver. In 1445, bankers were required to be present daily, two hours in the morning and two hours after dinner, with a penalty for irregularity, to prevent them from avoiding their depositors who might want their money. In 1467, an act limited to ten ducats the amount which banks could lend to any person upon a single obligation—presumably for purposes of diversification. The act also required that bankers show to any person the books containing his accounts and balances. In 1526, an act was passed defining how bank credits were to be written and transferred; and requiring bankers to pay in cash at once to those who wished to be paid. The restriction was aimed at what apparently was a common practice of sending creditors who wished payment to another bank with an order drawn on it, or to delay or refuse payment by announcing an error requiring that accounts be compared. Summary jurisdiction over issues between bankers and depositors was given to designated public officers by various acts from 1421 to 1523.

In some places, harsh penalties were imposed on money changers who did not meet their obligations. In Barcelona, the law barred from banking any money changer who failed, and provided that he be disgraced by public crier, and detained on a diet of bread and water until he satisfied all demands. In an age of "recreational homicide," this penalty was deemed insufficient. In 1321, a provision was added that if no . . . settlement were made they would be beheaded. In 1360 Francesh Castello, a failed banker, was beheaded in front of his bank.[56] Monetary crimes were crimes against the sovereign. In England, smelting, clipping, and counterfeiting coins, and later forgery of Bank of England notes, became punishable by death.[57]

### Public Banks

Despite regulation, recurrent banking problems created periodic economic and financial distress. Antagonism toward private banking grew in the fifteenth century.[58] Over the next two centuries, public authorities displaced private bankers with public banks.[59]

In the sixteenth century, public banks were established in Naples, Genoa, and Milan. In Venice, the public Banco della Piazza di Rialto was established in 1587; and then the Banco del Giro (Bank of Venice) in 1619.[60] The Exchange Bank of Amsterdam was established in 1609 and the Bank of Hamburgh in 1619. From the sixteenth century until the end of the eighteenth century, "the banking system on the European continent was made up of public banks."[61]

Some of the public banks extended credit and, like modern banks, offered notes and checks that served as money. Some made loans only to the government and selected organizations.[62] Many, including the Bank of Venice, and most notably, the Bank of Amsterdam, were intended to be transfer banks only, substituting "bank money" for coin. They were prohibited from lending, directly or by overdrafts, and required to hold all their deposits in precious metal. From the sixteenth century until the end of the eighteenth century, banking systems on most of the European continent were made up mainly of such "narrow" public banks.[63]

### *The Bank of Amsterdam: "100 Percent Money"*

The Exchange Bank of Amsterdam was established in 1609 as a result of recurrent currency problems.[64] The city authorities became convinced that "cash keepers," many of whom were merchants as well as money changers, and who had taken on a variety of banking functions, including the acceptance of deposits, the transfer of funds, and the extension of credit, caused the value of circulating silver coins to rise above the official rates, and create a scarcity of "good" coins. The problem, according to Adam Smith's account in *The Wealth of Nations*, was that trade had brought a large quantity of clipped and worn foreign coin to Amsterdam.[65] Freshly minted coins, with the standard amount of silver, disappeared from circulation quickly. Merchants could not always find a sufficient quantity of good coin to pay their bills; and the value of their debts became uncertain. In these circumstances, private bankers could earn a profit by segregating the best coins and selling them to merchants at a premium. Increases in the market value of the "good" coins placed pressure on the mint to raise the price of freshly minted coin, and made it impossible to sustain the official rate.

The Bank of Amsterdam was established to effect transfers of funds through "bank money," and to provide for multilateral clearing of international payments. The professions of money changing and cash keeping were officially abolished.[66] The bank accepted coin at its intrinsic value in return for a credit on its books in so-called "standard" or "bank money," the official standard of value. All merchant bills in Amsterdam above a minimum value (600 guilders) had to be paid in "bank money." Merchants were, thereby, obliged to keep deposits with the bank. They could transfer any amount in their accounts to a creditor, or pay in specie through the bank.[67] The city made itself liable for deposits. The operations of the bank restored the official standard of value, reduced uncertainty as to the value of debt, and provided the city with new revenues from a variety of fees.

The Bank of Amsterdam, established as a transfer bank, was seemingly immune to problems because it held all its assets in bullion and coin. It was an example of what, in the 1930s, was termed "100 percent money." The bank, Adam Smith wrote in 1776 in *The Wealth of Nations*, "professes to lend out no part of what is deposited with it, but, for every guilder for which it gives credit . . . , to keep in its repositories . . . money or bullion . . . for which it is at all times liable to be called upon."[68] The city of Amsterdam guaranteed the deposits of the Bank of Amsterdam. It should have been failure-proof.

At some point in the eighteenth century, however, without any change in law, the bank stopped paying specie on demand; "bank money" became inconvertible. The Commissioners of the Bank stabilized its value by currency purchases and sales.[69] Further, for many years the bank covertly extended credit to government and government-affiliated institutions, such as the Municipal Treasury, the Provincial States of Holland, the Masters of the Mint, the Bank van Leening, and the East India Company. Until 1781, the credits were not large.[70] However, with Holland's entry into the War of American Independence, the amounts of its lending increased substantially. Confidence was impaired when the Bank could not prevent a depreciation of "bank money."

With a liquidity crisis in 1790–1791 following a succession of problems and disclosure of its secret lending, it effectively failed in the last decade of the eighteenth century.[71] Even after the bank's liquidity had been impaired and its secret lending had been disclosed, it survived until 1816 when the Dutch King William I suppressed it and a new Netherlands Bank patterned on the Bank of England was established.

The failure of the Bank of Amsterdam resonated with the latter-day British and American economists. Alfred Marshall, the leading English economist, observed that "the fraud committed . . . was without the taint of private selfishness."[72] Charles Dunbar, the American banking historian, was not sympathetic: "For generations the peculiar constitution of the Bank had enabled the administration to hide this guilty secret and to stifle suspicion."[73] Irving Fisher, the prominent American economist of the early twentieth century and an advocate of "100 percent money," thought the bank's failure was an object lesson. In the 1930s, he wrote, "The only important difference between the abuse which ultimately wrecked the Bank of Amsterdam and the modern way of lending depositors' money (which nearly wrecked capitalistic civilization) is that the modern system is not secret . . . and is supposedly safeguarded by legal or other restrictions."[74]

The financial importance of banks to government and the assistance governments were prepared to offer banks was not confined to publicly owned institutions. An early example is provided by the Bank of England in 1696–1697.

### The Bank of England

By the last decade of the seventeenth century in England, difficulties faced by Parliament and the Crown in borrowing money resulted in the establishment of the Bank of England, a private, not a public, monopoly with broader but still restricted explicit powers than the Bank of Amsterdam, and with public functions.

Private banking in England, as described above, had developed principally through an extension of the goldsmiths' businesses in the seventeenth century, largely as an unintended consequence of sovereign misbehavior.[75] The advantages of the public banks on the continent were well-known in England in the seventeenth century. A number of proposals to establish a similar bank had been made early in the century, but not implemented. It was only in the desperate straights of a war with France (War of the League of Augsburg, 1689–1697), with the government urgently needing credit, at an affordable cost, that Parliament established the Bank of England in 1694.

The bank was established as a private corporation with a charter granted by Parliament, not a public bank like the Bank of Amsterdam. Its principal organizer, William Patterson, described his proposed bank candidly as "a simple association of public creditors . . . resembling the goldsmiths' banks . . . but without the hazard of bankruptcy."[76] There was no pretense about it being a transfer bank only. It was intended to make credit available to the government. The private organizers of the bank agreed to lend the entire capital of the bank (£1,200,000) to the government at a rate of 8 percent. In return, they received a corporate charter and authority to conduct a banking business, including issuing promissory notes payable on demand and other kinds of loans.

Patterson's expectation of a bank "without the hazard of bankruptcy" was given substance in the Bank of England's earliest experiences. In May 1696 the bank was confronted by a run and it was forced to suspend cash payments.[77] The bank's notes circulated at a discount and its stock fell in value. At the same time, the government, in need of funds to pay its armies in the field, pressed the bank for an additional loan. The bank's directors promised that they would do their best, and its general court voted an additional £200,000 in funds for the government.

The initial response from the government was reassurance. A grateful Chancellor of the Exchequer wrote "The bank notwithstanding all the hardships . . . are yet resolved to venture all for the Government and I hope what they do in our distress will not be forgotten in theirs." John Houblon, the first governor of the Bank of England, told his shareholders that the Lords of the Treasury had indicated that "neither the Government nor the trade of England can be carried on without creditt, and that they know if the creditt of the Bank be not maintained, no other creditt can be supported."[78]

The Lords promised to support the bank by buying its stock. While the results of their intervention were disappointing, the bank survived the crisis. In 1697, Parliament granted it a monopoly of note issue, exempted its property from taxation and, as noted above, like the King's money, designated forgery of its notes a felony punishable by death, the same as the penalty for clipping or coining the King's money.[79] For over a century thereafter, Parliament continued to help finance the government and repeatedly confirmed its monopoly of bank notes.

## SYMBIOSIS AND COMPETITION POLICY

From the late Middle Ages through the eighteenth century, modern banking in Europe was importantly shaped by political exigencies. The financial pressures on governments lead to politically beneficial banking policies that were also beneficial to both banks and their customers. In different times and locations there emerged an enduring tripartite relationship that was advantageous to all parties.

### Symbiosis

That governments often needed and sometimes established banks to obtain financial support is evident in the history previously reviewed. Even a transfer bank, like the Bank of Amsterdam, committed to hold all its assets in precious metal and coin, was covertly used to satisfy the financial demands of government and government-affiliated borrowers. The Bank of England was, of course, established explicitly to meet the government's financial needs. The support provided by banks through loans, however, was only part of the contribution banks made in meeting these needs. The banking system also provided new credit to business and a new payments arrangement, both of which tended to promote trade and economic growth and consequently, to contribute to higher tax revenues. If for no other reason, governments would be compelled to establish a distinctive policy for banks that would serve their own interests and the interests of banks.

Essential to the success of banks was public confidence; that is, customers, and in particular, depositors, had to accept banks as institutions in which it would be safe to deposit funds and with which to arrange for transfers to pay debts. Some minimum level of public confidence would, moreover, have to be general, if the new payments system was to work effectively. The early banks must have confronted "network externalities"; that is, the value of a bank's deposit account to any merchant increased as the number of merchants with bank accounts increased—like the value of having e-mail goes up with the number of people using e-mail.

Governments could and did assist in promoting public confidence. In the Mediterranean cities, municipal authorities assumed supervisory control. Among the earliest regulations were those to establish honest and fair dealings in Genoa, Lucca, Venice, and Barcelona. Even lending to the government may have helped. The nineteenth-century Italian political economist Francesco Ferrara believed that early Venetian banks were willing to lend to the government without compensation because the prestige thereby conferred increased their deposits.[80] The establishment of the Bank of Amsterdam, as a public bank, with the announced aim of holding its assets in bullion and coin, permitted the city to guarantee the Bank's deposits. It is clear that such measures were to the advantage of bank customers as well as to governments and banks themselves.

During this period the enduring problem for all three groups was recurrent bank failure, which undermined public confidence regardless of regulation or the prestige of a government affiliation. In fact, financing governments was part of the problem, at times because of an excessive concentration in this type of loan, and in part because governments were not necessarily good credit risks.

Nevertheless, the failure of private banks resulted in the establishment of banks with even a closer affiliation with governments; that is, the public banks that dominated the European continent for two centuries; and the quasi-public bank established in England to finance an ongoing war. In such cases, government support and assistance in times of trouble became a part of the arrangement.

### Competition Policy

While there appears to be little discussion of competition policy early in the development of banking, other government policies had implications for competition. In Barcelona in the fifteenth century restrictions on entry were justified as prohibiting banks that did not meet the regulatory standards.[81] In Venice, it was expected that private banks would disappear when the Bank of Venice was established. In Amsterdam, private banks were required, by law, to disappear when the Bank of Amsterdam was established. This suppression of competition can be viewed as an element in the effort to establish bank stability. In general, however, the reliance of governments on banks coupled with their periodic financial problems resulted in a historical progression toward competitive restriction, from private to public banks and, in England, to a private bank with monopoly privileges and public functions.

### Monopoly Privileges in England

In 1694, when the Bank of England was established, there had already been several centuries of struggle in England against exclusive grants by the Crown, and for the right of individuals to engage freely in any trade. The idea that government should not create monopolies had developed in the sixteenth and seventeenth centuries in England. It had been in the ascendancy in law and custom from this time; and during the seventeenth century was brought to the United States by the English colonists.[82] Complaints against monopoly as grants by government authority were not simply that it raised prices or lowered quality but that it violated the right of individuals to take up a trade of their choosing. In a well-known English court decision in 1614, it had been stated that "at common law, no man could be prohibited from working in any lawful trade."[83] The Statute of Monopolies in 1624 restricted the Crown from making monopoly grants.

Banking was not immune to the development of free enterprise. In the early seventeenth century the mercantilist merchant Geoffrey Malynes wrote that "The use of banks (unless they be countermined by other banks) are not to be suffered in any well ordered commonwealth, as time will manifest more and more." He goes on to say that "The French king Lewis the ninth, and Phillip the Faire did with great cause confiscate the bankers goods. . . . Phillip de Valoys did the like, and indicated them as cozeners of the commonwealth; for it is found that in a short time, with 24 thousand sterling, they had accumulated and gotten above two millions four hundred thousand pounds."[84] He believed Amsterdam established its public bank "to countermine" private bankers who, by charging high interest rates, accumulated financial resources that permitted them to monopolize commodities.[85]

Nevertheless, in 1694, the financial needs of the government dominated. The rights of individuals to engage in any trade, and the need for competition were not completely overlooked, but were at least partially sacrificed in Parliament's grant of a corporate charter to the Bank of England. Within a few years, the bank was granted exclusive privileges that were sustained and elaborated over the next century.

### *Monopoly Elements in the Corporate Charter*

In eighteenth-century England, it was not unusual for governments to delegate public functions to private individuals and groups. Delegation had long been a way to provide transportation, water, education, to collect taxes, and to meet military needs with mercenary armies. Such privatization reflected governments' lack of experience in public administration, policy making, and with erecting a large bureaucracy.[86] Perhaps, as is sometimes argued today, it was more efficient than having the government provide such services directly.

The charter was a mechanism for delegation; the charter was a grant of a franchise by a sovereign authority, a privilege, to run a specific enterprise or to trade in a particular area. Such delegations, as mentioned, were not unusual.[87] Each charter was a product of negotiation which was perceived as resulting in a contractual relationship.[88] In recent years regulation has, in general, been interpreted as a contractual arrangement that is (1) long term, (2) incomplete, and (3) has important implicit elements.[89] It originally included legislative (and later administrative) controls over key aspects of private market activity and involved both taxes and subsidies of various kinds.[90] It could be viewed as provided by government to assist politically influential groups and as a method of income redistribution.[91]

Those who did the work of the state, merchant adventurers, importers of clothing or playing cards, and providers of water or banks obtained the privilege of incorporation for a specified time. The grant meant that the corporate business could maintain its debts in the name of the corporation, which could sue and be sued on its own behalf, and continue to exist even though ownership and management changed. Judges inferred limited liability for stockholders from the fact that the corporation alone was liable for its debts. The grant typically included a monopoly of the specified activity for which it had been created.[92]

In granting privileges in return for services, governments also required certain safeguards for itself and other commercial interests. The activity of the corporation was defined and thereby limited in scope. The legal scholar, Adolph A. Berle, suggested that "In theory this was probably designed to prevent corporations from dominating the business life of the time."[93] But definition also permitted the stockholders to know how their investment was utilized. In addition, capital requirements were established to protect creditors against excessive leverage. Government took on a monitoring function.

### The Bank of England's Monopoly Privileges

The charter Parliament granted to the Bank of England was contractual in character in the sense that the bank received a number of privileges in return for pledging its capital to the government.[94] However in 1694 Parliament did not guarantee the Bank of England that it would grant no other banking charters. Subsequently, in 1696, it chartered the soon-to-fail National Land Bank to provide additional financing.[95] Nevertheless, the implicit monopoly element in the Bank of England's grant had provoked vociferous complaints in 1694 from both the banking goldsmiths and merchants. Goldsmiths were concerned about direct competition from a government-affiliated bank. Merchants were concerned that the bank would also undertake nonbanking businesses with which they would have to compete.

To assuage the complaining merchants, a provision was added to the 1694 act that restricted the bank's activities: "And to the intent that their Majesties subjects may not be oppressed by the said corporation by their monopolizing or engrossing any sort of goods, wares or merchandise be it further declared . . . that the said corporation . . . shall not at any time . . . deal or trade . . . in the buying or selling of any goods, wares or merchandise whatsoever."[96]

The concerns that lead to this restriction had been articulated by Malynes in his observation about the private bankers in Amsterdam who he believed had accumulated financial resources that permitted them to monopolize commodities. It may also have partially motivated the Venetian law that prohibited bankers from dealing in copper, tin, iron, lead, saffron, and honey.[97] This provision of the act that established the Bank of England found its way into early American bank charters and laws in the eighteenth and nineteenth centuries. It provided the foundation for a policy of separating banking from commerce that has, up to now, distinguished American banking from most of the rest of the world.

Soon after the crisis of 1696, the Bank of England took the position that to be useful to the government it must be the repository of cash for all of London. In other words, it must be the only institution of its kind. Its spokesmen argued that its notes would only circulate if the public had confidence in the Bank; competition caused distrust.[98] Parliament accepted this argument in 1697, amending the law to read that no other "Corporation, Society Fellowship Company or Constitution" would be allowed during the continuance of the Bank of England.[99]

This provision, however, left a loophole for the establishment of new banks through large partnerships. In 1708, Parliament amended the law again to prohibit all groups of six or more individuals "to borrow, owe, take up any sum . . . on their bills or notes payable at demand, or in any less time than six months from the borrowing thereof."[100]

In July 1720, in response to the collapse of the South Sea Company, Parliament passed the Bubble Act which prohibited the further establishment of unincorporated joint stock companies without its approval. The limitation remained on the books until 1856. It created a barrier to entry into banking, as well as other activities in America as well as in England.[101]

The bank's monopoly of note issue was reconfirmed and elaborated on a number of subsequent occasions through the eighteenth century and into the nineteenth:

| Date | Statute | Restriction/Rationale |
|------|---------|----------------------|
| 1694 | 5&6 Wm. & Mary, c.20 | Parliament grants corporate charter to establish Bank of England. Bank restricted from dealing in merchandise. No "exclusive privileges" provided. |
| 1697 | 8&9 Wm. III, c.20, s.28 | "During the continuance of the . . . Bank of England, no other bank, or |

| | | |
|---|---|---|
| | | any corporation, society, fellowship, company or constitution in the nature of a bank shall be erected or established . . . by Act of Parliament within this kingdom." |
| 1709 | 7 Anne, c.7 | Illegal for "any body politic or corporate . . . or for any other persons whatsoever united . . . in covenants or partnerships exceeding the number of six persons, in that part of Great Britain called England to borrow, owe, or take up any sum . . . on their bills or notes, payable at demand, or at any less time than six months from the borrowing thereof." |
| 1742–1826 | Various statute | Monopoly privileges reconfirmed. |
| 1826 | Statute 1826, c.46 | Monopoly of note issue restricted to sixty-five miles from London. |
| 1833 | Statute 1833, c.98 | Legality of joint-stock banks, operating on basis of checking deposits, affirmed. |
| 1844 | Statute 1844, c.32 (Peel's Act) | Right to issue notes confined to bankers who had privilege prior to 1844, and not to exceed levels established in 1844. Further restrictions imposed tending to eliminate all notes other than those of the Bank of England.[102] |

As had occurred elsewhere where competition is initially restricted, new banks ultimately found a way to circumvent the restrictions. In the second half of the eighteenth century, not long before the first bank was chartered in the American colonies, new banks had been organized on the periphery of the Bank of England's monopoly. "Country banks" developed without the advantages of limited liability provided by the corporate charter, and despite the law that limited banking partnerships in England to six people (Act of 1709). They grew by providing short-term credit to business; manufacturers obtained longer-term funds internally.[103] In 1776, Adam Smith observed that "The late multiplication of banking companies in both parts of the united kingdom, an event by which many people have been much alarmed, instead of diminishing, increases the security of the public."[104] Smith's view had no immediate effect on the government's position. Nevertheless, by the beginning of the nineteenth century, new joint stock banks found a way around the bank monopoly of notes by offering deposits. In the second and third decades of the century Parliament began the process of proscribing the Bank of England's monopoly and converting it from a commercial to a central bank.[105]

The tradition of restricted activities for banks was nevertheless maintained, even without explicit legal restriction. Today, in the absence of legal restrictions, the United Kingdom is sometimes listed as a country that permits very wide banking powers, including equity holdings in commercial firms.[106] Nevertheless, it has only been since the Big Bang in 1987 that commercial banks moved aggressively into securities trading and insurance through subsidiaries.[107]

This has been a case where the absence of restrictive law seems more than it actually is. Banks may own commercial firms and commercial firms may own banks, provided that they are considered to be fit and proper by the bank supervisor. However, the Bank of England, through moral suasion, has effectively constrained the mixture of banking and commerce. In practice, banks have not chosen, except through relatively small venture capital subsidiaries, to own commercial firms. The Bank of England has indicated that it would not favor controlling investments by industrial firms in major banks.[108]

### Symbiosis, Too Important to Fail, and Competition

Why did the Bank of England's monopoly privileges last for well over a century in which private enterprise and free markets were on the rise? The argument made by the bank in 1696–1697, was that competition causes distrust, and that the bank's notes would only circulate if the public had confidence in the bank. The argument must have been old when it was articulated. Clearly, it was in the interest of the government to promote public confidence in the bank, just as it had been in the interest of the city-states that had established public banks in the past. But Parliament, which could not obtain low cost loans from presumably competitive goldsmiths could not have much faith in competition for serving its needs. Its views, Geoffrey Malynes and Adam Smith notwithstanding, were probably closer to those of an anonymous English pamphleteer who wrote in 1695 that the Bank of England had "almost crush'd several sorts of Blood-suckers, mere Vermin and Gripers, Goldsmiths, Tally-Jobbers, Exchequer Brokers, and Knavish Money-Scriveners, and Pawn-Brokers, with their Twenty and Thirty per-cent."[109]

An early picture of the symbiosis and some of its effects on competition is apparent in thirteenth-century Genoa. The following excerpt from a paper by a well-known medieval scholar based on notarial minutes and offical records is indicative of the early relationship among banks, their customers, and government. He writes that bankers

were responsible to the Genoese government for converting domestic and foreign currencies into one another as the market required, ferreting out forged or forbidden coins, and generally watching over the circulation. The government soon required them to keep their cash and records available for inspection, and to obtain guarantors who would be answerable for their outstanding debts up to a cerain amount. In return for these restrictions, the government backed the bankers' credibility: it recognized entries in their books as legal proof of transactions carried out through them. Somewhat later, it ordered guardians of minors to deposit the wards' money in a bank. This gave the bancherii an advantage over ordinary merchants in conservative investments and small savings. Most citizens found it convenient to deposit some of their money in a bank account and receive a moderate interest . . . while using the account for receiving and making payments by written transfer in the banker's book. A reliable depositor was often allowed to overdraw his account within certain limits. The banker, in turn, was entitled to invest in his own trade the deposits of his clients.[110]

An even earlier articulation of the symbiosis and its competitive implications can be found in the experience of the tenth-century Jewish court bankers in the Abbasid Caliphate. These bankers were subject to the intense demands for funds by the government, as illustrated by the following message from a Vizier.

Do you want to avoid my inflicting penalties on you that may affect you and your heirs forever? . . . At the beginning of each month I need an amount of 30,000 dinars, which must be paid within the first six days to the infantry troops.[111]

In light of such dire threats, the bankers had a surprising longevity. This was explained in the following policy statement translated from a tenth-century document. The bankers "were never dismissed until their death; . . . The Caliph did not want to . . . in order to uphold the dignity of the office . . . , so that the merchants might . . . lend through the . . . jahbadh [banker]. . . . Were a jahbadh to be dismissed and another appointed . . . with whom the merchants had not yet had any dealings, the business of the Caliph would come to a standstill."[112]

Court bankers were protected to reassure depositors. New bankers would be suspect. The banker's benefit (lifetime tenure) and the government's (financing) were not a simple quid pro quo, but an enduring relationship that included merchants who were also depositors. From Jewish court bankers to the Bank of England there is recurrent evidence of government support that has made some banks too important to fail and that has collaterally suppressed competition.

Today it is understood that government safety nets confront banks with an incentive to take excessive risk; and this may have been understood in earlier times. But the persistence of the forces that compelled the symbiotic relationship should not be underestimated. Struggling and contentious states, under pressure, had to have the cheap credit that banks could provide. Leaders understood that prestigious banks, along with a stable payments system and a healthy commercial sector, provided banks with a larger supply of funds into which they could tap by borrowing and issuing securities, and government with higher tax revenues. They did not want merchants and others "to hide their gold and silver under the soil, in wells, in cisterns, in barns, among clothes, etc."[113] And so they supported banks that, in turn, supported them and a merchant economy simultaneously. The result was a three-way relationship between banks, their customers, and the government, in which banking was regulated but also assisted in times of need out of the needs of public finance and other elements of state policy.

## CONCLUSIONS

From its earliest modern beginnings in the twelfth and thirteenth centuries, banking served the interests of governments, frequently at war and typically short of funds, by making credit available as well as by promoting private commercial activity. Governments, in turn, implemented policies both to sustain depositor confidence on whom all else depended, and to regulate for safety and soundness. With recurrent failures, nevertheless, they established public and quasi-public banks entitled to direct government support. A unique and enduring mutually beneficial relationship developed among governments, banks, and bank customers.

Experience suggested that competition was incompatible with the interests of governments and, possibly, with bank stability. Public banks were established with the intention of replacing competitive private banks. The Bank of England obtained monopoly privileges shortly after it was established and thereafter aggressively opposed its rivals as they emerged.

Banking experience and policy in Europe were well known in the United States when, during the Revolution, the Bank of North America was chartered by Congress. It provided the boundaries of understanding within which this bank, and others after it, were structured. Despite the founders' strong commitment to free markets, monopoly turned out to be their default position for banking. In the next chapter, we turn to the consequences of that choice through the mid-twentieth century.

## APPENDIX: EARLY SCOTTISH BANKING

When, as mentioned in this chapter, Adam Smith wrote about "the late multiplication of banking companies in both parts of the united kingdom" he had referred, in part, to an increasing number of banks in Scotland. The free banking arrangement there constituted a prominent exception to government regulation and competitive restriction elsewhere. Banking in Scotland in the eighteenth century has suggested to a number of economists in recent years that competition among banks, without government intervention, could be beneficial.

Beginning about 1716 and lasting more than a century (to the Peel Act of 1844), easy entry into banking, without government restriction or assistance, resulted in relatively large numbers of well capitalized, and conservatively managed banks, whose notes circulated at par. While bank failures occurred, they did not result in serious losses to creditors, did not seem to spread to other banks, or have systemic consequences.[114]

Most of the Scottish banks were partnerships, and some have attributed their success to the unlimited liability of their stockholders who pledged all their assets though, unlike some before them, not their lives. They view "free banking" in Scotland as a natural experiment that provides evidence that competitive banking is not inherently unstable and that banking does not require government intervention.

Whatever the lessons of Scottish free banking, it originated in unique historical circumstances. During the period, there was no Scottish government authority with political aims comparable to those of other countries in Europe.[115] The British Parliament in London apparently did not view banking in Scotland as vital to its interest. While it protected the Bank of England with a monopoly of note issue, prohibiting partnerships larger than six persons throughout England, it did not satisfy the bank's request for an extension of its monopoly to Scotland.[116] Parliament also rejected the Bank of Scotland's petition against chartering its first rival, the Royal Bank of Scotland, in 1727.

In Scotland, there were no public finance needs to drive government intervention. There is also some dispute about how competitive the banking system in Scotland was. Scottish banking was dominated by three chartered banks whose stockholders had unlimited liability, whose notes were the only ones acceptable in payment of custom duties and that, from time-to-time, collaborated. Some economists have suggested that substantial barriers to entry existed, despite the appearance of free entry. It has also been suggested that self-regulation replaced government regulation.[117]

Scotland in the eighteenth century remains an interesting example of banking *sans* government, but one that is relatively unique and, quite possibly, idiosyncratic.

## NOTES

1. Helderman 1931, 146.
2. Hamilton's letter to Morris, 30 April 1781, as reprinted in Ferguson 1973, 32, 42–43.
3. Knox 1903, 2.
4. Dunbar 1904, 91.
5. This section and the following sections draw, in part, on Shull 1999. For the earliest emergence of banking functions, see Homer and Sylla 1991, Ch. 2.
6. Usher 1943, 5, 6.
7. Fischel 1937, 32–33; McNeill 1963, 434.
8. Lane and Mueller 1985, 79 ff.; *The Dawn of Modern Banking* 1979, 291 ff.
9. de Roover 1974, 201.
10. Lopez 1979.
11. Lane and Mueller 1985, 69–75; de Roover 1974, 210; Usher 1943, 264.

12. See Usher 1943, 12.
13. Blomquist 1979, 59–60.
14. Prestwich 1979, 99–100.
15. Usher 1943, 20; de Roover 1974, 202–238; Blomquist 1979, 78–79.
16. de Roover 1974, 214; Usher 1943, 3 ff.
17. See Holdsworth 1922, 183–188.
18. Lopez 1986, 1–4.
19. Spuford 1988, Chs. 2–4; Usher 1943, Ch. 7; Cippola 1967, 27 ff.
20. Hicks 1969, 81.
21. On the need of rulers in the last centuries of the Middle Ages for large and increasing amounts of credit, see Ehrenberg 1985, 59.
22. Commons 1957, Chs. 6, 7.
23. On the sources of war finance see Neal 1994, vol. I and, in particular, the "Introduction."
24. Mueller 1997, Ch. 10; Dunbar 1892, 314–315.
25. Lane 1937, 197–200.
26. Ibid., 205–206; Dunbar 1892, 314–315.
27. Neal 1994, vols. I, II.
28. See, for example, Goddard 1831, 10.
29. The myth was dispelled by the research of Lattes and Ferrara around 1870. For a review of the research that dispelled the myth, see Dunbar 1892, 308 ff. The myth lingered on, however, in at least some well-known banking histories in the United States. For a repetition of the story by an early twentieth-century Comptroller of the Currency, see Knox 1903, 2, 3.
30. Dunbar 1892, 325–327. Dunbar speculates on the confusions about the true origin of the Bank of Venice that permitted the "legend which . . . assigned to the Bank . . . a life of about six centuries."
31. de Roover 1974, 200–207.
32. Ibid., 225.
33. Mueller 1997, 122. On the problems of bank failure throughout Europe during these centuries, see de Roover 1974, 200–207.
34. Dunbar 1892, 312.
35. de Roover 1974, 219.
36. Neal 1994, vol. I, p. xiv. For a different view, see Hunt 1990, 149.
37. Marshall 1965, 298.
38. de Roover 1974, 228–229.
39. Goldsmiths were makers and sellers of gold and silver wares, and cutters and vendors of precious stones. For a discussion of the transformation of goldsmiths into bankers, see "Mystery of the New-Fashioned Goldsmiths or Bankers Discovered" 1676, 684–687; Richards 1929, 2–8.
40. "Mystery of the New-Fashioned Goldsmiths or Bankers Discovered" 1676, 684–687; Richards 1929, 2–8.
41. "Mystery of New-Fashioned Goldsmiths or Bankers Discovered" 1676, 686.
42. Ibid.
43. Bisschop 1910, 47–49.
44. Holdsworth 1918, 20.
45. de Roover 1974, 214, n. 53; see also Lane 1937, 187.

46. Mueller 1997, 125–128.
47. Kindleberger 1993, 78.
48. Ibid., 99.
49. de Roover 1974, 228–229.
50. Ibid.
51. On early restrictions in Lucca, see Blomquist 1979, 55, 61.
52. Lopez 1979, 11.
53. Mueller 1997, 46.
54. Usher 1943, 239 ff.
55. An extensive review of supervision and regulation in Venice can be found in Mueller 1997, Ch. 2. An earlier elaboration of Venetian banking regulation can be found in Dunbar 1892, 311–317.
56. Usher 1943, 240, 242.
57. See Bisschop 1910, 40, n. 1.
58. de Roover 1974, 219. In the fifteenth century the dukes of Burgundy adopted ordinances that forbade bankers to accept deposits and to make payments by transfer.
59. Rich and Wilson 1977, 312–313.
60. Ibid. Private banks did not disappear completely in Venice, though the Senate had contemplated that they would. See Usher 1934, 290.
61. de Roover 1974, 229.
62. Rich and Wilson 1977, 314.
63. de Roover 1974, 229; Lane 1937, 189, 201–203. An act of the Venetian Senate in 1587 establishing the Banco della Piazza di Rialto recited the problems resulting from the failure of the private banks along with the great need of a bank of some kind. The Banco del Giro absorbed the Bank of the Rialto in 1637.
64. van Dillen 1934, 82 ff.; Rich and Wilson 1977, 336–337.
65. Smith 1937, 446–455.
66. These professions were again legalized in 1621. See Rich and Wilson 1977, 343 ff.
67. In the second half of the seventeenth century the bank promoted its trade in gold and silver by making advances in bank money to the bullion traders who deposited precious metals. Van Dillen 1934, 102.
68. Smith 1937, 453.
69. van Dillen 1934, 101–102.
70. Ibid., 94 ff. and, in particular, 108–109. See also Heckscher 1934, 161–190.
71. de Roover 1974, 227–229. The bank continued to operate, however, until 1816, when King William I substituted a new bank patterned on the Bank of England.
72. Marshall 1965, 299–300.
73. Charles Dunbar, as quoted in van Dillen 1934, 109.
74. Fisher 1935, 36–37.
75. The operations of the public banks on the continent were well-known in England in the seventeenth century. See Holdsworth 1923, 183–185.
76. As quoted in Clapham 1945, 15.
77. The crisis of 1696 resulted from government recoinage made necessary by the clipping of British silver coins following the export of specie during the war. See Jones, in Neal 1994, vol. II.
78. Clapham 1945, 39–50.

79. Ibid., 50.
80. Mueller 1997, 427, 447.
81. Usher 1943, 246–250.
82. Letwin 1965, Ch. 2.
83. Ipswich Tailors' case, 11 Co. Rep. 53, Godbolt, 252 (1614).
84. Malynes 1636, Ch. 9, p. 272.
85. Ibid., Ch. 20, p. 96.
86. Hurst 1973, 152 ff.
87. See Berle and Means 1940, 128 ff.
88. The development of the modern corporate charter is traced in ibid.
89. Goldberg 1976, 427–429; Williamson 1985, Ch. 2.
90. Posner 1974.
91. Peltzman 1976; Stigler 1971; Gray 1940.
92. Berle and Means 1940, 128–129.
93. Ibid., 131.
94. A modern analysis of the banking charter as a contract can be found in Stanton 1994, 57–97.
95. 7 & 8 William & Mary, c. 31
96. 5 & 6 William & Mary c. 26.
97. It is also possible that public officials believed that these commodities were too risky for banks. See Dunbar 1892, 314.
98. Andreades 1966, 110.
99. Clapham 1945, 50.
100. 7 Anne c. 30.
101. Kindleberger 1993, 78.
102. Clapham 1943; Andreades 1966.
103. Cameron 1972, 11–12.
104. Smith 1937, 313. He had only two caveats: (1) that bankers be restrained from issuing bank notes under a given denomination, and (2) that bank notes be issued subject to the obligation of an immediate and unconditional payment in gold or silver on presentation.
105. Andreades 1966, 248–255, 258–262.
106. Barth, Nolle, and Rice 1997, Tables 4 and 5; Institute of International Bankers 1995, 16.
107. Llewellyn 1995, 2–3.
108. Institute of International Bankers 1995, 16; GAO 1994, 11. Another way of looking at conglomeration in the United Kingdom is to say that British banks have not taken advantage of the scope of their permissible powers. See Llewellyn 1995, 4–5; Goodman et al. 1984, 95 ff.
109. As quoted in Clapham 1945, 29.
110. Lopez 1979, 11.
111. Vizier Ali b. Isa to court banker in Baghdad, tenth century, as translated from Arabic historical sources in Fischel 1937, 23.
112. Nishwar al-Muhadara, in ibid., 28–29.
113. Ibid., 13, 14.
114. White 1984, 24–37.
115. Ibid., 25. The English and Scottish parliaments were unified in 1707.

116. Checkland 1975, 48–52.
117. See Gorton 1985, 274; Carr, Glied, and Mathewson 1989, 974 ff.

## REFERENCES

Andreades, A. 1966. *History of the Bank of England: 1640–1903*. 4th ed. London: Frank Cass & Co.

Bagehot, Walter. 1873. *Lombard Street*. New York: Scribner, Armstrong & Co.

Barth, James R., Daniel Nolle, and Tara Rice. 1997. "Commercial Banking Structure, Regulation and Performance: An International Comparison." Economics working paper no. 97-6, Office of the Comptroller of the Currency, Washington, D.C.

Berle, A. A., and G. C. Means. 1940. *The Modern Corporation and Private Property*. New York: Macmillan.

Bisschop, W. R. 1910. *The Rise of the London Money Market: 1640–1826*. London: P. S. King & Son.

Blomquist, Thomas W. 1979. "The Dawn of Banking in an Italian Commune: Thirteenth Century Lucca." In *The Dawn of Modern Banking*. New Haven: Yale University Press.

Cameron, Rondo. 1972. *Banking and Economic Development*. Oxford: Oxford University Press.

Carr, J., S. Glied, and F. Mathewson. 1989. "Unlimited Liability and Free Banking in Scotland: A Note." *Journal of Economic History* 49, no. 4: 974–978.

Checkland, S. G. 1975. *Scottish Banking, A History: 1695–1973*. London: Collins.

Cipolla, Carlo M. 1967. *Money, Prices and Civilization in the Mediterranean World*. New York: Gordian Press.

Clapham, John. 1943. *The Bank of England: A History*. Vol. 1. New York: Macmillan.

Commons, John R. 1957. *The Legal Foundations of Capitalism*. Madison: University of Wisconsin Press.

Copeland, M. A. 1974. "Concerning the Origin of a Money Economy." *American Journal of Economics and Sociology* 33, no. 1: 1–17.

Cranch, William. 1909. "Promissory Notes Before and After Lord Holt." In *Select Essays in Anglo-American Legal History*. Vol. 3. Boston: Little, Brown.

*The Dawn of Modern Banking*. 1979. New Haven: Yale University Press.

de Roover, Raymond. 1974. "New Interpretations of the History of Banking." In *Business, Banking and Economic Thought*. Ed. J. Kirshner. Chicago: University of Chicago Press.

Dunbar, Charles. 1892. "The Bank of Venice." *The Quarterly Journal of Economics* 6: 308–379.

———. 1904. *Economic Essays*. New York: Macmillan.

Ehrenberg, Richard. 1985 (1928). *Capital and Finance in the Age of the Renaissance*. Fairfield, N.J.: Augustus M. Kelley.

Ferguson, E. J., ed. 1973. *The Papers of Robert Morris*, 1781–84. Vol. 1. Pittsburgh: University of Pittsburgh Press.

Fischel, Walter. 1933. "The Origins of Banking in Medieval Islam." *Journal of the Royal Asiatic Society*.

———. 1937. *The Jew in the Economic and Political Life of Mediaeval Islam*. London: Royal Asiatic Society.

Fisher, Irving. 1935. *100% Money.* New York: Adelphi.

Goddard, Thomas. 1831. *A General History of the Most Prominent Banks in Europe.* New York: H. C. Sleight.

Goldberg, Victor P. 1976. "Regulation and Administered Contracts." *Bell Journal of Economics* 7: 426–448.

Goodman, Laurie S., et al. 1984. "Product Line Regulations for Financial Institutions." In *Proceedings of a Conference on Bank Structure and Competition.* Chicago: Federal Reserve Bank of Chicago.

Gorton, Garry. 1985. "Banking Theory and Free Banking History." *Journal of Monetary Economics* 16, no. 3: 267–276.

Government Accounting Office (GAO). 1994. *Bank Regulatory Structure: The United Kingdom.* No. 95-38. Washington, D.C.: GAO.

Gray, Horace M. 1940. "The Passing of the Public Utility Concept." *Journal of Land and Public Utility Economics* 16, no. 1: 8–20.

Heckscher, Eli F. 1934. "The Bank of Sweden in Connection with the Bank of Amsterdam." In *History of the Principal Public Banks.* Ed. J. G. van Dillen. The Hague: Martinus Nijhoff.

Helderman, L. C. 1931. *National and State Banks: A Study of Their Origins.* Boston: Houghton Mifflin.

Hicks, John. 1969. *A Theory of History.* Oxford: Oxford University Press.

Holdsworth, William S. 1922. *A History of English Law.* 3d ed. Vol. 8. London: Methuen.

Homer, Sidney, and Richard Sylla. 1991. *A History of Interest Rates.* 3d ed. New Brunswick, N.J.: Rutgers University Press.

Hunt, Edward S. 1990. "A New Look at the Dealings of the Bardi and Peruzzi with Edward III." *Journal of Economic History* 50, no. 1: 149–162.

Hurst, Willard. 1973. *A Legal History of Money.* Lincoln: University of Nebraska Press.

Institute of International Bankers. 1995. *Global Survey 1995: Regulatory and Market Developments.* New York: Institute of International Bankers.

Kindleberger, Charles P. 1993. *A Financial History of Western Europe.* Oxford: Oxford University Press.

Kirshner, J., ed. 1974. *Business, Banking and Economic Thought.* Chicago: University of Chicago Press.

Knox, John Jay. 1903. *A History of Banking in the United States.* New York: Bradford, Rhodes.

Kroose, Herman E., and Bernard Shull. 1996. "Banks and Banking: Origin and Development." *Encyclopedia Americana.* Rev. ed. Vol. 3. Danbury, Conn.: Grolier.

Lane, Frederick C. 1937. "Venetian Bankers, 1496–1533: A Study in the Early Stages of Deposit Banking." *Journal of Political Economy* 45, no. 1: 187–206.

Lane, Frederick C., and Reinhold C. Mueller. 1985. *Money and Banking in Medieval and Renaissance Venice: Coins and Moneys of Account.* Baltimore: Johns Hopkins University Press.

Letwin, L. 1965. *Law and Economic Policy in America.* New York: Random House.

Llewellyn, David T., 1995. "Universal Banking and the Public Interest: A British Perspective." Paper presented at the Conference on Universal Banking, New York University, 23–24 February, New York.

Lopez, Robert S. 1979. "The Dawn of Medieval Banking." In *The Dawn of Modern Banking*. New Haven: Yale University Press.

———. 1986. "An Aristocracy of Money in the Early Middle Ages." In *The Shape of Medieval Monetary History*. London: Variorum Reprints.

Malynes, Geoffrey. 1636. *Lex Mercatoria*. London: Adam Islip.

McNeill, W. H. 1963. *The Rise of the West*. Chicago: University of Chicago Press.

Marshall, Alfred. 1965 (1923). *Money Credit and Commerce*. New York: Augustus M. Kelley.

Mueller, Reinhold C. 1997. *The Venetian Money Market: Banks, Panics and the Public Debt, 1200–1500*. Baltimore: Johns Hopkins University Press.

*The Mystery of the New-Fashioned Goldsmiths or Bankers Discovered*. 1676. Reprinted in J. Thirsk and J. P. Cooper, eds. 1972. *Seventeenth-Century Economic Documents*. Oxford: Clarendon Press.

Neal, Larry, ed. 1994. *War Finance*. Vols. 1 and 2. Brookfield, Vt.: Elgar.

Peltzman, Sam. 1976. "Toward a More General Theory of Economic Regulation." *Journal of Law and Economics* 19, no. 2: 211–240.

Posner, R. A. 1974. "Theories of Economic Regulation." *Bell Journal of Economics and Management Science* 5, no. 2: 335–358.

Prestwich, Michael. 1979. "Italian Merchants in Late Thirteenth and Early Fourteenth Century England." In *The Dawn of Modern Banking*. New Haven: Yale University Press.

Rich, E. E., and C. H. Wilson, eds. 1977. *The Cambridge Economic History of Europe*. Vol. 5. London: Cambridge University Press.

Richards, R. D. 1929. *The Early History of Banking in England*. London: P. S. King & Sons.

Riu, Manuel. 1979. "Banking and Society in Late Medieval and Early Modern Aragon." In *The Dawn of Modern Banking*. New Haven: Yale University Press.

Shull, Bernard. 1999. "Banking, Commerce and Political Sovereignty: European Antecedents." In *European Monetary Union Banking Issues*. Ed. Irene Finel-Honigman. Stamford, Conn.: JAI Press.

Smith, Adam. 1937 (1776). *The Wealth of Nations*. New York: The Modern Library, Random House.

Spuford, Peter. 1988. *Money and Its Use in Medieval Europe*. Cambridge: Cambridge University Press.

Stanton, Thomas H. 1994. "Nonquantifiable Risks and Financial Institutions: The Mercantilist Legal Framework of Banks, Thrifts and Government-Sponsored Enterprises." In *Global Risk Based Capital Regulations*. Vol. 1. Ed. C. A. Stone and A. Zissu. Chicago: Irwin Professional Publishing.

Steuart, James. 1966 (1767). *An Inquiry into the Principles of Political Economy*. Vol. 2. Edinburgh: Oliver & Boyd.

Stigler, George. 1971. "The Theory of Economic Regulation." *Bell Journal of Economics and Management Science* 2, no. 1: 3–21.

Usher, A. P. 1943. *The Early History of Deposit Banking in Mediterranean Europe*. New York: Russell & Russell.

———. 1953. "The Origins of Banking: The Primitive Bank of Deposit, 1200–1600." In *Enterprise and Secular Trade*. Ed. Lane and Riemersma. Homewood, Ill.: Richard D. Irwin.

van Dillen, J. G. 1934. "The Bank of Amsterdam." In *History of the Principal Public Banks*. The Hague: Martinus Nijhoff.

White, Lawrence H. 1984. *Free Banking in Britain*. London: Cambridge University Press.

Williamson, Oliver E. 1984. *The Economic Institutions of Capitalism*. New York: The Free Press.

# 3

# Early Competition Policies
# in the United States

> The difference between England and the United States is simply this: in
> the former country, exclusive privileges are conferred on individuals who
> are called Lords; in the latter, exclusive privileges are conferred on cor-
> porations which are called Banks.
>
> William M. Gouge[1]

As indicated in Chapter 2, the importance of banking to both commercial
enterprise and governments was well understood by the leaders of the American Revolution. During the Revolutionary War, the Continental Congress,
with the Bank of England in mind, chartered the first American commercial
bank, the Bank of North America, to assist in financing the war. Over the next
two hundred years, tens of thousands of banks were chartered, under a variety
of government policies that alternately restrained and promoted competition.
The details notwithstanding, Congress and the states maintained distinctive
policies for banks throughout, separate from the generally procompetitive
policies developed for other private businesses.

This chapter describes the emergence of competition as a political and economic issue in banking and its relationship to regulation and supervision for
safety and soundness. It reviews the several policies undertaken in a succes-

sion of bank regulatory regimes from the late eighteenth century to the mid-twentieth century. At the end of this period, government had, for two decades following the massive bank failures of the early 1930s, suppressed bank rivalry with the aim of stabilizing the financial system. Thereafter, as addressed in the next chapter, competition in banking revived, with the assistance of new policies that for the first time applied antitrust law standards.

## THE COLONIAL PERSPECTIVE

While some English, Spanish, Dutch, and Portuguese coins circulated in the colonies, the inadequacy of the colonial payments system lead to a variety of experiments in paper currency, including the use of receipts against commodities like tobacco, the issuance by colonial governments of bills of credit which were, in essence, tax anticipation notes, and the issuance of bills by public and private "land banks." Whatever the form, notes were generally over-issued, and depreciated in value rapidly. In 1741, Parliament extended the Bubble Act to the colonies which restricted the issue of paper currency by land banks; it subsequently prohibited all paper currency.

Like other colonial powers, England viewed its colonies as useful to the extent they contributed to its own economic strength. Its mercantile policies aimed at transferring accumulations of gold and silver in the colonies to England itself. More generally the policy known as mercantilism, adopted by many European governments, aimed at building national states out of independent fiefdoms and towns. It included extensive government controls over production and prices, as well as trade. Manufacturing in the colonies was discouraged. The financing of trade was reserved for English merchants. Navigation acts required goods be shipped in British vessels, Enumeration acts listed articles that could only be exported to England, and the Molasses Act imposed duties on rum, sugar, and molasses from non-British sources.

These measures guaranteed the colonies would have a persistent trade deficit, and that gold and silver would flow to England in payment of the debt. In the colonies a variety of schemes were tried to retain coin, but were repeatedly frustrated by British countermeasures. Benjamin Franklin considered plans offered before 1764 to establish an American bank similar to the Bank of England, but thought it impractical because colonial trade "draws all the cash to Britain."[2]

By the time of the American Revolution, the advantages of commercial banking as a sound method for increasing paper currency beyond the limits of available gold and silver were widely appreciated. Comparing banks to the other great technological advance of that time, James Steuart, the Scottish economist, saw a bank as a "great engine" for improving trade and industry; and for reducing the interest burden of the crown.[3] Adam Smith saw the Bank of England as "a great engine of state."[4] For Alexander Hamilton, whose proposal ultimately led to the Bank of North America, who planned the First Bank of the United States, and who was instrumental in establishing the Bank of New York, banks were "the happiest engines that ever were invented for advancing trade."[5]

## FIRST POLICIES AND COMPETITIVE RESTRAINTS

Operating under the Articles of Confederation during the Revolution, the Continental Congress did not have power to tax, only to requisition the individual states, which might or might not meet the requisitions. It issued "bills of credit" which quickly depreciated in value because it had no capacity to meet its financial commitments. George Washington's army, according to Alexander Hamilton in 1780, had become "a mob . . . without clothing, without pay, without provision, without morals, without discipline."[6]

It was in this context that Hamilton urged the necessity of establishing a national bank.[7] He developed a detailed proposal for a bank in April 1781 in a letter to Robert Morris, who had been appointed superintendent of a newly created Department of Finance the previous year. Morris had announced that without a bank, he could make no progress in paying the army. In an insightful passage reminiscent of *Nishwar al-Muhadara* in the tenth century, Hamilton wrote,

The tendency of a national bank is to increase public and private credit. The former gives power to the state, . . . and the latter facilitates and extends the operations of commerce among individuals. Industry is increased, commodities are multiplied, agriculture and manufactures flourish, and herein consists the true wealth and prosperity of the state.[8]

The bank was to be a privately-run enterprise, like the Bank of England, not one owned and managed by the government like the Bank of Amsterdam. A decade later, in proposing to establish the Bank of the United States, Hamilton wrote,

It appears to be . . . essential, . . . that [the bank] . . . shall be under a private, not a public Direction, under the guidance of individual interests, not of public policy. . . . The keen, steady, and, as it were magnetic sense of their own interest as proprietors, in the direction of a bank, . . . is the only security that can always be relied upon for a careful and prudent administration.[9]

Hamilton resolved the issue in line with his intent to have wealthy merchants commit to the new government.

With its specie reserve borrowed from France, the Bank of North America was granted a charter by the Continental Congress in 1781. Because of uncertainty about the power of Congress to issue a charter, the bank also obtained charters from Pennsylvania, its home state; and also from New York and Massachusetts in whose principal cities it expected to do business. The new Bank extended a loan to the new government in the form of bank notes intended to circulate as currency.

The bank's charter was cryptic, with few powers or limitations specified. The prospectus for subscribers was more detailed. It indicated that the bank would issue notes, payable on demand in specie at the bank's offices, and that the notes would be receivable for duties and taxes in every state, and for requisitions made on the states by Congress; and that it would lend money to the government, as well as to businesses. Further, it acknowledged the legitimacy of public supervision in indicating that the Superintendent of Finance would, at all times, have access to the bank's records.[10]

Among the questions raised when Congress chartered the bank was whether it should be a monopoly. In the winter of 1779–1780, Alexander Hamilton had expressed opposition to granting monopoly privileges to the bank.[11] A year later he had changed his mind. In the plan he submitted to Robert Morris in 1781, he found monopoly necessary in that "other banks might excite a competition prejudicial to the interests of this and multiply and diversify paper credit too much."[12] Congress accepted this view, and expressed its intention that no other bank would be chartered during the War.[13] The bank secured similar promises from the states in which it was chartered.[14]

Many in the United States believed that one bank would be sufficient.[15] However, with states as successors to the sovereign power of the crown, a federal monopoly could barely be established and could not be sustained. After the war, the Bank of North America reverted to its Pennsylvania charter. Other states began to charter new banks. All were established through legislative grants that implied more or less exclusive privileges.

As noted in Chapter 2, corporate charters originally provided the exclusive privilege of engaging in the activity specified. Banks already in existence frequently assumed that no other banks would be chartered. They put pressure on state legislatures to keep out unchartered competitors. As soon as bank notes became a prominent a form of currency, states began passing "restraining laws," reserving banking functions for chartered banks and overriding the common law rights of individuals to issue their own notes.[16] Massachusetts prohibited banking associations not authorized by law in 1799. New Hampshire passed a law prohibiting private banking in the same years. In 1804 New York enacted a law specifying that only corporations could issue notes that circulated as currency. Other states followed suit.[17]

Between 1781 and 1816, three banking charters were issued by Congress: In addition to the charter for the Bank of North America, it provided charters to the First Bank of the United States (1791–1811), and the Second Bank of the United States (1816–1836). All others were issued by state legislatures. In 1836, there were 713 state-chartered banks in the United States (Table 3.1).

Exclusive privileges, if not actual monopoly, raised serious questions in principle and, as discussed below, in actuality. Why, in a country energized by freedom of opportunity for individuals to engage in any business, and founded on an aggressive opposition to trade restrictions, was banking held out as an exception? Perhaps because of European experience and in particu-

**Table 3.1**
**Numbers of the Banks, 1781–1960**

| Year | Bank Classification | | |
|---|---|---|---|
| | State Banks | National Banks | Private Banks |
| 1791* | 4 | 1 | |
| 1794* | 18 | 1 | |
| 1800* | 29 | 1 | |
| 1804* | 45 | 1 | |
| 1811* | 88 | 1 | |
| 1820* | 307 | 1 | |
| 1830* | 329 | 1 | |
| 1834 | 506 | 1 | |
| 1836 | 713 | 1 | |
| 1840 | 901 | 0 | |
| 1850 | 824 | 0 | |
| 1860 | 1,562 | 0 | |
| 1863 | 1,466 | 66 | |
| 1864 | 1,089 | 467 | |
| 1865 | 349 | 1,294 | |
| 1866 | 297 | 1,634 | |
| 1870 | 325 | 1,612 | |
| 1880 | 650 | 2,076 | 2,573 |
| 1890 | 2,250 | 3,484 | 4,305 |
| 1900 | 5,007 | 3,731 | 5,178 |
| 1910 | 14,348 | 7,138 | 3,669 |
| 1920 | 20,635 | 8,024 | 1,736 |
| 1929 | 16,728 | 7,530 | 685 |
| 1930 | 15,798 | 7,247 | 598 |
| 1933 | 8,908 | 4,897 | 330 |
| 1940 | 9,238 | 5,164 | 57 |
| 1950** | 9,163 | 5,992 | |
| 1960** | 8,942 | 4,530 | |

Sources: Board of Governors of the Federal Reserve System, 1941, *Banking Studies* (August), 418, except where otherwise identified. *Historical Statistics of the U.S., Colonial Times to 1957*, Part 2, Banking (Washington, D.C.: U.S. Department of Commerce, 1960).

*Bray Hammond, *Banks and Politics in America* (Princeton, N.J.: Princeton University Press, 1957), 144ff.

**Banking and Monetary Statistics: 1941–70* (Washington, D.C.: Board of Governors of the Federal Reserve System, 1976).

lar, England's success. Revolutionary leaders in the American colonies and Alexander Hamilton in particular, had available important reference works on European banking.[18] Moreover, they also had firsthand knowledge of the debilitating effects of an overproduction of paper currency from competing sources; and, like others before them, may have been concerned that competition would undermine depositor and note holder confidence.

## THE AMERICAN BANKING MODEL: BENEFITS, COSTS, AND PERENNIAL ISSUES

Modeled on the Bank of England, the first American banks were private establishments employed as public agents.[19] They obtained important privileges or benefits from the governments that chartered them in return for the services they provided. Monopoly was a benefit, such as it was. But more or less exclusive grants by government raised serious economic issues that, over the course of the nineteenth and twentieth centuries, were raised repeatedly, resolved, and then resolved again. These included questions regarding new entry into banking, restrictions on banking activities, the pricing of banking services, and mergers. In this section we examine the mutuality underlying the banking model that was adopted and the enduring competitive issues that it raised. In the following section we follow the course of these competitive issues through a series of bank regulatory regimes.

### Mutuality

According to the historian Bray Hammond, "The realistic view was that the community, whether shrewdly or not, had adapted private initiative and wealth to public purposes, granting privileges and exacting duties in return."[20] This, of course, was what European governments had been doing for about 300 years. In early nineteenth-century United States, each bank charter was subject to bargaining between applicants and legislatures in ways that today would be scandalous. Everything was negotiable, including the length of the charter, capitalization, branching restrictions, and the price to be paid by the applicant.[21] The government–bank relationship of the early charters was defined through a number of elements, most importantly including what banks were expected to do for the government and what the government would do for them in return. In general, the benefits provided by the early charters to banks and the services provided the chartering governments, under successive banking regimes, are outlined in the following list:

**Initial Policies: 1787–1830s**

*Principal Public Benefits*
- Extension of credit to government
- Increase in currency (bank notes) beyond available gold and silver

*Principal Bank Benefits*
- Corporate status
- Right to issue promissory notes payable on demand
- Monopoly privileges/competitive restrictions
- Some expectation of ad hoc assistance for troubled banks

*Elements of Competition Policy*
- Competitive restrictions imposed by chartering process

## Free Banking: 1837–1863

*Principal Public Benefits*
- Improved market for state securities
- Uniform currency statewide
- Value of currency stabilized by collateralization

*Principal Bank Benefits*
- Corporate status
- Banks notes countersigned by state official
- Exclusion of nonchartered firms from issuing currency

*Elements of Competition Policy*
- Lowered legal barrier to entry in free banking states
- Restrictions on branching

## National Banking: 1863–1913

*Principal Public Benefits*
- Improved market for treasury securities
- Uniform national currency
- Value of currency stabilized by collateralization and by government guarantee
- Expectation of lower risk for deposits through reserve requirements

*Principal Bank Benefits*
- Corporate status
- National bank notes issued by Comptroller of the Currency and guaranteed by federal government
- Expectation of ad hoc government assistance through shifting treasury deposits

*Elements of Competition Policy*
- Barriers to entry high as a result of high capital requirements and limits on volume of national bank notes
- Branching prohibited
- Unplanned growth in numbers of state banks and development of trust companies

### Federal Reserve Act, 1913

*Principal Public Benefits* (banking system)
- Provision for an elastic currency
- Promote development of commercial paper market for better geographic allocation of credit to rural areas and farmers
- Promote development of bankers' acceptance market to promote foreign trade
- Assist in improved payments system

*Principal Bank Benefits*
- Low cost credit at discount window
- Clearing and settlement facilities
- Expectation of emergency assistance

*Elements of Competition Policy*
- No liberalization of branching restrictions
- Established Federal Reserve as competitor for private clearing house associations
- Some liberalization of national bank lending and investing powers

### Banking Acts, 1933–1935

*Principal Public Benefits* (banking system)
- Reduction in failure rate
- Congressional sanction for use of open market operations as key monetary policy tool
- Banks positioned to support substantial increase in federal borrowing

*Principal Bank Benefits*
- Establishment of interest rate maximum on time and savings deposits
- Prohibition of interest payments on demand deposits
- New restrictions on entry by new charter
- Federal deposit insurance

*Elements of Competition Policy*
- Restrictions on competition indicated as bank benefits above
- Cooperation supported by bank regulatory agencies
- Separation of commercial and investment banking
- Minor liberalization of branch banking for national banks, providing equality with state-chartered banks

The early banks, like the Bank of North America, the Bank of New York and the Bank of Massachusetts, as well as the Bank of the United States, were expected to lend to the governments that chartered them, along with operating as private, profit-making corporations providing banking services to merchants. The Bank of New York took pride in the accommodation it could provide the state and the federal government.[22] In Pennsylvania each bank chartered was required to lend to the state as a condition of the charter.[23]

Mutuality was repeatedly a subject of contention. For example, when Andrew Jackson vetoed the bill to recharter the Second Bank of the United States in 1832, he argued that the bank's charter involved the sale by the government of an exclusive privilege for which the government was not exacting "as much as [it] is worth on the open market."[24]

Competitive restrictions imposed by government, in granting exclusive privileges and by passage of restraining acts, supported the franchise values of chartered banks, but presumably benefitted government as well by enhancing bank stability. Government assistance for troubled banks can be similarly interpreted. It clearly benefitted bank owners and creditors, but from the government's point of view, the costs of assistance might be far less than the costs of failures. The costs of failure would include not simply the loss of banking services to merchants, but to the government itself; and also the loss of the government's relational-specific investment in the failing bank—to say nothing of the potentially large costs to the economies of the community, region, and/or nation associated with any systemic event that might follow failure. Competitive restraints and troubled-bank assistance can be thought of as providing reciprocal benefits, within an implicit contractual framework, that reflect the underlying symbiosis.

We now understand that competitive restraints produce inefficiencies; and that once the government provides assistance, an expectation of future assistance is likely to be created that encourages excessive risk-taking. The adverse effects of competitive restraints did not escape the public, as is discussed in the next section; nor, at least intuitively, did the effects of a safety net.

### Development of Perennial Issues

In a market economy, the geographic domain of a firm, the scope of its activities, the duration of its operations, and its prudent management are determined by individual owners and managers operating under market constraints imposed by demands for their products and services, costs of production, the state of technology, and the degree of competition. With the grant of exclusive privileges, limits on market competition becomes a governmental decision. The government, in one form or another, is likely to determine the number of firms that can operate, their geographic locations, the scope and limits of their activities and, since rivalry is limited, the peripheral protections, if any, that will be afforded customers. Since, by definition, the chosen industry is of particular importance to the government, the prudent management of its firms and their safety and soundness require the establishment of standards (regulation) and monitoring (supervision). These decisions, being political, are open to political debate. With exclusive privilege being an anomaly in a free market economy, it is hardly surprising that their specific character has been repeatedly challenged. The result has been two-hundred years of revisiting the same issues.

The origin of the issues is discussed next. Their recurrence through repeated legislative change is discussed in the following section.

### Chartering and Numbers

The legislative chartering process in the early nineteenth century raised a legal barrier to entry. Restrictions notwithstanding, the numbers of chartered banks grew rapidly. In 1794 there were eighteen banks in the United States; and by 1800, twenty-nine in twenty-four cities. By 1804 it was estimated that there were forty-five banks throughout the country, and by 1811 there were eighty-nine.[25] An act passed in Pennsylvania in 1814 granted identical charters to forty-one banks (see Table 3.2).

When Congress did not recharter the Bank of the United States in 1811, there was a substantial upsurge in the number of state-chartered banks. By 1820, there were 307 banks. With the establishment of the Second Bank of the United States in 1816, and its exercise of effective restraints on state bank notes in the early 1820s, the growth in numbers of state banks slowed down. There were still only a little over 300 by 1830.

Andrew Jackson's veto of a bill to recharter the Second Bank of the United States in July 1832 combined with a speculative boom resulted in another upsurge in numbers of state-chartered banks. By the time the Second Bank's charter expired in 1836, there were over 700 state banks in existence.

In addition to chartered banks, private banking firms thrived even though prohibited from issuing bank notes. Stephen Girard in Philadelphia and Alexander Brown in Baltimore operated successful nonchartered banks. In the Western states, the numbers grew substantially before the Civil War. It has been estimated that there were about 400 private banks in 1853 and over 1,000 in 1860.[26] Some of these private banking partnerships developed, later in the century, into well-known investment banking houses.

There is little available information on the extent to which the increasing numbers of state-chartered banks affected competitive conditions in local communities in the first four decades of the eighteenth century. Whatever their impact, the perception of chartered banks as government-established monopolies remained.

### Branch Banking

The slow development of branch banking in the United States is typically attributed to the primitive transportation and communication technology that existed in the nineteenth century and the long distances between population centers. However, in some states branching was probably discouraged by laws that referred, in the singular, to a bank's place of business.

Branch banking, nevertheless, did develop early. The First Bank of the United States had its home office in Philadelphia and branches in eight other cities; the Second Bank of the United States also had its head office in Philadelphia, and branches in twenty-five other cities.[27] These were necessary to facilitate the banks' function as a fiscal agent for the federal government. The Bank of the State of South Carolina and the State Bank of Indiana also had networks of branch offices prior to the Civil War.

Branch banking by the Second Bank of the United States precipitated a federal–state conflict whose high points included the landmark Supreme Court decision in *McCulloch v. Maryland* holding unconstitutional Maryland's attempt to tax the Baltimore branch of the bank. Justice Marshall's opinion found the Maryland tax unconstitutional on the grounds that a federal government with responsibility for declaring and conducting war and raising armies and navies must also be able to charter a bank that would create credit and money immune from attacks by the states. His reference to the inextricable connection between the "the sword and the purse" concisely summarized centuries of banking history. "It may, with great reason, be contended, that a government entrusted with such ample powers . . . must also be intrusted with the ample means for their execution."[28]

President Andrew Jackson understood the sword better than the purse. He found the branches of the Second Bank objectionable. In his veto message, he wrote that "it cannot . . . be 'necessary' or 'proper' to authorize the bank to locate branches where it pleases to perform the public service, without consulting the Government and contrary to its will."[29] When a bill to establish a Third Bank of the United States was passed by Congress in 1841, President Tyler vetoed it, stating that he would oppose any bank created by Congress having the power to establish branches in the states without their consent.[30]

### Activity Limits

The charters of early U.S. banks were not always specific in their definition of banking, but they did limit bank activities. There were two reasons. The first, already mentioned, was the concern that the franchise would permit banks to dominate other businesses. The second was to prevent banks from investing in illiquid and risky assets.

Many of the early charters included a prohibition on dealing in merchandise.[31] This restriction provided some assurance bank lending would be "arms length," and not simply directed toward nonbanking enterprises that the bank owned. Some charters included restrictions on owning real estate.[32]

In 1785, the state of Pennsylvania repealed the charter it had granted to the Bank of North America, in part on the grounds that there were insufficient limits on the bank's powers. The bank was rechartered in 1787, with limits on its activities, including a restriction on dealing in merchandise. The limits, in fact, were suggested by the bank's proponents.[33] In New York, none of the bank charters issued before 1825 defined the scope of what a bank could do. The legislature relied on restrictive clauses inserted in each charter. In each case, the charters it issued contained a clause indicating that trading or dealing in stocks (securities), goods, wares, and merchandise was not included within the scope of banking.[34]

In 1825 however, in granting two bank charters the New York legislature included a definition of banking powers that was, in substance, to be adopted by other states and in subsequent federal legislation. Banks would

possess all incidental and necessary powers to carry on the business of banking—by discounting bills, notes and other evidences of debt; by receiving deposits; by buying gold and silver, bullion and foreign coins; by buying and selling bills of exchange, and by issuing bills, notes and other evidences of debt; but the said Company shall have and possess no other powers whatever, except such as are expressly granted by this act.[35]

This specification was incorporated into general law in 1827. From 1829 to 1838, when New York's General Banking Act (free banking law) was passed, the legislature, "notwithstanding the express prohibition [in state law against dealing in merchandise, etc.] from abundant caution, inserted in each of these charters, an express prohibition against these banks, dealing or trading in . . . goods, wares, merchandise, commodities."[36] An important court decision held that "independently of the general Bank Act [of 1838], these banks have no corporate existence, and they are thus created with restricted and limited powers, for a special purpose."[37]

The restrictions on banking were always under pressure. Reserving bank services for governments and merchants proved too narrow a definition of "public function." Commercial groups such as farmers, cotton growers, lumbermen, and mechanics were able to persuade legislatures that it was in the public interest to charter banks to serve their special needs. States needing to build roads, canals and, later, railroads chartered banks to finance internal improvements.[38] A notable example of granting more expansive powers involved the rechartering of the Second Bank of the United States by Pennsylvania after its federal charter expired in 1836. The bank thereafter invested heavily in securities, attempted to support the market for cotton, and failed in 1841.[39] The bank's failure was followed by a grand jury indictment of its President (Nicolas Biddle) for conspiracy to defraud his shareholders; the indictment was quashed. In a review of the issue fifty years later, it was concluded that he was not guilty of anything but bad banking.[40] In 1857 the New York Court of Appeals acknowledged that the state's banking act did not list all authorized powers, which included, but were not necessarily limited to, those implicit powers needed to exercise the powers that were explicitly listed. In particular, the court decided that banks had the right to borrow money by issuing bonds, even though this power was not specified in the act.[41]

In New York however, bank powers, whether explicit or implicit, did not include the power to engage in mercantile enterprises. As late as 1854, banking legislation introduced in the New York state legislature to establish standards for the formation of banking corporations included the provision that the corporation "shall not, directly or indirectly, deal or trade in buying or selling any goods, wares, merchandise or commodities. . . ." Even at that time, the provision apparently existed in all bank charters.[42]

The essence of the New York definition of banking powers was widely adopted elsewhere and in particular by the National Banking Act. It remains to this day a description of banking powers for national banks. Over the next 175 years, the meaning of its terms were repeatedly disputed as banks were confronted by changes in institutions, technology, and by new, less restricted competitors.

### Regulation, Supervision, and a "Safety Net"

As noted, supervision and regulation were implicit in the early charter grants, as had been the case in Europe. The dependency of both business and government on bank stability and the implicit government assurance of assistance in exigent circumstances made necessary both monitoring by official bodies, and regulatory restrictions to minimize the likelihood of failure and instability. Such assurances, however vague, in and of themselves tended to encourage risk-taking by banks and further exposed bank customers and the government to risk.

The close affiliation of banks with the governments that chartered them implied that they could expect assistance when in trouble. When, in 1796, the Bank of New York found it was overextended and pressed for payment in specie by the First Bank of the United States, it asked Secretary of the Treasury Oliver Wolcott for assistance. In a stance similar to that of the British Treasury during the Bank of England's troubles in 1696 (discussed in Chapter 2) and foreshadowing the future of government–bank relationships in the United States, he wrote "The Bank . . . might rest assured of as full and cordial assistance from him as was in his power." At the same time, he may have recognized the problem his seemingly necessary response created. He privately observed that "these institutions have all been mismanaged; I look upon them with terror. They are at present the curse, and I fear they will prove the ruin of the Government."[43]

### COMPETITIVE ISSUES IN CHANGING REGIMES

With governments, state and/or federal, making decisions about the numbers of banks that would exist, the geographic limits of their office locations, the scope of their activities, and the quality of their management and operations, it is not surprising that comprehensive overhauls of the regulatory/supervisory system were periodically necessary. With governments needing well-functioning banks for both monetary and fiscal reasons and imposing a pattern of control to meet their needs, they took responsibility for preventing financial crises and bank failures long before taking responsibility for overall economic stability. The latter imperative was a product of the twentieth century.

Crises and failures notwithstanding, the exclusive privileges granted banks also created a continuing incentive for nonbanking firms to invade traditional banking markets through financial innovations and thereby diminish the franchise value of banks. And banks, similarly motivated by profit, were impelled to find ways to expand their geographic and product scope. Bank regulators, on their own initiative, might make minor adjustments in support of an industry whose safety and soundness they were mandated to protect. Major adjustments, at least in the nineteenth and early twentieth centuries required new legislation.

The result was periodic legislative reforms that altered the character of banking and its regulation. These included pre–Civil War free banking laws, the National Banking Act passed during the Civil War, the Federal Reserve Act passed in 1913, and the banking reforms of 1933 and 1935. At each of these junctures, the perennial issues were revisited, and for a time, resolved. The role of competition in banking was a recurrent theme. In the several sections that follow, we review the competitive questions that developed in successive banking regimes.

### Free Banking

Corporate charters for banks continued to be legislative grants until passage of "free banking" laws beginning in the late 1830s that established administrative processes for chartering and made obtaining charters relatively easy. Free banking legislation was passed in eighteen of the thirty-three states prior to the Civil War, though free banks were chartered in only ten. In some states, such as Texas and Arkansas, where "hard money" views prevailed and bank money was an anathema, note-issuing banks were simply not chartered. In others, like Wisconsin, legislation made banking unlawful. In still others, like Indiana and Iowa, banking became a state-run enterprise. Even though restricted in its geographic scope, the impact of free banking on subsequent developments was profound.

The first free banking laws were a response to economic distress. Widespread speculation in the early 1830s had been followed by panic and depression in 1837. In January of 1838, all the banks in New York and most throughout the country had suspended specie payments. Large numbers of banks failed. A free banking law was enacted in Michigan in 1837, and a more influential one was enacted in New York in 1838. Free banking laws spread to over half the states before the Civil War.

The General Banking Act of 1838 in New York served as a prototype. Its centerpiece was a new plan to support the notes then commonly issued by banks in making loans. Banks were compelled to purchase government securities and transfer them to the Comptroller in New York state to obtain that promissory notes, payable on demand they could then lend to their customers. The notes, countersigned by the state official, were collateralized by the securities.

Paralleling the Bank of England scheme discussed in Chapter 2, the free banking plan had the practical effect of improving the market for government securities. Initially, the securities to be transferred were limited to the public debt of the United States, the state of New York and other states approved by the New York Comptroller. In 1840, however, the act was amended to allow the Comptroller to receive, for circulating notes, only the "public stock issued, and to be issued by this State."[44]

Of particular importance, free banking laws removed the bank chartering decision from state legislatures. State banking officials and/or agencies, such as now exist in every state, were established to evaluate applications and supervise banks. They were to issue charters on the basis of relatively simple conditions that could be easily met. No limits were set on the numbers of charters they could issue.

Free banking laws moved the banking business toward the economic mainstream of free enterprise. Henry Charles Carey, a prominent economist, provided a rationale:

Governments have arrogated to themselves the task of regulating the currency, and the natural effect is that nothing is less regular. . . . Were government to regulate the markets as they do the currency, there would be a succession of oversupplies, during which vast quantities of provisions would be spoiled, followed by a succession of scarcities, when double prices would be paid for the necessaries of life, precisely as is now the case with money. . . . There is no more propriety or necessity for regulating who shall or who shall not issue his note, to be exchanged with those who are willing to take it, than there is for regulating who shall or who shall not grow potatoes or make shoes.[45]

It would be a mistake, however, to attribute the free banking reform to economics alone. There were social and political motives as well. In proposing passage of New York's law, Governor William L. Marcy proclaimed that "monopolies are undoubtedly incompatible with the equality of civil rights which is the great object of a free government."[46] William Leggett, a well-known New York journalist of this era, expressed the political objective as follows:

The great object which we desire . . . is the utter and complete divorcement of politics from the business of banking. We desire to see banking divorced not only from federal legislation, but from state legislation. Nothing but evil, either in this country or others, has arisen from their union. . . . Men want no laws on the subject, except for the punishment of frauds . . . no laws except such as are necessary for the protection of their equal rights.[47]

Over a century later, Bray Hammond, a Secretary of the Federal Reserve Board and historian, summed up the motivation as follows: "A feeling also arose that banking should not be a privilege granted to a few favored persons but a business like any other, open to anyone able to engage in it."[48] He suggested that "free banking was an application of laissez faire to the monetary function."[49]

Perhaps so! But free banking laws did not make banking "a business like any other business." Each bank remained a differentiated "monied corporation" with a grant to run an enterprise with limited powers. This was the case even as states began passing general incorporation laws that produced the modern corporate charter, "readily available and a right to conduct any lawful business."[50]

The free banking law in New York, as in a number of states, established an elaborate system of regulation and supervision. Among other things, the New York law provided for reporting and examinations, imposed minimum capital requirements and, initially, reserve requirements. As a New York court stated, the business of banking is an exercise of "public powers," and "public powers are never granted without some *public object* in view: especially is this true, in respect to banking corporations, whose operations affect the currency, and thus the whole community."[51]

As discussed, the restrictive specification of banking powers had been dealt with in New York prior to its free banking legislation in 1838. The separation of banking from other forms of commercial activity was repeatedly confirmed.

While free banking laws did not substantially modify the traditional government–bank association, it did eliminate an important barrier to new entry in banking. Easy chartering has been the characteristic most often emphasized. In twenty months after passage of the New York law, 134 new free banks were chartered.[52]

The actual number of banks in the United States did increase from about 900 to 1,500 between 1840 and 1860. On the basis of a state-by-state analysis, however, one recent study contends that neither the numbers of banks nor bank assets systematically rose as the result of free banking laws, *except in New York*.[53] However, it is necessary to keep in mind that a decline in the legal barrier to new entry in banking is not necessarily inconsistent with little change in *actual* new entry. The legal barrier is not the only determinant. As will be discussed more fully in Chapter 6, other demand and supply factors that affect expected profits make it possible for the legal barrier to new entry to fall, and actual entry to rise, fall or remain unchanged. Nevertheless, the decline in the legal barrier itself would tend to intensify competition by threatening established banks and thereby influencing their behavior and performance.

On the other hand, free banking laws may have discouraged branch banking. The New York law contained a mandate that "the usual business of banking shall be transacted at the place where such banking association shall be located." The term "at the place," being in the singular, was subject to the interpretation that a bank could have only one office. The substance behind the legalism was probably an effort to discourage so-called "wildcat banks" that issued notes from convenient home offices, but only redeemed them in specie at branches in remote locations. State policies aimed also to constrain "shaving shops," the branch offices of a bank where its own notes were redeemed at a discount.[54] The dodge was not new. It will be recalled that in 1445, Venice found it necessary to require bankers to be at their place of business daily to keep them from avoiding creditors who might want their money.

Free banking laws were, without doubt, a major reform that ushered in a new kind of banking regime in the United States. Most importantly, they made charters easily available. Despite the classical liberalism of many of its proponents, however, they did not divorce banking from government. The banking charter remained limited, and state governments did not relinquish the traditional use of banks in the service of public finance. Not only did free banking laws provide support for state securities, but many states also obtained substantial revenues by investing funds in bank stocks, from taxes on banks, and from "chartering bonuses" which they collected from applicants.[55]

### The National Banking System

The critical financial exigencies of the Civil War, along with congressional dissatisfaction with a currency system dependent on a wide variety of differentially functional banks whose notes fluctuated in value with their ability to redeem them in specie—and were unevenly regulated and supervised by the several states—led to the establishment of the National Banking System. Legislation in 1863, 1664, and 1865 established the new system. It constituted a return of the federal government to active involvement in banking, for the first time since the demise of the Second Bank of the United States.

In providing for the chartering of national banks by the federal government, it also effectively abolished state banking for a time. Senator John Sherman, the principal author of the 1863 act, noted that the state systems did not provide the federal government with the financial support that was necessary during the Civil War.[56] Later, when the legality of the National Banking Act was challenged, the Supreme Court affirmed that banks "are instruments designed to be used to aid the government in the administration of an important branch of the public services."[57]

The new National Banking System followed free banking precedent by creating an administrative officer in the Treasury Department, the Comptroller of the Currency, to charter and supervise national banks. It provided for a new uniform national currency by establishing national bank notes. When Congress found large numbers of state banks refusing to convert to national bank charters, it imposed a prohibitive tax on their notes that took the profit out of their business.[58] As can be seen in Table 3.1, the numbers of state banks declined precipitously in 1865 after the tax measure was passed.

National bank notes were to be stable at their face value, regardless of the issuing national bank. In addition to being secured by the bank's assets, they were secured by the Treasury bonds each bank had to purchase and deposit in order to obtain the notes. If a national bank failed, its notes were to be immediately paid by the Treasury, even if the prices of the underlying bonds were depressed. In other words, the full faith and credit of the government was also pledged for redemption.[59]

To encourage prudent operations and sustain safety and soundness, the law established a rigorous system of supervision and regulation, including lending and investing limits. Maximums were imposed on loans to single borrowers and on total borrowing. Minimum capital requirements were established. The New York banking law had been amended in 1846 to impose double liability on bank stockholders, making them liable not only to the extent of their shares, but for an additional amount equal to their shares. The National Banking Act followed suit. The framers of the law believed that they could also make national bank deposits, as opposed to notes, more secure and therefore more attractive by establishing reserve requirements. In practice, Treasury operations also provided assistance to banks during periods of financial stress by shifting deposits and bank reserves where needed.[60]

While these regulatory restrictions imposed costs on national banks, there were also benefits (see page 49). National banks were designated as depositories for public funds. The rate at which they obtained notes in exchange for government bonds was intended to yield a profit and, for a time, did.[61] In the latter part of the nineteenth century the profitability of national bank notes declined as interest rates fell and bond prices rose.[62] National banks were easily and favorably identified by having the term "national" as a required part of their name, and prohibiting the use of the term "national" in the name of any other bank. Membership in the system was intended to inspire confidence in customers. The Comptroller of the Currency would of necessity have an interest in both their safety and profitability. A bank's circulating notes, with its name, also constituted a form of advertising.[63]

National bank powers, and the limits placed upon them, were patterned after New York banking law. National banks were authorized to "issue circulating notes, discount bills, notes, and other debt, receive deposits, buy and sell gold and silver bullion, foreign coins, and bills of exchange, loan money, and to exercise such incidental powers as shall be deemed necessary to carry on the business of banking;" they were restricted to "discounting and negotiating promissory notes, . . . and other evidences of debt; . . . loaning money on personal security."[64] The law did not permit them to make mortgage loans. In litigation it was determined that they could not, in general, invest in real estate; that they could accept corporate stock as collateral and as payment for debt, but could not deal in or purchase stock as an investment; that they could not, under any circumstances, become a partner in a business in which they could incur unlimited liability; further, it was beyond their power to engage in the operation of a business, even if it had been acquired in satisfaction of a debt.[65]

Competition would presumably be served in the same way it had been under the state free banking laws. Charter requirements were to be relatively easy, and there were no restrictions on the number of banks the Comptroller could charter. However, the capital requirements that had been established, and perhaps unintended limits on the volume of national bank notes which were tied to a declining federal government debt, restricted the number of national banks for decades. Comptrollers were also choosy about applicants. For years they required that an application for a new charter be endorsed by a congressman, or accompanied by character references from prominent citizens.[66] The Comptroller also required that prominent citizens vouch for the needs in the community where the bank was to be located.

The issue of branching was not explicitly addressed in the legislation establishing the National Banking System. The absence of explicit consideration is typically attributed to a lack of interest among bankers in having more than one office. According to a recent Treasury Report, "Apparently, unit banks had a comparative advantage over branch banks."[67] There is, however, little evidence on this issue. In any event, Congress adopted the phraseology in the New York banking law, referring in the singular to the place of business of the bank. In 1911, the Comptroller of the Currency requested an opinion of the Attorney General as to whether national banks were permitted to have branch offices. The opinion was that they could not. In subsequent litigation, the Supreme Court came to the same conclusion.[68]

With the procompetitive effects of easy entry by new charter limited by regulatory restrictions, and branch banking frustrated by court interpretation, new competition for national banks emerged from outside the system. State banks, as can be seen in Table 3.1, revived in the 1870s and 1980s. They found, as had the British joint stock companies earlier in the century, that they didn't have to issue promissory notes payable on demand in making loans to operate effectively; deposit banking was a convenient, and in a number of ways, a preferable substitute. Along with trust companies and unincorporated banks, state banks emerged as new competitors. All were less regulated competitors who not only competed by offering traditional banking services, but by offering services not permitted to national banks.[69] In general, state banks had lower capital and reserve requirements and were less restricted in lending and investing. In addition, they were not as well supervised or examined.[70]

A rivalry in chartering new banks developed between the Comptroller of the Currency and state banking supervisors. In 1891 the Comptroller dropped a requirement that prominent citizens vouch for the needs in the community.[71] At the Comptroller's urging, Congress lowered the tax on national bank currency in 1900 and permitted currency to be issued up to 100 percent of the par value of the bonds securing it. When Congress lowered capital requirements in 1900 for banks in small rural towns (under 3,000 people) the number of newly chartered national banks increased significantly.[72]

These changes, however, did not reinvigorate the system. Between 1900 and 1914, the number of state banks grew by over 12,000; while the number of national banks increased by about 4,000.[73]

The branching issue was raised seriously with the development of new population centers in the mid- and far-west at the beginning of the twentieth century. States typically prohibited banks in other states from opening branch offices. Between 1910 and 1930, many states passed legislation that restricted branch banking. While some states prohibited branching completely, others limited branching to restricted areas such as counties, while others didn't restrict it at all.

In Midwestern states, in particular, rural banks that opposed the expansion of large, urban-based banks as competitive threats were influential in obtaining legislation that prohibited it entirely. By 1939, thirteen states prohibited branching or had no legislation authorizing it; and seventeen states limited branching to home office cities, counties, or other restricted geographic areas within the state.[74] Among the more popular concerns was the fear that deposit funds accumulated by branch offices in rural communities would be shifted to home offices in large urban areas where they would be loaned and invested—an early concern about "redlining."

The result in those states that restricted branching was that the expanding needs for banking services were met by newly chartered banks. The number of banks increased to a peak of about 30,000 in 1921.

National banks, which were not permitted to have branch offices, were at a competitive disadvantage in states that permitted their own banks to branch. It was not until passage of the McFadden Act of 1927 and its amendment in 1933 that national banks were granted the authority to branch, and then only to the same extent as the laws in their home states permitted.

The bank holding company emerged in the early years of the twentieth century as a way to circumvent restrictive branching laws. Banks in states with restrictive branching laws could organize holding companies that, in turn, could own and control as many banks as it could charter or acquire. Moreover, multiple-bank holding companies could acquire banks in multiple states.

Few states prohibited both branching and multiple-bank holding companies. Illinois was one of the few states that prohibited both holding companies and branch banking. When the Continental Illinois Bank, one of the largest in the United States at the time with $47 billion in assets, failed in 1982, it had only one office in the Chicago loop.

Ross Robertson, the economic historian who authored the official history of the Office of the Comptroller of the Currency, viewed the period from 1880 to 1907 as one in which banking was nearer to the free market model than it ever has been in the United States—as close to "free banking as the country has ever experienced."[75] He had in mind the intensification of competition emerging out of increased numbers of banks, and the circumvention of legal and regulatory restrictions.

Limitations on banking powers in the National Banking Act were overcome by large banks at the beginning of the twentieth century. National banks that wanted to engage in investment banking and other activities were faced by adverse court decisions precluding them from investing or dealing in corporate stock. The Comptroller of the Currency brought the adverse court decisions to their attention in letters. Excerpts of at least one can be found in his *Annual Report* for 1915.[76] In response, large national banks in New York and Chicago organized state-chartered affiliates. Principally owned *pro rata* by bank stockholders and controlled by bank management, the affiliates often had powers that permitted almost any kind of transaction. Realty, insurance, and mortgage company affiliates were also acquired and frequently had their main offices in the same building as the bank.[77]

George Baker, chairman of the board of First National Bank of New York, in candid testimony in 1913 before the Congressional committee, "To Investigate the Concentration of Control of Money and Credit" (Pujo Committee), indicated what had happened. The story unfolded in his response to the questions of Louis Untermeyer, counsel for the committee:

UNTERMEYER: "Mr. Baker, what was the purpose of organizing the security company?"

BAKER: "For doing business that was not specially authorized by the banking act. We held some securities that in the early days were considered perfectly proper, but under some later decisions of the courts the holding of bank stock or other stock was prohibited; *at any rate the comptroller prohibited it.*"

And a little later in his testimony,

BAKER: "The purchase of bank stocks or any other stocks for years and years was never questioned by the comptroller."

UNTERMEYER: "Until when?"

BAKER: "Until probably 10 years ago."

UNTERMEYER: "And for how many years did you continue to carry stocks in the First National Bank after the right to do so was questioned?"

BAKER: "Probably for five or six years; but after we were told that we absolutely must not do it, we stopped it."[78]

The Comptroller of the Currency accepted the development of affiliates as beyond his capacity to challenge. He took the position that "security companies are corporations . . . with which I have nothing to do. . . . They are not under my jurisdiction in any way, shape, or form."[79] His position effectively removed the security activities of national banks from regulation, at least for a time, without any measures to insulate the national banks from problems arising in their affiliates, or to lessen potential conflicts of interest.

The report of the committee "To Investigate the Concentration of Control of Money and Credit" complained about the unregulated expansion of bank activities through affiliates, condemned control by investment bankers of commercial and industrial firms, and offered proposals to correct the problems that it saw. Bankers considered the hearings and deliberations of the committee hostile and unfair. Some of the partners of J. P. Morgan & Co. attributed the subsequent death of J. P. Morgan to the pressures imposed by the committee's interrogation of him in 1912.[80]

The committee's opposition to the development of bank affiliates and the unrestricted expansion of bank powers nevertheless had little legislative impact at the time. Two decades later, however, in 1933, with the banking system in shambles and the country in depression, similar arguments helped shape the Glass–Steagall Act.

The latter years of the nineteenth century and early years of the twentieth century are similar to recent decades in the circumvention of old regulatory restrictions and the development of new competitors. In the former period, however, banking competition was muted by industry self-regulation principally through clearinghouse associations. Associations had organized in local areas for the efficient exchange, clearing, and settlement of checks. The New York Clearing House Association, the first, had been established in 1857. Over the years, associations took on additional functions. They assumed the authority to expand currency during periods of financial stress by issuing clearinghouse certificates. They prescribed accounting and reporting standards, liquidity and capital requirements, and conducted examinations of their members.[81] In addition, they formulated competition policy for their members by prohibiting interest payments on deposits and fixing interest rates on loans, prohibiting banks from accepting customers of other banks and regulating advertising. Violators were threatened with expulsion from membership and the withdrawal "of indispensable privileges."[82]

With all its changes, the National Banking System continued the distinctive legal treatment of commercial banks under the traditional limited purpose banking charter. It dealt with the perennial issues by reaffirming earlier resolutions or by making changes. The federal government explicitly aimed to improve the market for the sale of its securities while upgrading the currency system. In addition to their corporate privileges, national banks were provided with a secured currency, a new prestige as secure institutions and initially, restraints on competition. By the turn of the twentieth century market changes had altered the cost–benefit arrangement considerably. By the time the Federal Reserve Act was passed in 1913, it was clear that national banks were not getting what they had bargained for in the 1860s.

### The Federal Reserve System

Competition from less regulated banks and trust companies increased pressure for changes in the National Banking Act. In a statement that, with minor variation, might have been written by the Comptroller of the Currency in the 1960s, 1970s, or even in the 1990s, the Pujo Committee in 1913 stated that, "We have been much embarrassed . . . by the fact that banks and trust companies organized under State laws . . . have other powers which are denied to national banks. We are reminded that if the activities of the national banks are . . . too severely circumscribed they may be converted into State institutions."[83]

A series of financial crises, culminating with a panic in 1907, precipitated congressional action that culminated in passage of the Federal Reserve Act in 1913.[84] Like the National Banking Act before it, the Federal Reserve Act was designed to remedy a currency disorder that had contributed to crises. National bank notes, while secure, could not expand with increased public demands for currency which occurred during banking crises. The Federal Reserve was to provide an "elastic currency" that expanded and contracted with public demand. Congress accomplished this by authorizing Federal Reserve Notes that would enter into circulation through the banking system.

The act did not alter the chartering and supervisory authority of either the Comptroller under the National Banking Act, or state bank supervisors under state banking statutes, but it did, of necessity, alter the cost–benefit arrangement (see page 50).

National banks, compelled to be members of the Federal Reserve System, were faced with a substantial increase in costs. The placement of their required reserves against deposits was of particular importance. Under the National Banking Act, national banks had kept their reserves in interest-bearing deposit accounts at other banks. Along with other funds, these reserve accounts from banks throughout the country "pyramided" in New York and Chicago where there was a ready outlet in the "call loan market" when interest rates were high. In an attempt to forestall the precipitous withdrawal of excess reserves in times of crisis, particularly from New York, the Federal Reserve Act provided that required reserves be kept in noninterest-bearing accounts at Federal Reserve Banks. Many national banks threatened to convert to state charters. Ross Robertson concluded that "their remonstrances . . . helped . . . forge a statute that would be tolerable."[85]

Among other things, reserve requirements were lowered under the Federal Reserve Act. The act also permitted national banks for the first time to make some types of mortgage loans, to accept time and savings deposits, to open trust departments, and foreign branches. Further, the aim of an "elastic currency" was to be met through banks—the ready availability of Federal Reserve Notes that member banks could obtain by withdrawing deposits from Federal Reserve Banks and by borrowing from their new discount windows. The credit offered by the Federal Reserve Banks, originally, long-term as well as short-term, was at below-market rates.[86] Finally, member banks were given a new, and presumably superior, differentiation through membership.

The Federal Reserve Act did nothing to curb the growth of state banks and trust companies. However, some national bank restrictions, such as a limit on loans to one borrower, capital requirements, and reserve requirements, were applied to state banks who chose to be members of the Federal Reserve, and thereby tended to level the playing field.

Government benefits, which included overall financial and economic gains, were to be achieved, in part, through the Federal Reserve's contribution to economic stability and resource allocation. The Federal Reserve Act was not simply designed to eliminate periodic crises. It also included measures to improve the geographic distribution of credit, channel additional credit to domestic businesses by promoting the commercial paper market, and to foreign trade, through Federal Reserve support in the market for bankers' acceptances.[87] More direct gains were soon realized with the entry of the United States into World War I. The Federal Reserve served as fiscal agent for the Treasury and it developed policies aimed at making credit available for the purchase of Treasury securities to finance the war.[88]

The Federal Reserve Act also had procompetitive objectives. The historian Arthur Link has suggested that Woodrow Wilson proceeded with banking reform on the basis of two assumptions: (1) banking was "so much a public business that the government must share with private bankers in making fundamental financial decisions"; and (2) that the so-called "money trust" (the affiliation of large investment and commercial banks in New York and Chicago) had the power to destroy economic freedom. He supported the Federal Reserve bill because "it provides . . . for public instead of private control." Further, he believed that "we will correct the evil we are most bent upon correcting—that of the present concentration of reserves and control at the discretion of a single group of bankers."[89]

It is noteworthy that the concern about concentration had not persuaded Congress to adapt the constraints of the Sherman Antitrust Act of 1890 to banking; and that when the Clayton Act, with its more specific constraints on particular anticompetitive practices, was passed in 1914, its impact on banking was minimal. The underlying reason was that banking was "so much a public business" that Congress felt obliged to deal with it differently. How this approach ultimately changed is the subject of Chapter 4. The Federal Reserve Act nevertheless may have made anticompetitive agreements more difficult by providing banks with the Federal Reserve as an alternative source of essential clearinghouse services.[90]

Branch banking remained beyond the powers of national banks. Congress explicitly rejected branch banking (along the national lines that had been adopted in Canada) as a way of dealing with the problem of financial crises. The reason stated in the House Report on the Bill for the Establishment of Federal Reserve Banks is worth quoting because it reflects a perception of competition identified with free banking that is uniquely associated with small banks having few or no branches.

The successful introduction of the branch system would almost necessarily have meant the abandonment of the idea of free banking. While it would not necessarily have been requisite to abandon free banking in theory in order to introduce the Canadian principle, it would have been practically true that the power of establishing branch banks, if widely exercised by large national institutions, would have entailed the contracting of the number of independent banks in the United States and a corresponding limitation of the perfect freedom of competition which exists today. . . . That the country was prepared for so profound a modification, not to say transformation, of the basic ideas upon which the national banking system has been developed, the committee did not believe and it was therefore led to the abandonment of all thought of attempting a plan of banking reform based upon the conception of large privately managed institutions operating unrestrictedly and with great numbers of branches.[91]

Modifications of branch banking restrictions began in the 1920s. With the approval of the Comptroller in 1922, national banks had established teller windows to circumvent branching restrictions. The McFadden Act of 1927 began the long legislative process of liberalizing the restrictions on branching by national banks. It permitted national banks to open in-city branch offices in states that permitted branch banking. As noted, an amendment in 1933 permitted national banks to branch to the same extent as state banks in their home states.

Both securities affiliates and holding companies also developed further as mechanisms for the combination of banking and commerce. The McFadden Act of 1927 gave national banks explicit authority to buy and sell marketable debt obligations.[92] The Comptroller ruled that national banks could underwrite all debt securities, and that their affiliates could underwrite both debt and equity securities. The circumvention of both branching and activity restrictions was accomplished through the bank holding companies that were largely unregulated. Transamerica Corporation was symbolic. Organized in 1928 to control the banking and nonbanking firms of A. P. Giannini, by 1954 it controlled banks in five Western states in addition to nonbanking subsidiaries that included insurance companies, real estate and oil development companies, a fish packing company, and a metal fabrication company.[93]

### The Great Depression and Return to First Policies

The achievements of the Federal Reserve System in securing banking and financial stability in the 1920s came to an abrupt halt in a succession of banking crises in the early 1930s. At the time, many in Congress and the federal banking agencies blamed the massive numbers of bank failures, about 9,000 between 1929 and 1933, at least in part, on intense banking competition.[94] It was argued that easy entry by new charter had produced a large number of banks that were too small to be efficient and too local to be adequately diversified.[95] During the 1920s, the Comptroller of the Currency had attempted to restrict competition by limiting new charters and simply by encouraging banks not to compete.[96]

With a general collapse of the financial system, Congress again instituted major banking reform. The Banking Act of 1933 provided trade-offs for banks in limiting bank powers and restricting competition (see page 50).

Table 3.2
Banking Structure and Performance, 1940–1960 (Dollar Amounts in Millions)

| Banking Characteristic | Year 1940 | 1950 | 1960 |
|---|---|---|---|
| No. of Insured Commercial Banks | 13,438 | 13,446 | 3,115 |
| Total Assets of Insured Commercial Banks | $70,720 | $166,792 | $256,323 |
| No of Unit Banks | 13,334 | 12,830 | 11,1433 |
| No of Commercial Banks Operating Branches | 954 | 1,291 | 2,329 |
| No. of Branches | 3,489 | 4,832 | 10,559 |
| No. of Bank Holding Companies | 41 | ------ | 47 |
| No of Banks Controlled by Bank Holding Companies | 427 | ------ | 427 |
| Newly Organized Commercial Banks | 36 | 67 | 125 |
| Average Concentration of Deposits in Two Largest Banks in All Metropolitan Areas | ------ | ------- | 64.0% |
| Profits of Commercial Banks [Net Profits-to-Capital(%)] | 7.0 | 8.3 | 10.0 |
| No. of Commercial Bank Failures | 43 | 4 | 1 |
| No. of Savings & Loan Associations | 7,521 | 5,992 | 6,276 |
| Total Assets of Savings & Loans | $5,733 | $16,893 | $71,489 |
| No. of Insured Savings Banks | 53 | 194 | 330 |
| Total Assets of Insured Savings Banks | $1,984 | $15,907 | $37,065 |
| No of Credit Unions | 3,756 | 4,984 | 9,905 |
| Total Assets of Credit Unions | $72.5 | $406 | $2,670 |
| No. of States With Holding Companies | 31 (1941) | ---- | 31 |
| No. of Unit Banking States | 18 | 18 | 18 |
| No of Limited Branching States | 17 | 17 | 17 |
| No of Statewide Branching States | 16 | 16 | 16 |

Sources: Bernard Shull and Paul M. Horvitz, "Branch Banking and the Structure of Competition," *The National Banking Review* 1 (1963): 301–341; FDIC, *Historical Statistics on Banking: 1934–1992* (Washington, D.C.: FDIC, 1993); FDIC, *Annual Report, 1995* (Washington, D.C.: FDIC, 1995); Leon T. Kendall, *The Savings & Loan Business* (Englewood Cliffs, N.J.: Prentice Hall, 1962); *Annual Report* of National Credit Union Administration, 1978. Board of Governors of the Federal Reserve System, *Banking & Monetary Statistics 1914–41 and 1941–70* (Washington, D.C.: Board of Governors of the Federal Reserve System 1970).

Risk was constrained by limiting banking powers. The twenty-year-old critique of the Pujo Committee regarding the risks involved in bank affiliates underwriting securities, whether or not valid at the time, seemed prescient. The powers that had been granted by the McFadden Act in 1927 were revoked by the Glass–Steagall provisions in the Banking Act of 1933.

The Glass–Steagall composed Sections 16, 20, 21, and 32 of the Banking Act of 1933. Section 16 limited bank dealing and underwriting to specified types of securities including obligations of the United States and general obligations of states and political subdivisions. It did permit banks to provide brokerage services to customers. Section 20 prohibited banks from having affiliates principally engaged in dealing in securities. Section 21 prohibited any business that deals in securities from being in the business of receiving deposits, and Section 32 prohibited interlocks of directors and officers for securities firms and banks.

Separation of investment banking from commercial banking was thereby effected. Many affiliates surrendered their charters and liquidated their assets. In some cases, affiliates separated from parent banks and continued as independent organization; for example, First Boston Corporation from First National Bank of Boston. Private investment banks had to choose between accepting deposits and dealing in securities; J. P. Morgan split into Morgan Guaranty and Morgan Stanley.

The Banking Act of 1933 also instituted new controls on bank holding companies. The 1933 restrictions required corporations owning more than 50 percent of the stock of one or more Federal Reserve member bank to apply to the Federal Reserve for permits to vote their stock. The act also added Section 23A to the Federal Reserve Act, imposing restrictions on interaffiliate transactions. The ineffectiveness of these restrictions was reflected in the failure of holding companies to subject themselves to federal authority. By 1954, only 18 of the 114 bank holding companies identified by the board had registered.[97] The imposition of effective restrictions in the Bank Holding Company Act of 1956 are discussed in detail in the next chapter.

In a fragmented system, still with thousands of banks, the new legislation could not establish monopoly conditions thought desirable in the late eighteenth century, but it did effectively cartelize the industry. Among other things, entry by new charter was restricted through the establishment of a "needs test" for new banks. A group wanting a charter would have to show that the community in which its bank was to be located would be able to support the bank without injuring existing banks. The Banking Act of 1933 gave the Federal Reserve authority to limit the rate of interest paid by member banks on time and savings deposits and prohibited interest payments on demand deposits. Of equal importance, legislators and bank regulators propounded the view that cooperation among banks was preferable to competition.[98] Regulatory officials, at times "advised, stimulated, and occasionally required, cessation of competition among state banks." New York banking law, for example, required that the Banking Department supervise and regulate to "eliminate unsound and destructive competition among banking organizations."[99] Interstate branch banking, however, remained beyond the pale. Congress amended the McFadden Act, but only to let national banks branch to the same extent as state banks. Holding companies continued unregulated expansion across state lines until they, also, were effectively limited to their home states by the Bank Holding Company Act of 1956.

The Banking Act of 1935 reorganized the Federal Reserve System, giving the Board in Washington greater authority to support the financial system through open market operations and to regulate the extension of credit at the discount windows of the Federal Reserve Banks. It provided commercial banks with permanent federal deposit insurance to bolster the confidence of depositors.

Passage of the Federal Home Loan Bank Act of 1932, the Home Owners Loan Act of 1933, and the National Housing Act of 1934 reorganized the savings and loan industry and expanded the orbit of federal government supervision, regulation, and support to a new class of depository institution. Just as government had visualized commercial banks as serving public functions, now S&Ls were also chosen as instruments to meet a national objective to expand home ownership.[100]

The regulatory regime established in the 1930s reaffirmed the Hamiltonian view of banks as private businesses serving public purposes. It reconstructed the bank–government affiliation, redefining the public benefits provided by banks and offering them new benefits in return. Part of the new benefit package was the elimination of competition.

## BANKING STRUCTURE AND COMPETITION IN THE MID-TWENTIETH CENTURY

The revised regulatory design of the 1930s helped produce a stable banking industry in the 1940s and 1950s. The Federal Reserve provided the bank reserves needed to maintain a stable pattern of low yields during World War II, permitting the banking system to finance a substantial portion of the huge increase in the federal debt that financed the war. At the war's end in 1945, Treasury securities accounted for about 56 percent of bank assets. With most of their resources in safe securities, and with the guarantees of federal deposit insurance, the threat of runs had been substantially eradicated from depositor consciousness. The FDIC, looking back on the postwar experience in its *Annual Report for 1960*, reflected:

The record of events since 1933 has substantiated the belief that deposit insurance, together with other banking reforms, would revive and maintain confidence in the nation's banks. . . . From 1946 to 1960, inclusive, only 42 insured banks were closed because of financial difficulties requiring disbursements by the Corporation, with no more than five in any one year. Most of the closings were due to defalcations.[101]

The other banking reforms, to which the FDIC statement refers, involved the suppression of competition for deposits, severe restrictions on new charters, continuing restrictions on multiple-office banking, and the new marketplace ethics established by government regulation that muted competition for all other banking services. Commercial banks did not, and were not expected by bank regulators, to compete vigorously.

Competition was also suppressed by the legal and regulatory balkanization of the financial services industry along functional lines. Commercial banks provided short-term credit, checkable deposits, and invested in safe securities. Savings and loans and mutual savings banks were confined by law and regulation to personal savings. While savings banks were regulated by the states and were permitted to invest in a variety of long-term assets, S&Ls were permitted only residential mortgage loans. Law and regulation prohibited insurance companies and investment banks from offering deposit services and prohibited banks from providing most types of insurance and investment banking services.

The bank failures of the Depression and the reforms that followed produced a safe and sound banking system that seemed, for a while, resistant to change. The principal structural features of the system are described in Table 3.2. As can be seen, neither the number of banks, number of offices or holding companies changed very much between 1940 and 1960.

The failures of the 1930s, and the reforms that followed, created monopoly and oligopoly in local banking markets. Rural communities in which only one or two banks existed were widespread. There were more banks in metropolitan areas, but concentration among the largest was high. Along with the new regulatory restrictions, noncompetitive behavior was the norm.

As shown in Table 3.2, the proportion of deposits owned by the largest two banks in all metropolitan areas was, on average, 64 percent. In most local markets, neither entry by new charter nor by branching could alter the competitive conditions materially. Bank profits were not high, but this was probably attributable to banks not fully exploiting their favorable competitive positions. With little competitive pressure, a good life could be secured notwithstanding inefficiency, passiveness, and extreme risk-adverse behavior. To the extent deficiencies in competition produced safe and sound banking, however, it did so at the expense of small business and consumer customers who were largely confined to banks in their local markets.

Beginning around 1950, Congress began to consider procompetitive measures that could affect commercial banks. In addition, market forces also began to erode the competitive restrictions that legislation and regulation had erected. In particular, S&Ls competing for deposit funds to finance the postwar boom in home building initiated new competitive pressure in deposit markets. Both S&L competition for deposits and new legislation would soon have profound effects on competition in banking markets, disturbing the stable framework that had been constructed in the 1930s. As demonstrated repeatedly over American banking history, legal and regulatory restrictions on competition in a free market system are subject to a principle something like the second law of thermodynamics. Over time, they progress from order to disorder, but at midcentury, the coming "perennial gale of creative destruction," to use Joseph Schumpeter's phrase, was no more than a whisper in the wind.

## CONCLUSIONS

Banking and banking policy in the United States was forged out of a need to finance the revolution. The model on which the early banks were based was the Bank of England, similarly established to help finance a war.

The original bank charters in the United States reflected a symbiosis that tied together governments and banks. Both obtained benefits and incurred costs. The unique arrangement raised a number of issues that were repeatedly addressed through successive bank regulatory regimes.

The extent to which competition should be promoted or suppressed, both among banks and between banks and other financial institutions, was one of these issues. An initial decision to establish the first banks as monopolies was subsequently modified by legislation and through market developments in the nineteenth and early twentieth centuries. Following the banking crises of the early 1930s, Congress returned to severe competitive restraint that survived, intact, through World War II and into the 1950s.

Throughout, competition policies for banking were developed separately from competition policy for private sector firms in general, and reflected distinctive public purposes for chartering banks. Banking, as discussed in detail in the next chapter, was largely immune to the antitrust laws. The passage of the Sherman Act in 1890 had no applicability. For the most part, the Clayton Act of 1914 also bypassed banking. The distinctive treatment afforded banks was implicit in the symbiotic arrangement that characterized the bank–government relationship from the beginning.

By midcentury, the anticompetitve legislative and regulatory framework of the 1930s seemed to have established a permanently stable banking system. But even then, new competitive forces were beginning to emerge.

## NOTES

1. Gouge 1968, 44.
2. Syrett 1962, 240.
3. Stewart 1966, 477, 541.
4. Smith 1937, 304.
5. The quote can be found in Hamilton's letter to Robert Morris, 30 April 1781, reprinted in Ferguson 1973, 43.
6. As quoted in Hammond 1957, 40.
7. Syrett 1962, 237 ff.
8. Ferguson 1973, 43.
9. Hamilton, "Second Report on the Further Provision Necessary for Establishing Public Credit" ("Report on a National Bank") 1790, reprinted in Syrett 1962, 331.
10. Hurst 1973, 6, 7.
11. Hamilton to Robert Morris, 1780, in Lodge 1904, 340–341.
12. Hamilton to Robert Morris, 30 April 1981, in Ferguson 1973, 43.
13. Hurst 1973, 7.

14. Redlich 1968, 7–8, 21.
15. Ibid., 7–8, 21; Syrett 1962, 246.
16. Hurst 1973, 152–153.
17. For the various ways in which states framed these restrictions, see Dewey 1910, 143–150.
18. The books Hamilton found useful included Geoffrey Malynes's *Lex Mercatoria*, Malachy Postlethwayt's *Universal Dictionary*, and Adam Anderson's *Origin of Commerce*. See "Introductory Note" in Syrett 1962, 236–256.
19. Dunbar 1904, 91.
20. Hammond 1957, 67.
21. Dewey 1910. See also Ng 1988, 886–887; Stanton 1994.
22. "The Early Days of the Bank of New York" n.d., 13–19.
23. Dewey 1910, 209 ff.
24. Jackson, in Commager 1938, 270–271.
25. Hammond 1957, 144 ff.
26. Sylla 1975, 26.
27. U.S. Treasury Department 1991, XVII–4.
28. *McCulloch v. Maryland*, 4 Wheaton 316 (1819).
29. Commager 1938, 273.
30. Fischer 1968, 14–15.
31. Dewey 1910, 43; Hammond 1957, 129–131, 593. Also see Shull 1983, 1994.
32. Hammond 1957, 63; Dunbar 1904, 91.
33. Syrett 1962, 243–244.
34. *Legislative History of Banking* 1855, 10–11.
35. Ibid., 19–20.
36. Ibid., 53.
37. Ibid., 111; for a more recent analysis, see Symons 1983, 691 ff.
38. A compilation of the various purposes for which bank charters were put to use can be found in Dewey 1910, 48–51. See Hammond 1957, 528 ff.
39. Hammond 1957, 467 ff.
40. White 1897, 12.
41. *Curtis v. Leavitt*, 15 N.Y. 2 (1857). For an analysis of this and related court decisions in New York with respect to powers clause in the Banking Act of 1838, see Symons 1983, 694–698.
42. For example, New York Assembly 1854.
43. Wolcott's letter of 8 December 1796 is reprinted in Syrett 1974, 435–436. An earlier call for help to the Treasury by the Bank of New York, as a result of specie withdrawals, is reported in Hammond 1957, 84. Another early request for Treasury help by a Pennsylvania bank is described in Holdsworth 1910, 67–68.
44. *Legislative History of Banking* 1855, 84.
45. Carey 1838, 117–119.
46. As quoted in Redlich 1968, vol. 1, p. 190.
47. Leggett 1984, 123.
48. Hammond 1963, 6, 7.
49. Hammond 1957, 573.
50. Berle and Means 1940, 135–136.
51. *Bank of Utica v. Smedes*, 3 Cowen 684, as reproduced in *Legislative History of Banking* 1855, 112.

52. Hammond 1957, 596.

53. Ng 1988, 877–889.

54. Chapman and Westerfield 1942, 59.

55. Sylla, Legler, and Wallis 1987, 391–403.

56. Sherman 1895, vol. 1, pp. 282 ff.; Redlich 1968, vol. 2, chs. 15, 16; Robertson 1968, 37; Hurst 1973, 179–180.

57. *Farmers & Mechanics National Bank v. Dearing*, 91 U.S. 29, 33 (1875).

58. Redlich 1968, vol. 2, pp. 112–113.

59. Ibid., 105.

60. Friedman and Schwartz 1963, 149–152.

61. Cagan 1963, 22.

62. Ibid., 22–23.

63. Robertson 1968, 64.

64. 12 Stat. 665 (1863); 13 Stat. 99, 101 (1864). Also see Hammond 1957, ch. 18.

65. For reviews of court decisions, see *Harvard Law Review* 1920, 718–721; Symons 1983, 701–719.

66. Robertson 1968, 67.

67. U.S. Treasury 1991, XVII–5.

68. *First National Bank in St. Louis v. State of Missouri*, 263 U.S. 640 (1924).

69. Barnett 1911, 12–14, 34, 199–204.

70. Robertson 1968, 64–66.

71. Ibid., 47.

72. Sylla 1969, 659; Robertson 1968, 66–69.

73. Robertson 1968, 64–67.

74. Cagle 1941, 114–116.

75. Robertson 1968, 66.

76. Comptroller of the Currency 1915, 15, 36–39.

77. See Peach 1941, 46–47, 51–52; Redlich 1968, vol. 2, pp. 390 ff.

78. U.S. House 1913b, part 20, pp. 1424, 1432 (emphasis added). See also U.S. House 1913, 152. Kaufman and Mote who, in 1992, argued that "there is no evidence that the Comptroller actually issued . . . a ruling, . . . in 1902 . . . that forced national banks to transfer some of their securities to special security affiliates," were in error with respect to the true nature of the Comptroller's involvement in the matter.

79. U.S. House 1913b, part 19, pp. 1407.

80. Chernow 1990, 158.

81. Redlich 1968, vol. 2, p. 283.

82. Cannon 1913; Redlich 1968, vol. 2, pp. 284–285; some of these measures were publicized by the "Pujo Committee Report" (U.S. House 1913c, 18–32). See also Gorton 1985.

83. U.S. House 1913c, 153.

84. Sprague 1910.

85. Robertson 1968, 93.

86. Shull 1968.

87. Hackley 1973, 20, 43, 53.

88. Anderson 1965, 10–13; Friedman and Schwartz 1963, 216 ff.

89. Link 1956, 211–212.

90. Ibid., 199.

91. U.S. House 1913a.

92. Peach 1941, 40 ff.
93. U.S. Senate 1955, 62–63.
94. Linke 1966, 461–462; Chandler 1938, 10–11.
95. FDIC 1960, 27, 36.
96. Robertson 1968, 95; Beatty 1969, 21.
97. U.S. Senate 1955, 8.
98. Fischer 1968, 251.
99. Berle 1949, 595.
100. Teck 1968.
101. FDIC 1960, 3.

# REFERENCES

Anderson, Clay J. 1965. *A Half-Century of Federal Reserve Policy-Making, 1914–1964*. Philadelphia: Federal Reserve Bank of Philadelphia.

Bank of New York. n.d. "The Early Days of the Bank of New York."

Barnett, George E. 1911. *State Banks and Trust Companies Since the Passage of the National Banking Act*. U.S. Senate National Monetary Commission.

Beatty, Richard S. 1969. "What Are the Legal Limits to the Expansion of National Bank Services?" *The Banking Law Journal* 86, no. 1: 3–34.

Berle, A. A. 1949. "Banking under the Antitrust Laws." *Columbia Law Review* 49: 589–606.

Berle, A. A., and G. C. Means. 1940. *The Modern Corporation and Private Property*. New York: Macmillan.

Cagan, Phillip. 1963. "The First Fifty Years of the National Banking System—An Historical Appraisal." *Banking and Monetary Studies*. Ed. Deane Carson. Homewood, Ill.: Richard D. Irwin.

Cagle, C. E. 1941. "Branch, Chain and Group Banking." *Banking Studies*. Board of Governors of the Federal Reserve System. Baltimore: Waverly Press.

Cannon, J. G. 1913. "Clearing Houses and Currency." Address given at the Chamber of Commerce, Syracuse, New York, 27 March.

Carey, H. C. 1838. *The Credit System in France, Great Britain and the United States*. Philadelphia: Carey, Lea & Blanchard.

Chandler, Lester V. 1938. "Monopolistic Elements in Commercial Banking." *Journal of Political Economy* 46, no. 1: 1–22.

Chapman, John M., and Ray B. Westerfield. 1942. *Branch Banking*. New York: Harper & Bros.

Chernow, Ron. 1990. *The House of Morgan*. New York: Simon & Schuster.

Commager, Henry Steele. 1938. *Documents of American History*. New York: F. S. Crofts & Co.

Comptroller of the Currency. 1915. *Annual Report*. Washington, D.C.: Comptroller of the Currency.

Dewey, Davis R. 1910. *State Banking before the Civil War*. Washington, D.C.: National Monetary Commission.

Dunbar, Charles. 1904. *Economic Essays*. New York: Macmillan.

"The Early Days of the Bank of New York." n.d.

Federal Deposit Insurance Corporation (FDIC). 1960. *Annual Report*. Washington, D.C.: FDIC.

Ferguson, James E., ed. 1973. *The Papers of Robert Morris, 1781–84*. Vol. 1. Pittsburgh: University of Pittsburgh Press.

Fischer, Gerald F. 1968. *American Banking Structure*. New York: Columbia University Press.

Friedman, Milton, and Anna J. Schwartz. 1963. *A Monetary History of the United States*. Princeton, N.J.: Princeton University Press.

Gorton, Gary. 1985. "Clearing Houses and the Origin of Central Banking in the United States." *The Journal of Economic History* 45 (June): 277–283.

Gouge, William M. 1968 (1833). *A Short History of Paper Money and Banking*. New York: Augustus M. Kelley.

Hammond, Bray. 1957. *Banks and Politics in America*. Princeton, N.J.: Princeton University Press.

————. 1963. "Banking before the Civil War." *Banking and Monetary Studies*. Ed. Deane Carson. Homewood, Ill.: Richard D. Irwin.

Hackley, Howard. 1973. *Lending Functions of the Federal Reserve Banks: A History*. Washington, D.C.: Board of Governors of the Federal Reserve System.

*Harvard Law Review*. 1920. Vol. 33, no. 5: 718–721.

Helderman, Leonard C. 1931. *National and State Banks*. Boston: Houghton Mifflin.

Holdsworth, John T. 1910. *The First and Second Banks of the United States*. U.S. Senate National Monetary Commission. 61st Cong. 2d Sess., S Doc. 571.

Hurst, Willard. 1973. *A Legal History of Money, 1774–1970*. Lincoln: University of Nebraska Press.

Kaufman, George G., and Larry R. Mote. 1992. "Commercial Bank Security Activities: What Really Happened in 1992." *Journal of Money, Credit and Banking* 24: 370–374.

Leggett, William. 1984. *Democratic Editorials*. Ed. L. H. White. Indianapolis: Liberty Press.

*The Legislative History of Banking in the State of New York, from 1791–1841*. 1855. New York: Wm. C. Bryant.

Link, A. S. 1956. *Wilson: The New Freedom*. Princeton, N.J.: Princeton University Press.

Linke, C. M. 1966. "The Evolution of Interest Rate Regulation on Commercial Bank Deposits in the United States." *The National Banking Review* 3, no. 4: 449–469.

Lodge, Henry Cabot. 1904. *The Works of Alexander Hamilton*. Vol. 3. New York: G. P. Putnam & Sons.

New York Assembly. 1854. *An Act to Authorize the Forming of Corporations for Banking Purposes*. No. 128. 28 March.

Ng, Kenneth. 1988. "Free Banking Laws and Barriers to Entry in Banking." *Journal of Economic History* 38, no. 4: 877–889.

Peach, W. Nelson. 1941. *The Security Affiliates of National Banks*. Baltimore, Md.: Johns Hopkins University Press.

Robertson, Ross. 1968. *The Comptroller and Bank Supervision*. Washington, D.C.: Office of the Comptroller of the Currency.

Redlich, Fritz. 1968. *The Molding of American Banking*. Vols. 1, 2. New York: Johnson Reprint.

Sherman, John. 1895. *Recollections: An Autobiography*. Vol. 1. Chicago: Werner.

Shull, Bernard. 1968. *Report on Research Undertaken in Connection with the Reappraisal of the Federal Reserve's Discount Mechanism*. Washington, D.C.: Board of Governors of the Federal Reserve System.

————. 1983. "The Separation of Banking and Commerce: Origin, Development and Implications for Antitrust." *The Antitrust Bulletin* 18, no. 1: 255–279.

————. 1994. "Banking and Commerce in the United States." *Journal of Banking and Finance* 28, no. 2: 255–270.

Smith, Adam. 1937 (1776). *The Wealth of Nations*. New York: Random House.

Sprague, O.M.W. 1910. *History of Crises under the National Banking System*. Washington, D.C.: National Monetary Commission.

Stanton, Thomas H. 1994. "Nonquantifiable Risks and Financial Institutions: The Mercantilist Legal Framework of Banks, Thrifts and Government-Sponsored Enterprises." In *Global Risk Based Capital Regulations*. Vol. 1. Ed. C. A. Stone and A. Zissu. Chicago: Irwin Professional Publishing.

Steuart, James. 1966 (1767). *An Inquiry into the Principles of Political Economy*. Vol. 2. Edinburgh: Oliver & Boyd.

Sylla, R. E. 1969. "Federal Policy, Banking Market Structure and Capital Mobilization in the United States." *Journal of Economic History* 29, no. 4: 657–686.

Sylla, R. E. 1975. *The American Capital Market*. New York: Arno Press.

Sylla, R. E., J. B. Legler, and J. J. Wallis. 1987. "Banks and State Public Finance in the New Republic: The United States, 1790–1860." *Journal of Economic History* 47, No. 2: 391–403.

Symons, Edward L. 1983. "The Business of Banking in Historical Perspective." *The George Washington Law Review* 51: 676–726.

Syrett, Harold C., ed. 1962. *The Papers of Alexander Hamilton*. Vol. 3. New York: Columbia University Press.

————. 1974. *The Papers of Alexander Hamilton*. Vol. 20. New York: Columbia University Press.

Teck, Alan. 1968. *Mutual Savings Banks and Savings and Loan Associations: Aspects of Growth*. New York: Columbia University Press.

U.S. Department of the Treasury. 1991. *Modernizing the Financial System*. Washington, D.C.: U.S. Department of the Treasury.

U.S. House. 1913a. "Changes in the Banking and Currency System of the United States." 63d Cong., 1st Sess., 5 January.

————. 1913b. *Pujo Committee Hearings before a Subcommittee of the Committee on Banking and Currency. Money Trust Investigation*. 62d Cong., 2d Sess.

————. 1913c. *Report of the Committee to Investigate the Concentration of Control of Money and Credit. Pujo Committee Report*. 62d Cong., 3d Sess., Rept. 1593.

————. 1955. *Report of the Committee on Banking and Currency. Bank Holding Company Act of 1955*. 84th Cong., 1st Sess., H. Rept. 609.

U.S. Senate. 1955. *Report of the Committee on Banking and Currency. Control of Bank Holding Company Act*. 84th Cong., 1st Sess., S. Rept. 1095.

White, H. 1897. "The Second United States Bank. Part II: The Bank War." *Sound Currency* 4, no. 18: 1–12.

# CHAPTER 4

# Banking and Antitrust

The Congress of the United States has determined to deal with banking
in a manner different from other forms of "commerce."

Adolph A. Berle, Jr.[1]

The anticompetitive measures imposed on banking in the 1930s were indeed
draconian. As reviewed in Chapter 3, Congress accepted the view that excessive competition was a principal cause of the massive failures that had occurred. Free banking was abolished through the establishment of a needs test
for newly chartered banks; interest payments were prohibited on demand deposits, and the Federal Reserve was given authority to limit the rate of interest paid by member banks on time and savings deposits. Both the law and its
implementation by bank regulators advanced the view that cooperation among
banks was preferable to competition. As mentioned, New York banking law
required that the Banking Department supervise and regulate to "eliminate
unsound and destructive competition among banking organizations." Moreover, regulatory officials "advised, stimulated, and occasionally required, cessation of competition."[2]

Both the restrictions and their implementation by bank regulators survived
World War II and for a number of years thereafter, but, by the early 1940s the

bank failure problem had run its course. With recovery and stabilization of the economy following the war, the anticompetitive restrictions of the 1930s increasingly came into question.

From the 1950s through the 1970s, as a result of both court decision and legislative initiative, a new bank competition policy was developed and integrated with the antitrust laws. This integrated policy still exists, though in a form somewhat modified by deregulation in the 1980s. Its origin, development, and modification is examined in this chapter.

## BEGINNINGS OF ANTITRUST ENFORCEMENT IN BANKING

Through the first half of the twentieth century banking was effectively exempt from the antitrust laws.[3] Its exemption from the Sherman Act of 1890 derived from nineteenth-century Supreme Court decisions which held that money transactions were not in interstate commerce and, therefore, beyond the reach of federal law.[4] As late as 1960, Senator J. William Fulbright pointed out in the congressional debate that "it seems clear that John Sherman and the 51st Congress did not expect or intend banking to be covered by an act applicable to interstate commerce."[5]

In 1914, the Clayton Act outlawed certain specific practices perceived as having anticompetitive effects. The explicit purpose was "to prevent as far as possible control of great aggregations of money and capital."[6] It eased the government's burden in enjoining the specified practices by requiring only that it show that they probably would injure competition, not that they actually had.

For the most part, banking again escaped. The Clayton Act's prohibition on price discrimination (Section 2) and on tying and reciprocal agreements (Section 3) did not apply to financial services, only to commodities. The merger prohibition (Section 7) only included those mergers consummated through stock transactions; bank mergers were typically accomplished through asset acquisition. Only the section on interlocking directorates (Section 8) clearly applied to banks. In this case, as with other sections to the extent relevant, enforcement authority for banking was vested in the newly established Federal Reserve Board (Section 11). As discussed below, the Federal Reserve did not think very much of this new restraint and, through interpretation, minimized its effect.

As a result, through the mid-1940s, banking's effective immunity from the antitrust laws was unquestioned. In 1944, however, a Supreme Court decision in an insurance case abruptly undercut what had appeared settled principle. In *U.S. v. South-Eastern Underwriters Association*, it reversed its long-held position on money transactions, and found that the insurance business was in commerce and therefore subject to the Sherman Act.[7] By implication, so were banks.

The *South-Eastern* decision raised understandable concerns in the banking industry. As discussed in Chapter 3, price-fixing agreements among banks had long existed. In 1929, a survey by the American Bankers Association revealed that 58 percent of the responding banks set rates on deposits in accordance with clearinghouse association rules, and another 14 percent by direct agreement with other banks.[8] In 1946, in the wake of the *South-Eastern* decision, the General Counsel of the American Bankers Association wrote to member banks that "it would seem to be a safer practice for clearinghouses not to attempt to establish uniform service charges."[9]

His advice was sound. Almost immediately after the decision, the Justice Department began to challenge price-fixing agreements among large financial institutions, including banks. Nevertheless, anticompetitive practices, particularly among smaller banks in rural areas, continued to exist for some time. Through the early 1960s, price-fixing and market-sharing agreements were not difficult to find, as evidenced by the following excerpt from a Juniata County (Pennsylvania) Banker's Association brochure, freely distributed in 1963: "The banks of . . . [this county] invite you to continue using their facilities. . . . In the interest of uniformity in their services to you, the banks . . . have agreed upon the rates, charges, and practices set forth in this leaflet. We are confident you will find them fair."

The Court's decision in the *South-Eastern* case coincided with new congressional deliberations on amendments to the Clayton Act's merger prohibition (Section 7) that had become moribund, in part because of its limitation to stock transactions. The initial bills in the House and Senate would have extended Section 7 to asset acquisitions of all corporations engaged in commerce with exceptions for regulated industries, including banks. In March 1945, Mariner Eccles, then Chairman of the Board of Governors of the Federal Reserve System, wrote to the Chairman of the House Judiciary Committee requesting that the House bill be amended to require prior approval by the Federal Reserve of bank mergers through asset as well as stock acquisitions.[10] Over the next five years, in the course of congressional debate on amending Section 7, the Federal Reserve repeatedly requested that its powers over bank mergers be extended to include asset acquisitions. Immediately before passage in 1950 of the Celler–Kefauver Amendment to Section 7 that extended the prohibition to asset acquisitions, the board wrote to Congressman Celler calling his attention to a "weakness in Section 7 of the Clayton Act . . . where applicable to banks."[11] The letter pointed out that all other regulatory agencies with enforcement responsibilities under Section 7, including the Civil Aeronautics Authority, the Federal Communications Commission, the Federal Power Commission, the Maritime Commission, the SEC, and the Secretary of Agriculture had authority over asset as well as stock acquisitions, and that when the amendment passed, so would the Federal Trade Commission. The bank regulatory agencies would be the only exception.

Congress rejected the board's appeal. The amendment became law with its new restrictions on asset acquisitions explicitly applicable only to corporations subject to Federal Trade Commission jurisdiction and therefore not to bank mergers that were subject to Federal Reserve jurisdiction under Section 11 of the Clayton Act. In its 1949 report on the bill that became Section 7, the House Banking Committee offered the simple explanation that "there is no disposition to change the present arrangements regarding [banks]." The 1965 legislative history on bank merger legislation, prepared for the Senate Banking Committee, indicated "Congress knew of the problem of bank mergers and reached a deliberate decision not to attempt to deal with them in the amendment. . . . It may well have been based on the feeling that the addition of such a provision would have resulted in the defeat of the bill."[12]

## THE BANK HOLDING COMPANY AND MERGER ACTS

The failure of Congress to deal with bank mergers in 1950 ushered in a decade of deliberations on bank acquisitions and consolidation. In addition to large bank mergers in major metropolitan areas, large bank holding companies, for the most part unregulated, had also embarked on a series of banking and nonbanking acquisitions.

Congressional review was undertaken in the context of the widespread belief that the antitrust laws were largely inapplicable to banking. A legislative history developed for the Senate Banking Committee in 1965 indicated that in the 1950s no responsible government official took the position that bank mergers were subject to the Clayton Act. Representatives of the Antitrust Division of the Justice Department had testified on six separate occasions beginning in 1955 that the Clayton Act did not apply; and officials continued to state this belief almost to the time when the Justice Department filed its complaint in the Philadelphia–Girard Trust merger case. They also testified that the Sherman Act, while applicable to bank mergers, was not a practical constraint. The belief that the Sherman Act could not be effectively used was based on the Supreme Court's 1948 decision in *U.S. v. Columbia Steel*, 344 U.S. 495. In that case, the Court upheld the acquisition of the largest producer of rolled steel products in the United States by the largest independent steel fabricator on the West Coast. In doing so, it established a formidable "rule of reason" that looked to factors such as the percentage of business controlled, the strength of the remaining competition, the purpose of the transaction, probable industry development, consumer demand, and other market characteristics.[13]

The validity of these views notwithstanding, substantial numbers in Congress took the position that the kind of competition visualized by antitrust standards was impractical and/or inappropriate for banking. The underlying belief was that "a bank failure is a community disaster, however, wherever, and whenever it occurs. [Therefore,] it is impossible to require unrestricted competition in the field of banking, and it would be impossible to subject banks to the rules applicable to ordinary industrial and commercial concerns, not subject to regulation and not vested with a public interest."[14]

## The Bank Holding Company Act of 1956

While bank stability was paramount, the potential anticompetitive effects of mergers and acquisitions required attention. Congress decided to deal with bank holding company acquisitions first. Senator Robertson, Chairman of the Banking Committee, justified this priority, arguing as follows:

There has been much discussion in and out of Congress of bank mergers. I believe there is substantially greater danger of abuse through the bank holding company device. . . . Imagine what a New York City bank with deposits of $7 billion could do in the way of competition with other banks if it also controlled a vast industrial empire worth $1 billion, and had unlimited ability to establish banks throughout New York State and in any other State.[15]

Limited restrictions on bank holding companies had been established by the Banking Act of 1933. Corporations owning more than 50 percent of the stock of one or more Federal Reserve member bank were required to apply to the Federal Reserve to secure permits to vote their stock. These registration requirements proved to be inadequate. Holding companies, through a variety of devices, avoided registering, thereby subjecting themselves to federal authority. By 1954, only 18 of the 114 bank holding companies identified by the Federal Reserve had registered.[16] In its 1943 *Annual Report*, the Federal Reserve Board stated that there was no effective control over the expansion of bank holding companies and recommended immediate legislation to prevent further expansion.

The holding company issue was symbolized by the expansion of Transamerica. Organized as a bank holding company in 1928 to control the banking and nonbanking companies acquired by A. P. Giannini, the founder of Bank of America, it came into serious conflict with the Federal Reserve. By 1954 it controlled banks in eleven western states. In addition, its nonbanking subsidiaries included insurance companies (Occidental Life and others), real estate, oil development companies, a fish packing company, and a metal fabricating company.[17]

In 1948, the Board had issued a complaint against Transamerica, charging that it violated Section 7 of the Clayton Act by acquiring the stock of banks in five western states: California, Oregon, Nevada, Arizona, and Washington. In 1952, the board issued an order requiring Transamerica to divest itself of the stock of forty-seven banks.[18]

On appeal, the Third Circuit set the Board's order aside. The court objected to the board's determination of the five state area as the relevant geographic market. It stated "No valid reason is shown for taking five states rather than one, the seven included in the [12th] Federal Reserve district, or all 48. . . . It may well be in the public interest to curb the growth of this banking colossus by appropriate legislative or administrative action. This, however, is not for us to decide."[19]

What the Board could not accomplish by litigation, it achieved through legislation. The Bank Holding Company Act, passed in May 1956, required bank holding companies, defined as companies owning two or more banks, to register with the Federal Reserve. The act prohibited registered bank holding companies from acquiring banks in states other than the state of their principal office (home states), unless the acquisition were specifically authorized by statute in the state of the bank to be acquired (Douglas Amendment). The Act also prohibited bank holding company control of almost all nonbanking firms. Under the act, activities were to be "of a financial, fiduciary, or insurance nature" and "so closely related to *the business of* banking or managing or controlling banks as to be a proper incident thereto."[20] The Federal Reserve Board narrowly interpreted the term "the business of banking" to mean a relationship between the customers of specific banks and their nonbanking affiliates. The term "the business of" was eliminated in the 1970 Amendments to make clear that nonbanking activity should be related to banking in general and not to the business of specific institutions.[21] Because Transamerica decided to retain control of its nonbanking subsidiaries, it found it necessary to spin-off its banks (with one exception) to the newly established Firstamerica Corporation. Further, severe restrictions were imposed by Section 6 of the act on transactions between banks and their holding company affiliates. Nearly all were prohibited. The Section 6 restrictions exceeded those of Section 23A of the Federal Reserve Act that had been added by the Banking Act of 1933. When the Bank Holding Company Act was amended in 1966, Section 6 was repealed and Section 23A again became binding.

The Federal Reserve was given general supervisory authority under the Act, and prior approval authority over holding company acquisitions of banks. In evaluating acquisitions, it was directed to consider a number of specific factors: (1) the financial history and condition of the holding company and/or its banks; (2) their prospects; (3) the character of management; (4) the convenience, needs, and welfare of the areas concerned; and (5) whether the effect of the proposal would be to expand the size of the holding company beyond limits consistent with sound banking, the public interest, and the preservation of competition (Section 3[c]). The first four were generally referred to as banking factors. The fifth, which included "preservation of competition," was termed the competitive factor. However, Congress provided no explicit standards for evaluating the preservation of competition. At the same time, the Act indicated that nothing therein should be construed as constituting a defense in any antitrust proceeding (Section 11).

In passing the Bank Holding Company Act, Congress made clear that it was concerned with the growth of large banking organizations and the resulting concentration of financial resources in the country; that is, with aggregate concentration in the nation and/or in particular states. It seemed less concerned with competition in local areas. In the course of the debate on the Douglas Amendment, there was a revealing exchange between Chairman

Robertson of the Senate Banking Committee and Paul Douglas of Illinois, a member of the committee and a former president of the American Economic Association. Robertson opposed the Douglas Amendment that effectively prohibited bank holding companies from acquiring banks across state lines. He asserted that the amendment would limit new entry into highly concentrated local banking markets and "create tremendous monopolies and freeze the big banks into favored positions."[22] Douglas, concerned about the elimination of small banks whether they had market power in local areas or not, and opposed to substituting large multimarket banking organizations, responded by stating

The Senator from Virginia . . . yesterday . . . criticized my amendment on the ground that, by making further interstate expansion more difficult, it would freeze the present situation and would aid monopoly. . . . Basically the argument . . . seems to be that the way to check monopoly is (by) permitting other competing banking concentrations (to) take over independent banks. . . . I am not interested in having . . . two banks in a State competing with each other. I am interested in a . . . situation in which there are a large number of banks with no monopoly and with a dispersion of power.[23]

Douglas seems to have visualized holding company affiliates replacing independent banks with no change in local market concentration, but higher state and national concentration. In 1956, Douglas's views and amendment prevailed. The majority emphasis on the growth of large banks and increases in aggregate concentration was subsequently reflected in Federal Reserve decisions under the act.

An example is provided in the board's denial of a 1962 proposal by Morgan Guaranty to affiliate with six substantial upstate New York banks, each located in a separate local area. In rejecting the proposal, the Board stated "The impetus for . . . enactment (of the Holding Company Act) was the need for control of affiliations of banks through the holding company device because uncontrolled, such activity could lead to 'undue concentration' of banking resources and the attendant power to restrain or inhibit competition." The Board concluded that the Morgan application "would have serious adverse consequences for the competitive banking structure of the state."[24]

### The Bank Merger Act

After passage of the Holding Company Act, Congress turned its attention to mergers. There had been over 1,300 between 1950 and 1959, in what was considered a massive merger movement at the time.[25] As in the case of holding companies, however, Congress focused on the growth of large banking organizations. Large bank consolidations in New York City, including the merger of Chase National and Manhattan Bank, and National City Bank and First National, both in 1955, and the merger of Crocker National and Anglo National in California in 1956 became focal points.

Mergers in the major financial centers could hardly have done more than reproduce the highly concentrated banking structures that existed in most rural towns where one or two banks were frequently all that were available to local customers. But many viewed further increases in concentration in metropolitan areas objectionable.

Beyond the question of local market concentration, influential congressmen argued that large bank growth and rising concentration in metropolitan areas would also injure competition among business customers of banks. In their "Supplemental Views" on the bill that became the Bank Merger Act, Senators Douglas, Clark, Proxmire, and Muskie echoed complaints, discussed in Chapter 3, that were prominent in the first decade of the twentieth century: "As the banking resources of the various cities become more and more concentrated with these banks closely affiliated . . . with local business companies, the more difficult it will be for competing concerns to get the credit which they need to compete. Financial concentration . . . promotes . . . industrial concentration."[26]

Senator O'Mahoney went further, suggesting that bank mergers were associated with poverty, broken marriages, and juvenile delinquency, a perspective exceedingly strange to modern views.

In 1958, 20 million families in the United States had annual incomes of less than $4,000. . . . This is one of the reasons, I believe, why so many husbands . . . find themselves compelled to hold two jobs . . . why so many wives, . . . must seek employment, . . . why families are broken, . . . why their children wander the streets without care or supervision . . . for the increase in juvenile delinquency. . . . We allow the economy . . . to be handled by the few who are at the head of the great economic organizations. . . . We allow numerous bank mergers to take place.[27]

Of particular importance in the congressional deliberations on a new bank merger law was the role, if any, for the antitrust laws. In 1955, Congressman Celler had introduced a bill that would have rectified the omission in the 1950 Celler–Kefauver Amendment, and made the revised Section 7 of the Clayton Act applicable to banks. The Senate and House banking committees, however, preferred that the agencies not be constrained by antitrust standards. Senator Robertson took the position that the federal banking agencies should take into consideration only whether the effect of a merger "may be to lessen competition *unduly*" (emphasis added). The Senate Report on the bill that ultimately became the Bank Merger Act 1960 stated that the word "unduly" was used to show that any lessening of competition had to be weighed by the banking agency as just one of several factors."[28] The House dropped the word "unduly" as potentially confusing in that it might suggest that mergers could be approved even if they "unduly" lessened competition, regardless of other effects. It intended that a merger be approved only in the case of a showing of net public benefits. The report of the House Banking Committee stated that the term "substantially lessen competition" was not used because it would suggest that Clayton Act standards were applicable and that the competitive factor might be taken as decisive, rather than one of several factors in a public benefits test.[29]

The Bank Merger Act, passed in 1960 as an amendment to the Federal Deposit Insurance Act, was dazzling in its simplicity.[30] It was contained in a little over 600 words. In general, it followed the pattern of the Bank Holding Company Act by establishing a set of banking factors, as well as a competitive factor to be evaluated in merger cases. The former included the financial condition of each of the banks involved, their capital adequacy, future earnings prospects, the character of their managements, and the convenience and needs of the communities to be served. The competitive factor was specified as "the effect of the transaction on competition (including any tendency toward monopoly)." In contrast to the Bank Holding Company Act, prior approval authority was divided among all three federal bank regulatory agencies: the Office of the Comptroller of the Currency (OCC), the Federal Reserve (Fed), and the FDIC, in accordance with the regulatory status of the resulting institution. In each merger case, the appropriate agency was to request advisory opinions on competitive issues, normally due in thirty days, from the other two and also from the Justice Department. Exceptions were provided for emergency cases where a banking agency had to act quickly "to prevent the probable failure of one of the banks."

While the Bank Merger Act made Justice Department advisory opinions mandatory, the federal banking agencies were not bound by the Department's views. It simply stated that the agencies "shall not approve the transaction unless, after considering all such factors, it finds the transaction to be in the public interest." Again, Congress provided no standards or weights. As in the case of the Holding Company Act, the agencies were on their own.

It proved to be of particular importance that neither the House nor Senate reports made clear as to whether the federal banking agency decisions would be immune from challenge under the antitrust laws. Both indicated that the bill "would not in any way affect the applicability of the Sherman Act or the Clayton Act to bank mergers."[31] However, since Congress had passed the Bank Merger Act with the understanding that neither had been of practical applicability, this seemed a strange statement. The House Report did state that

Because banking is a licensed and strictly supervised industry that offers problems acutely different from other types of business, the bill vests the ultimate authority to pass on mergers in the Federal bank supervisory agencies, which have a thorough knowledge of the banks, their personnel, and their types of business.[32]

This type of statement persuaded the federal banking agencies and many others that the Act "left final authority over bank mergers in the banking agencies. . . . It left bank mergers not subject to the antitrust laws except to whatever extent the courts may ultimately hold that the Sherman Antitrust Act is applicable.[33]

## INTEGRATION OF BANKING POLICY AND ANTITRUST

Senator Douglas and colleagues, in their "Supplemental Views," to the 1959 report of the Senate Banking Committee on the bill that became the Bank Merger Act, indicated a preference to block bank mergers whenever the Justice Department believed competition might be substantially reduced. They hoped that the Justice advisory opinion would spotlight issues and force the federal banking agencies to take the views expressed into account. They did not explain precisely how or why this might occur.[34] As matters turned out, the Supreme Court provided the answer in a decision on the proposed merger of two large Philadelphia banks in 1963.

### The Philadelphia Decision

Shortly after the Bank Merger Act was passed, disagreements arose between the Department of Justice and the Comptroller of the Currency about the competitive effects of several mergers. Justice challenged OCC approvals of large bank mergers in Philadelphia and Lexington by issuing complaints under Section 7 of the Clayton Act and Section 1 of the Sherman Act.

The *Philadelphia* case involved the merger of the Philadelphia National Bank, the second largest in Philadelphia, and Girard Trust, the third largest. The resulting bank would be the largest. Judge Clary, for the District Court, dismissed the complaint, finding that Section 7 was not applicable to the bank merger because it was not a stock acquisition, and even if it were, the Justice Department had failed to prove that the merger was unlawful. Moreover, he suggested that competition might even be more vigorous after the merger. Finally, *a fortiori*, the merger did not violate Section 1 of the Sherman Act.[35]

On appeal, the Supreme Court ruled that Section 7 was, in fact, applicable and that there was sufficient evidence to indicate that the merger would substantially lessen competition, and therefore violated the law.[36] As a result, the Court found it unnecessary to consider whether the merger was also a Sherman Act violation. The *Philadelphia* decision initiated a series of events that in a few years established effective antitrust enforcement in bank merger cases.

In retrospect, the most innovative element of the Supreme Court's majority decision was its analysis of why Section 7 was applicable. From 1914 on, bank mergers had seemingly been immune. They were generally understood to be asset acquisitions; and Congress had intentionally excepted banks from the Celler–Kefauver amendment in 1950. Nevertheless, the Justice Department in 1960 reversed its long held position that Section 7 did not apply to bank mergers and entered suit when Philadelphia National Bank and Girard Trust proposed merger. Justice Harlan began his dissent to the Court majority's decision with the comment that "no one will be more surprised than the Government to find that the Clayton Act has carried the day for its case in this Court."[37]

The Justice Department argued that bank mergers were not really asset acquisitions; they differ from "the ordinary purchase of assets" which do not necessarily represent "the complete disappearance of one of the corporations [and] may involve no more than a substitution of cash for some part of the selling company's properties."[38] The banks, on the other hand, argued that the merger was not a stock acquisition, and that "the only transfer which will occur in the proposed merger will be the transfer by operation of law of the assets of Girard to the resulting bank."[39]

The Supreme Court commended both sides for the merit of their arguments and concluded that a bank merger fit neither the asset acquisition nor stock transaction category neatly. With the determination that the literal terms of Section 7 did not dispose of the issue, it would have to interpret congressional intent.[40] It did so by finding that the 1950 amendment was intended to "give Section 7 a reach which would bring the entire range of corporate amalgamation, from pure stock acquisitions to pure assets acquisitions, within the scope of Section 7." It excluded only asset acquisitions that did not result in the elimination of one of the firms.[41] Since a bank merger, however accomplished, was an amalgamation, it could not be excluded. Moreover, the Court pointed out, if Congress had intended the Bank Merger Act to immunize banks from Section 7, it would have been explicit.[42]

It did not matter that Congressman Celler had testified in support of bank merger legislation in 1959, in part on the grounds that the 1950 Amendment to Section 7 did not apply to banks.[43] Nor did it matter that, following the *Philadelphia* decision, he commented that neither he nor Senator Kefauver were aware that their amendment would cover bank mergers.[44] Courts do not necessarily accept authors of bills as the final arbiters of congressional intent.

The decision went on to establish a framework for bank merger analysis. The area within which the competitive effect of a merger had to be evaluated was the market, which had a product and a geographic dimension. The Court defined the product dimension in banking as "the cluster of products . . . and services . . . denoted by the term commercial banking;" that is, as including the variety of financial services unique at the time to commercial banks. It defined the geographic dimension as the "area in which the seller operates and to which the purchaser can practicably turn for supplies"; that is, local service areas bounded by the location of the customers of a group of banks. These were admittedly pragmatic compromises, and in a number of respects simplistic.[45] Finally, the Court held that "a merger which produces a firm controlling an undue percentage share of the relevant market and results in a significant increase in the concentration of firms in that market, is so inherently likely to lessen competition substantially that it must be enjoined in the absence of evidence clearly showing the merger is not likely to have such anticompetitive effects."

The Court then fit the proposed merger into this framework. It found that the combined Philadelphia National Bank and Girard Trust, controlling about

30 percent of the market, and with the next largest bank, raising the two-bank share from 44 to 59 percent, raised "an inference that the effect . . . may be substantially to lessen competition" and thereby violated the law.[46]

The following year the Supreme Court reviewed a merger of the largest and fourth largest of six banks in Fayette County, Kentucky that the Comptroller of the Currency had approved despite advisory reports from each of the other banking agencies and the Justice Department indicating that there would be substantial anticompetitive effects (the *Lexington* case). The resulting institution would have had over 50 percent of deposits in the local market and about 95 percent of trust assets. The Court found this merger to create an unreasonable restraint of trade under Section 1 of the Sherman Act.[47] It thereby made clear that the Sherman Act, as well as Section 7, could effectively prevent bank mergers.

### The 1966 Amendments

The legal framework that resulted from these decisions was at best impractical. A bank merger could now be approved by a federal banking agency under Bank Merger Act standards, consummated, and then challenged by the Justice Department under antitrust standards. Moreover, the Justice Department could conceivably move against any bank merger completed after 1950. In fact, it had brought suit in three important mergers consummated before the *Philadelphia* decision, including the merger in Lexington, the mergers of Manufacturers Trust and the Hanover Bank in New York City, and the merger of Continental Illinois and City National Bank in Chicago. The Manufacturers Hanover merger had been found unlawful by the District Court in New York in 1965. At the time of the 1966 amendment, the Continental Illinois case was pending. The Justice Department had also brought suit in three other cases where the mergers had been consummated after the *Philadelphia* decision.[48]

Congress could have resolved the problem through legislation exempting bank mergers from the antitrust laws, leaving future proposals subject only to banking agency evaluation under the Bank Merger and Holding Company Acts. In fact, Senator Robertson proposed an amendment to this effect in 1965.[49] Alternatively, legislation repealing the Bank Merger Act would have left bank mergers subject to the antitrust laws and to whatever authority had previously resided in the banking agencies.[50]

The 1966 amendments to the Bank Merger Act effected a compromise.[51] The language of the revision prohibited the banking agencies from approving mergers that violated the standards of Section 2 of the Sherman Act, and also prohibited approving mergers "whose effect may be to substantially lessen competition" or "which would be in restraint of trade" unless "the anticompetitive effects of the proposed transaction are clearly outweighed in the public interest by the probable effect of the transaction in meeting the convenience and needs of the community to be served." Further, the federal banking agencies were to "take into consideration the financial and managerial resources and future prospects of the existing and proposed institutions." The amended act gave the Justice Department authority to obtain an automatic injunction to stay an approved merger if it entered suit within thirty days after the appropriate banking agency had approved it. It also provided that mergers consummated before the *Philadelphia* decision (June 17, 1963) and prior to the amendment (February 21, 1966) were presumed, conclusively, not to be in violation of Section 7 of the Clayton Act and Section 1 of the Sherman Act, but not Section 2 of the Sherman Act that made monopolization unlawful. The mergers affected included the Lexington and Manufacturers Hanover mergers which had already been found unlawful by the courts, and the Continental Illinois merger which had not yet been tried. Mergers consummated after the *Philadelphia* decision in which the Justice Department had entered suit, but which had not yet been resolved, remained exposed. The Philadelphia National Bank–Girard Trust merger, which had not been consummated, was not immunized by the 1966 amendment.

Shortly after passing the Bank Merger Act amendment, Congress also amended the Bank Holding Company Act to include the same language for holding company acquisitions of banks; that is, to establish standards that conformed.[52] Issues remained to be resolved in the courts, but the 1966 amendments largely completed twenty years of legislative debate and legislation on bank mergers and the antitrust laws.

## EARLY ENFORCEMENT AND THE EVOLUTION OF POLICY

The early years of antitrust enforcement were characterized by discordant banking agency policies, agency conflicts with the Justice Department, periodic litigation, and a number of additional Supreme Court and lower court decisions. Nevertheless, the aims of Congress and the Court to block large bank combinations and restrain increases in banking concentration were quickly met.

### Early Issues

Among the issues raised after the amendments in the late 1960s and early 1970s were how the banking agencies were to weigh and relate projected benefits from a merger stemming from improvements in "convenience and needs" against projected anticompetitive effects; what standards governed the evaluation of potential competition; and could an agency deny a merger on the basis of a finding that competitive effects were serious, but not serious enough to violate Section 7 of the Clayton Act? Through litigation, the role of convenience and needs as an offset justifying merger approval was limited, as was the significance of potential competition as a factor justifying denial; it was determined that the federal banking agencies could not reject mergers that did not violate the standards established by Section 7. By the mid-1970s, the scope and limits of the new integrated approach had been delineated by court decision.[53]

As well as the disappearance of open price fixing and market sharing, a key economic result of the new policy was the disappearance of large horizontal bank mergers. As a result, concentration, which had increased in a number of large urban areas in the 1950s, stopped rising.[54] Nevertheless, the new policy did little or nothing to reduce concentration. As late as the mid-1970s, concentration remained high in most local markets, arguably at levels of effective monopoly.[55]

On the other hand, between 1960 and 1980, the proportion of deposits held by the top 10, 25, 50, and 100 banking organizations actually declined.[56] This decline was in line with the objectives of the traditional, pre-antitrust competition policy that aimed at sustaining large numbers of small banks and constraining the expansion of large organizations.

### The Impact of Deregulation

In the 1970s and 1980s, the reconstructed bank merger policy confronted a rapidly changing financial environment characterized by inflation and rising interest rates that created profit opportunities in the circumvention of existing laws and regulations. The result was a systematic failure of long-existing anticompetitive restrictions. New types of checkable deposits that paid interest, including NOW (Negotiable Order of Withdrawal) accounts offered by S&Ls and savings banks, and credit union share drafts, developed; money market mutual funds emerged to compete with the demand, time and savings deposits offered by depository institutions. Securities firms developed the capacity to combine checkable deposits with related investment services through money market mutual funds and cash management accounts.

A direct incursion into banking by commercial firms was made possible by a loophole created by the redefinition of the term "bank" in the amendments to the Bank Holding Company Act in 1970. The Bank Holding Company Act of 1956 had defined "bank" as "any national banking association or any state bank, savings bank or trust company." National and state banks and trust companies might offer demand deposits and/or other kinds of deposits, and/or commercial loans, and/or other kinds of loans and investments. In amending the Holding Company Act in 1966, to avoid coverage of savings banks, Congress changed the definition of a "bank" to include only institutions that offered demand deposits. In amending the Holding Company Act in 1970, to avoid including trust companies that accepted demand deposits but did not make commercial loans, and in particular Boston Safe Deposit and Trust, Congress again redefined the term "bank" to include only institutions that offered both demand deposits and commercial loans. Thus national and state banks that offered only one or the other could avoid the restrictions imposed by the Bank Holding Company Act.

In 1980, large conglomerates and major securities and insurance firms began acquiring banks that would either divest their commercial loans or shed their demand deposits, remaining banks with national or state charters, but not banks under the Holding Company Act. These were termed "nonbankbanks." By the mid-1980s, Gulf + Western, General Electric, JCPenney, ITT, Prudential Bache, and Merrill Lynch, among others, owned such nonbank banks.[57]

The circumvention of regulatory restrictions compelled Congress to eliminate or modify the restrictions themselves. In the deregulation legislation of the early 1980s, it eliminated interest rate maximums on time and savings deposits and authorized the provision of the newly developed checkable deposits by savings banks, savings and loans, and credit unions. It simultaneously expanded the lending powers of noncommercial bank depository institutions. The nonbank bank was permanently forestalled by the Competitive Equality Banking Act of 1987 which once more changed the definition of bank in the Holding Company Act to include institutions having deposit insurance, thus temporarily blocking entry into banking by other businesses. However, the Federal Reserve Board, through favorable interpretation of the Glass–Steagall Act and Section 4(c)(8) of the Bank Holding Company Act, provided bank holding companies authority to deal in and underwrite a wide variety of securities, thus opening an entry into investment banking for commercial banks. Securities restrictions on banks were further relaxed by an FDIC determination that the Glass–Steagall Act did not apply to affiliates of nonmember insured banks. Numerous states authorized affiliates of such banks to deal in securities beyond the limits established by federal law and regulation.[58]

Passage of the Gramm–Leach–Bliley Act in 1999 has recently created opportunities for new "financial holding companies" and new "financial subsidiaries" of national and state banks to engage in a wide range of nontraditional banking activities. It facilitates the affiliation of banks, securities firms, and insurance companies.

Beginning in the 1980s, states that had long prohibited or restricted branching began to change their laws. Many organized compacts to permit reciprocal interstate expansion through holding company acquisitions. Passage of the Riegle–Neal Interstate Banking Act of 1994 effectively eliminated most of the McFadden Act constraints, first imposed in 1927, that had effectively prohibited interstate branching. The liberalization of geographic restrictions on both intrastate and interstate expansion opened up opportunities for mergers that had previously been impossible.

### Merger Policy Adaptations

Deregulation meant more competitors for commercial banks in traditional banking markets, and promised a substantial intensification of both actual and potential competition. If the pragmatically simplistic product and geographic market definitions of the Supreme Court's *Philadelphia* decision ("commercial banking" and "local service area," respectively) were mechanically applied, the impact of these changes would have been blunted. In part, this result was avoided through a revision of the Justice Department's *Horizontal Merger Guidelines* in 1982.[59] The revised *Guidelines* outlined an economically sophisticated method for determining markets in merger cases that legitimized federal banking adjustments to changes in economic and institutional conditions. Further, it diluted the effect of any given concentration level, such as indicated by the Court in *Philadelphia*, by establishing a set of concentration thresholds with varying implications for competition and a set of factors that would limit their significance.

The geographic market area for banking had been established as something comparable to the merging banks' "service area"—the area from which the banks obtained most of their deposits—by the Supreme Court's *Philadelphia* decision. Under the *Guidelines*, the geographic market area was expanded through consideration of the likely effects on competition through customers shifting their business in response to differences in prices, and to the potential for such shifting implied by commutation patterns.[60]

The product market had been established by the decision as "commercial banking." Under the *Guidelines*, it was expanded to include other savings institutions that offered similar services—"thrifts." The Federal Reserve has typically weighted the deposits of thrifts at 50 percent in calculating market concentration.

The Justice Department, however, has also narrowed the definition of the product market by adopting specific banking products less comprehensive than represented by commercial banking. In evaluating mergers it has focused on small business loans and transactions accounts. In the most recent litigation in which the Justice Department's departure from the *Philadelphia* definition was raised, a court declined to accept the narrower market Justice proposed.[61] The Justice Department has nevertheless continued to use loans to small and medium-sized businesses to determine geographic markets, and has continued to negotiate divestitures based on the resulting competitive analysis. Because the Federal Reserve has continued to base its analysis on the Supreme Court's *Philadelphia* definition of the product market; that is, commercial banking, it has reached different results in some in important cases. For example, in one case the Federal Reserve found that the relevant geographic market for commercial banking was the entire Cleveland metropolitan area. Focusing on the availability of loans to locally-limited small business borrowers, the Justice Department took the position that the relevant geographic markets were confined to the home county of the merging banks.[62]

Relying on the Herfindahl–Hirschman Index (HHI) that utilizes information on the market shares (relative size) of all firms in the market, the *Guidelines* established concentration thresholds for classifying markets as highly concentrated, moderately concentrated, and unconcentrated. They specified threshold levels and changes in the HHI that would lead Justice to enter suit. Thus, in markets where the postmerger HHI was less than 1,000 (unconcentrated), the Justice Department would be unlikely to challenge the merger. In markets where the HHI was between 1,000 and 1,800 (moderately concentrated), it would be unlikely to challenge a merger unless it increased the HHI by 100 points or more; and in making its decision would consider a number of other factors that throw additional light on actual competition in the market. Finally, in markets where the HHI was 1,800 or more (highly concentrated), it would likely challenge any merger that increased the HHI by 100 points or more. (The HHI and the thresholds are more fully discussed in the Appendix to this chapter.)

In 1985, the Justice Department modified its threshold standards for challenging bank mergers. It gave official recognition to the competition offered by nonbank financial institutions for some banking products in informing the federal banking agencies that it would generally not challenge a merger unless the postmerger HHI was at least 1,800, and the merger raised the HHI by more than 200 points.[63]

The federal banking agencies have, more or less, adopted the Justice Department's threshold levels for screening merger applications, but the Federal Reserve Board, the principal agency passing on large bank mergers, typically consummated through holding company consolidations, has made clear that it will not adhere to them rigidly in denying mergers that exceed the Justice Department's standards.[64]

A typical result of the new market determination analysis is that the local banking markets, as defined, are likely to have lower levels of concentration than in the past. The New York City market provides an example of an expanded market with lower concentration. In 1970, the Federal Reserve Bank of New York could only tentatively suggest that suburban counties might be competitively integrated with the city of New York in one local banking market; and it did not contemplate the inclusion of thrifts.[65] The New York City market today is routinely defined by the Federal Reserve to encompass a good portion of Long Island, New Jersey, and Connecticut. In 1992, it included about 190 commercial banks and 200 thrifts.

As a result, the 1992 merger of Chemical Banking Corporation (third largest in the area) and Manufacturers Hanover (fourth largest) had negligible effects on concentration in a market that, on the basis of Justice Department *Guidelines*, was unconcentrated to begin with. With thrifts weighted at 50 percent, it increased the HHI from 537 to 643.[66] The 1996 combination of Chemical Banking Corp., with close to $200 billion in assets, and Chase Manhattan, with $119 billion in assets, established the "New Chase," at the time the largest banking organization in the United States, with 4.5 percent of total U.S. banking assets. In the metropolitan New York–New Jersey market, the merger increased the HHI by 240 points, but only to the still unconcentrated level of 776.

The new merger analysis further reduces the probability of denial by establishing mitigating factors when the concentration thresholds are violated. These have included the existence of potential competition, the existence of a substantial number of firms remaining in the market, improvements in efficiency and related convenience and needs considerations. Any or all may be invoked to counter the effect of increases in concentration.[67] Of particular importance, liberalization of interstate banking laws introduced new potential competitors for local markets that could serve to mitigate any increase in concentration. This liberalization has, moreover, created opportunities for market-extension mergers that do not increase concentration directly and therefore rarely raise competitive issues.

On the other hand, once it is determined that concentration levels are not exceeded, all other possible effects can be ignored. For example, the 1995 merger of Chase Manhattan and Chemical Banking Corporation did not raise concentration to high levels. As noted, it only raised the HHI in the New York–New Jersey market to 776. The Federal Reserve did consider alternative geographic and product market definitions. But it concluded that the merger did not raise concentration beyond threshold levels in any of the nine banking markets in which they competed directly.[68] In the context of current policy standards, there was no reason to investigate further into the possible adverse impact of the merger on potential competition or on any other structural factor.

A distinguishing characteristic of current policy is that it systematically facilitates mergers by negotiated divestitures. The settlement of banking cases by divestiture is not completely new. As discussed, Transamerica was compelled to spin-off all but one of its banks after passage of the Bank Holding Company Act of 1956. In 1958, a California holding company, Firstamerica Corporation, was established for the purpose of acquiring them. The Justice Department challenged the proposed acquisitions and the suit was resolved by a negotiated divestiture that established First Western Bank & Trust.[69]

When merging banks compete directly in some of the same geographic market areas, objections can be eliminated through the divestiture of competing offices.[70] Divestitures have become an element of policy, enforced by the underlying threat of denial or suit. Because they reflect agreements hammered out through negotiations between the staffs of the federal agencies and bank officials, the effect has been to eliminate the phenomena of merger denials, contested by the merging banks and ultimately litigated in court.

The current systematic use of divestiture agreements raise a number of issues, the most important having to do with whether or not they have successfully eliminated the anticompetitive effects that motivated them. This issue has not been fully evaluated.[71]

Given the changes in competition policy since the early 1980s, it is not surprising that merger denials by the agencies have been infrequent, despite consolidation of some of the largest banking organizations in the United States.

Between 1972 and 1982, the Federal Reserve Board denied sixty-three proposed acquisitions on competitive grounds. From 1983 to 1994, with far greater numbers of proposals, it denied only eight.[72] Denials on competitive grounds, when they have occurred, have generally involved small banks in small markets. Litigation resulting in court decisions has, for the most part, disappeared.

The diminished significance of competition as a factor in deciding merger cases is reflected in the decisions of the Federal Reserve. Between 1980 and 1994, it decided over 70 percent of the bank acquisition cases reviewed by the federal banking agencies. Among those cases, as shown in Table 4.1, only an infinitesimal number have raised competitive problems; and an even smaller number have been denied. By far the most important reason for denial has been convenience and needs issues, and particularly those arising out of failure of one or both of the merging banks to meet their Community Reinvestment Act obligations.

It is sometimes suggested that lower denial rates result from the discouragement of applications that would have been submitted under the more ambiguous standards of the past and denied. While the relative ambiguity of past and present standards is moot, current practice is distinguished by discussion between applicant banks and agency staff that permit the latter to point out problems, for example, the substantial impact that the merger might have on concentration that would require such extensive divestiture for approval that the combination would not be feasible. There is, however, no empirical evidence supporting the argument that changes in informal procedures are significant in reducing the denial rate.

Further, there is some question as to whether there is, at present, any absolute level of concentration that would preclude Federal Reserve approval. So, for example, in 1997 the board approved a merger that raised the market share of the resulting bank to about 64 percent in the local Columbus, Ohio market.[73] The merger of NationsBank Corp. and Barnett Banks, Inc. in 1997 raised similar questions in several Florida markets, including Tampa Bay, Fort Meyers, and Daytona Beach where competition was direct. In this case, both banks were among the largest in the markets and, despite required divestitures, the HHI after the merger exceeded the 1,800 level threshold.[74]

The sharp drop in denial rates over the last two decades has been a product of changes in both the regulatory environment and merger policy. Deregulation aside, the new policy standards have accommodated large bank mergers. A question can be raised as to whether, even in the old regulatory environment, a Supreme Court in 1963, following current standards, would have found the Philadelphia National Bank–Girard Trust merger to have violated Section 7 of the Clayton Act. Granted, the HHI in the four-county Philadelphia, Pennsylvania metropolitan area, identified by the Court in 1963 as the relevant geographic market, was very high, and the HHI increase produced by the merger was substantial. But under current standards, the geographic market would have been defined differently. It would not ignore the competi-

Table 4.1
Principle Merger Decisions of the Federal Reserve Board, 1994–1996

| Acquiring Organization Cases (Size Deposits) | Cases | Approvals | Denials | Reasons for Denials | | | Issues Raised | | |
|---|---|---|---|---|---|---|---|---|---|
| | | | | Comp | C&N | F&MR | Comp | C&N | F&MR |
| Over $1 billion | 92 | 92 | 0 | 0 | 0 | 0 | 8 | 41 | 0 |
| $100 million to $1 billion | 57 | 56 | 1 | 0 | 1 | 0 | 2 | 15 | 0 |
| Under $100 million | 55 | 53 | 2 | 0 | 1 | 1 | 1 | 13 | 2 |
| All Cases | 204 | 201 | 1 | 0 | 2 | 1 | 11 | 69 | 2 |

*Source*: 77–79 *Federal Reserve Bulletin* (1994–1996).
*Note*: Comp = Competition
C&N = Convenience and Needs
F&MR = Financial and Managerial Resources

tive significance of important nearby banks in New Jersey and Delaware (and commutation patterns between, for example, Philadelphia, communities in south and central New Jersey, and Wilmington) and, of course, the presence of other nonbank financial institutions. Further, the Court gave no consideration to mitigating factors, such as possible improvements in efficiency and the large number of banks remaining after the merger (forty-one commercial banks in the four-county area alone). An analogy would be the easy approval of the Chemical–Chase merger in 1996 that combined the second and third largest banks in the New York market to become the largest banking organization in the United States.

Because the adaptations to bank merger policy have effectively precluded large bank merger denials, the courts have been effectively eliminated, not simply from the evaluation of bank mergers but from the evaluation of the adaptations adopted by the federal bank regulatory agencies and the Justice Department. With neither changes in the law nor relevant judicial decisions, the federal agencies have been on their own in crafting new approaches to evaluating the competitive effects of bank mergers. As shown in the following list, there has not been a meaningful court decision in a bank merger case since 1985. The last one was a Circuit Court decision in 1987 that dealt with a suit brought by the Justice Department in 1982:

**Supreme Court Decisions**
*U.S. v. Philadelphia National Bank* et al., 374 U.S. 321 (1963).
*U.S. v. First National Bank & Trust Company of Lexington*, 376 U.S. 665 (1964).
*U.S. v. First City National Bank of Houston*, 386 U.S. 361 (1967).

*U.S. v.Third National Bank in Nashville et al.*, 390 U.S. 171 (1968).

*U.S. v. Phillipsburg National Bank & Trust Company*, 399 U.S. 350 (1970).

*U.S. v. Marine Bancorporation et al.*, 418 U.S. 602 (1974).

*U.S. v. Connecticut National Bank et al.*, 418 U.S. 656 (1974).

*U.S. v. Michigan National Corp. et al.*, 419 U.S. 1 (1974).

*U.S. v. Citizens & Southern National Bank et al.*, 422 U.S. 86 (1975).

**Circuit Court Decisions**

*Washington Mutual Savings Bank v. FDIC*, 482 F.2d 459 (9th Cir. 1973).

*County National Bancoporation v. Board of Governors*, 654 F.2d 1253 (8th Cir. 1981).

*Mercantile Texas Corporation v. Board of Governors*, 638 F.2d 1255 (5th Cir. 1981).

*Republic of Texas Corporation v. Board of Governors*, 649 F.2d (5th Cir. 1981).

*U.S. v. Central State Bank*, 817 F. 2d 22 (6th Cir. 1987).

**District Court Decisions Since 1980**

*U.S. v. First National State Bancorporation*, 479 F. Supp. 793 (D. N.J. 1980).

*U.S. v. Virginia National Bankshares*, 1982-2 Trade Ca. (CCH) Para. 64,871 (W.D. Va. 1982).

*U.S. v. Central State Bank*, 621 F. Supp. 1276 (W.D. Mich. 1985).

From the mid-1960s through the 1970s, a number of important federal banking agency denials and Justice Department challenges had been litigated. The court decisions that resulted provided interpretations of the Supreme Court's earlier decisions and shaped banking agency decision making. As the elimination of denials has precluded court-litigated suits, there has been a transfer of responsibility for final determinations to the federal agencies and, in particular, to the Justice Department.

The transfer is significant in that federal agency determinations were never routinely sustained by the courts; and, in the most recent cases, have been consistently overturned. Between 1960 and 1970, merger approvals by the Comptroller of the Currency were repeatedly challenged by the Justice Department and reversed by Supreme Court decision (*Philadelphia, Lexington, First City National Bank of Houston, Third National, and Phillipsburg*).[75] Thereafter, court decisions have routinely gone against the Justice Department (Supreme Court decisions in the *Marine Bancorp, Connecticut National Bank, Citizens & Southern* cases; and in lower court decisions in *Virginia National Bankshares* and *Central State Bank*). Further, when lower courts have had their chances, they have exercised a restraining influence on the Federal Reserve and the FDIC (*Washington Mutual, County National Bankcorporation, Mercantile Texas,* and *Republic of Texas*). The last two lower court decisions in 1982 and 1985 (1987) (*Virginia National Bankshares* and

*Central State Bank*, respectively) rejected the Justice Department's market determinations. From 1974 to the last court decision in 1987, the Justice Department, the Federal Reserve and the FDIC have not won a case.

Without merger denials, the judiciary has not had an opportunity to review the policy it was instrumental in establishing thirty-five years ago; nor, since the early 1980s, to sanction, modify or effectively reject the changes the federal agencies have made. A hint of what might have occurred had litigation continued was provided by the District court decision in the *Central State Bank* case in 1985. The court rejected the Justice Department's product market definition that, by focusing on services the banks provided to small customers, deviated from the Supreme Court's 1963 "cluster of services" definition. The lower court decision was upheld on appeal to the 6th Circuit in 1987. Without further appeal, and with no further litigation, the Justice Department has been able to continue using its distinctive product market definition.

One result, as noted, has been uncontested differences in analysis between the Federal Reserve and the Justice Department in defining the relevant product market. In contrast to the Justice Department's focus on transaction deposits and small and medium-sized business loans, the Fed has continued to use the Supreme Court's 1963 "cluster of services" definition. Because differences in definition can imply differences in the extent of geographic markets and competitive effects under current practice, the two agencies may require a different set of divestitures. There have been times when merging banks have been confronted with one set required by the Fed and another by the Justice Department.[76]

## OTHER ELEMENTS OF COMPETITION POLICY

Other elements of bank competition policy have also been modified in recent years. Interlocking directorates, analogous to mergers, can have anticompetitive effects. Restrictions, to be enforced by the Federal Reserve, were imposed by the Clayton Act in 1914. They were modified in legislation in 1978. The Clayton Acts' restrictions on tying and other conditional agreements were never applicable to banks. In amending the Bank Holding Company Act in 1970, Congress devised a new prohibition on tying and reciprocal agreements that was applicable.

### Interlocking Directorates

The Democratic party platform of 1908 proposed that interlocking directorates among competing corporations be abolished. In 1912 it called for the prohibition of all interlocking directorates. Woodrow Wilson, in his inaugural address, asked for laws that would prevent interlocks of the "great corporations—banks and railroads, industrial, commercial and public service bodies—as in effect making those who borrow and those who lend practically one and the same." A prominent historian of the period has stated that it was only to save Carter Glass's Federal Reserve System bill from radical changes proposed by the agrarian wing of the Democratic party that President Wilson promised to include a provision in the Clayton Act restricting interlocking bank directorates.[77]

Section 8 of the Clayton Act did not go very far. It did prohibit interlocks where individuals served as directors or officers of two or more competing companies, where the elimination of competition between the companies would be a violation of the law. Section 11 of the act gave enforcement authority with respect to commercial banks to the newly created Federal Reserve Board.

Wilson's rhetoric notwithstanding, the restrictions did not apply to vertical interlocks involving banks and their customers. The Federal Reserve Act, however, does restrict insider loans to related interests.[78] These restrictions are implemented by the Fed's Regulation O, and limit the extension of bank credit to firms where directorates are interlocked with the bank. The direct aim of these restrictions, however, is to sustain bank safety and soundness, not promote competition.

The board appears to have had little sympathy for the Clayton Act restriction on interlocking directors. Parker Willis, who had been the economic adviser to Senator Carter Glass, a principal developer of the Federal Reserve Act, and served as secretary of the Federal Reserve Board between 1914 and 1918, had nasty words for Section 8. He wrote in 1923

The Clayton Act was a blemish upon the system of banking legislation. . . . It . . . protected no one, aggravated rather than cured the evils at which it was aimed, and caused continual annoyance and embarrassment to those in charge of the federal reserve system. . . .

[In consequence, the Federal Reserve had] relaxed the operation of the measure to a maximum extent. This was not difficult to do because of the extraordinarily loose and vague character of the language.[79]

Willis argued that because the restriction on interlocking directorates in the Clayton Act was applicable to all members of the Federal Reserve System, state members as well as national banks, it would have tended to restrict the growth of membership in the system had not the Board relaxed its administration.

Interlocks were again at issue in the early 1930s in the wake of the stock market crash. Section 32 of the Banking Act of 1933 prohibited interlocks of directors and officers of securities firms and banks. With other sections, generally referred to as the Glass–Steagall Act, the effect was to separate commercial and investment banking.[80]

By the late 1970s it had become clear that interlocks among financial institutions were extensive.[81] A new Depository Institutions Management Interlocks Act was passed in 1978.[82] The restrictions on interlocks that had applied to Federal Reserve member banks was expanded to all nonaffiliated depository institutions (banks, thrifts, credit unions, and industrial banks) and to bank holding companies in the same metropolitan area, or in the same or adjacent cities, towns, or villages. For an institution with more than $1 billion in assets and another with more than $500 million, the restriction applied without geographic limit. A number of exclusions and exemptions were created, and administrative, regulatory, and enforcement authority was divided among the several federal bank regulators.

Aside from exemptions in the law and exceptions provided by regulation, certain interlocking relationships were prohibited regardless of actual competitive impact. The federal banking agencies review formal requests by banks for interpretative rulings applicable to specific cases. Presumably in granting exemptions and providing interpretations, they rely on the same competitive standards as are used in merger decisions. However, the competitive analysis in this decision-making process has never been completely clear. Nor has it been clear that the practices of the several federal banking agencies are consistent.

In April 1994, Henry Gonzales, the chairman of the House Banking Committee, expressed a concern about a Federal Reserve proposed amendment to its regulation governing interlocks (Regulation L) that would permit banks in the same local areas to share management officials if the combined institutions controlled no more than 20 percent of the deposits of the area. The chairman of the Federal Reserve Board argued that the proposal would not have serious anticompetitive effects, and in some instances have procompetitive effects by permitting smaller institutions to attract management and directors from a larger group of individuals."[83]

The practices of the federal banking agencies in constraining anticompetitive interlocks has not raised serious public policy issues in the same way that mergers have. The process of exemption and interpretation in individual cases, and the difficulties of obtaining and evaluating relevant data, has largely precluded careful analysis.

### Tying and Reciprocal Agreements

A requirement sometimes imposed by sellers that buyers of a particular good or service also purchase other goods or services was seen by many as an anticompetitive aimed at leveraging power in one market to another.[84] With the tying prohibition of Section 3 of the Clayton Act not applicable to commercial banks that provided financial services, not commodities, Congress saw a problem when bank holding companies began to expand into new activities.[85] It formulated a new antitying provision for banks in conjunction with amending the Bank Holding Company Act.

#### The Legal Restraint

As discussed earlier, the Bank Holding Company Act of 1956 severely restricted the financial and nonfinancial activities in which affiliates of bank holding companies could engage. But, for purposes of the Act, holding companies were defined as companies controlling two or more banks. Congress viewed the "two-bank" definition as reasonable in that one-bank holding companies were generally inconsequential. They mainly included small companies owning small banks and other affiliates in rural areas, and a relatively few large commercial firms that owned small banks for the convenience of their employees.

In 1968 and 1969 however, some of the largest banks in the country became one-bank holding companies in order to expand into new activities that were impermissible to both banks themselves under existing legislation and to multiple-bank holding companies under the Bank Holding Company Act. It was widely conceded that bank diversification would intensify competition in some of the new markets their affiliates entered, permit banking organizations to become more efficient, and contribute to customer convenience. However, Congress—supported by the federal banking agencies, the Justice Department, and nonbank trade groups, including insurance and securities firms— became concerned that unregulated expansion would provide large banks with opportunities to coerce or induce agreements by conditioning the availability of credit on the purchase of services from other bank holding company affiliates. Such agreements could permit the leveraging market power in banking to other industries and injure competitors in the new lines into which banks were entering. A number of observers, including President Nixon, expressed the fear that several large bank holding companies might achieve Zaibatsu-like status, becoming the center of an extended family of commercial and industrial firms, as had been the case for large Japanese banks prior to World War II.[86]

In general, the 1970 amendments to the Bank Holding Company Act were an attempt to reconcile such concerns with the advantages of diversification. In doing so, it eliminated the one-bank holding company exemption, but gave the Federal Reserve Board authority, under legislative guidelines, to establish permissible lines of activity and permit an expansion into these lines by holding company affiliates. In doing so, the board was required to consider competitive effects, among other factors. The permissible lines were to be "closely related to banking" and "a proper incident thereto." The latter phrase established a "net public benefits test" that required the Board to consider the effect of a new activity on competition, unfair methods of competition, efficiency, convenience, concentration, and bank soundness.

At the same time, Congress enacted an explicit prohibition of certain tying, reciprocal and exclusive dealing arrangements (Section 106). It indicated that "Section 106 . . . will largely prevent coercive tie-ins and reciprocity. . . . But the dangers of "voluntary" tie-ins and reciprocity are basically structural and must be dealt with by the Board in determining the competitive effects of bank holding company expansion . . . under Section 4(c)(8).[87]

Under Section 106, bank holding companies and their subsidiaries were prohibited from extending credit, leasing or selling property, furnishing services or fixing the consideration for such on the condition or requirement that

1. the customer obtain some additional credit, property, or service from the bank, the bank holding company, or any of its subsidiaries; that is, a tying agreement. There is an explicit exemption applicable to banks, but not bank holding companies or their other affiliates, for loans, discounts, deposits, or trust services ("traditional banking services"). (Sec. 106[b][1][2]).

2. the customer provide some additional credit, property, or service to the bank, the bank holding company, or any of its subsidiaries; that is, a reciprocal agreement. There is an explicit exemption applicable to banks, but not bank holding companies or their affiliates for loans, discounts, deposits, or trust services "usually provided" (Sec. 106[b][3][4]).

3. the customer shall not obtain some additional property, credit, or service from a competitor of the bank, the bank holding company, or any of its subsidiaries; that is, an exclusive dealing agreement. There is an explicit exemption for reasonable restrictions to insure the soundness of the credit extended (Sec. 106[b][5]).

In addition to the exemptions indicated, the Federal Reserve was given authority to permit additional exemptions "as it considers will not be contrary to the purposes of the Section." The Justice Department was authorized to enforce the prohibitions by entering suit. Private parties could also sue, and if injured, for treble damages.

Some lower courts (the Supreme Court has yet to decide a case) have interpreted Section 106 as establishing a more restrictive prohibition on conditional agreements than the antitrust laws. Because it does not include any reference to market power or effect on competition, a favored interpretation has been that conditional agreements in banking are per se unlawful, without any need to provide evidence that a bank has market power or that the effect of the agreement is anticompetitive.

This interpretation, seemingly accepted by the Federal Reserve, assumes that banks have sufficient market power by virtue of high concentration in local markets and regulatory restrictions on entry permit them to impose anticompetitive conditional agreements—a far cry from the assumption long motivating bank merger analysis. Over the years, bank regulators repeatedly suggested that Section 106-type restrictions were necessary precautions in permitting bank diversification.[88] The Federal Reserve extended the prohibitions to bank holding companies and their nonbank affiliates in 1971. Congress passed parallel prohibitions for other depository institutions.[89]

It was not until 1990 that the Federal Reserve exercised its authority to establish an exemption under the tying prohibition.[90] The Justice Department has yet to enter a suit. There have been, however, a substantial number of treble damage cases brought by private parties. The published decisions in these cases contain the only information readily available on the factual circumstances precipitating suits, the nature of the allegations, and the role of the statute in supporting competition.

As would be expected, plaintiffs have typically argued that there is no legal need to show market power or anticompetitive effects; defendants have argued the opposite. With the issue of what Congress intended frequently in dispute, standards imposed by courts have varied. Some have taken the position that Section 106 does not require a showing of market power over the tying product.[91] Others have moved closer to the current Supreme Court position on tying under the antitrust laws, arguing that "it is all but impossible to define a 'tie' apart from inquiry into competitive conditions."[92] Still others have made pronouncements that can, at best, be judged mysterious: Plaintiffs "are not required to prove actual anticompetitive effects . . . such as a bank's dominance or control over the tying product market. . . . However [they] must show that the practice complained of is anticompetitive."[93]

Tying cases elicit considerable detail about who said what to whom and when. The charges brought in Section 106 cases, moreover, are frequently coupled with other complaints, based on other statutes or common law producing similar contradictions. What a District Court observed in one case appears to be fairly typical of all: "There exists a monumental morass of conflicting conclusionary claims and allegations concerning the parties' actions."[94]

A substantial proportion of the decisions rendered by the courts between 1973 and 1992 (forty-four unrelated federal court cases) were reviewed several years ago. The findings were classified in a table reproduced here as Table 4.2. The results of the table's classification indicate the following:

1. Most (over 61 percent) of the suits have been precipitated by the default of the borrower. Another 11 percent have been related to loan restructuring, typically the result of borrower distress.

2. In all but one case where it could not be determined, the tying or strong product has been a bank loan of one kind or another.

3. The tied-product or condition has varied, but in none of the cases was it associated with a closely related activity permitted by the Federal Reserve under Section 4(c)(8) of the Bank Holding Company Act. The cases do not reflect the concerns about leveraging that motivated the 1970 Amendments.

4. In general, few if any of these cases appear to have had any competitive significance. There have been some (about 7 percent) in which market power in the tying product market has been evident. None of these cases has provided any evidence of injury to competition in the tied-product market. Only a few (less than 5 percent) provides any evidence of injury to competitors in any market.

5. In only a few of the cases (about 7 percent) was there any evidence that the bank was attempting to secure some type of competitive advantage in any market.

6. In most cases (about 64 percent) the principal motivation of the bank in instituting the condition was to protect or improve its position as a creditor.

7. No violations were found in about 70 percent of the decisions, typically as a result of the explicit exemptions for traditional banking services or protection of the creditor position.

8. Violations were found in only four of the forty-four decisions (about 9 percent). A number of the decisions were, however, on intermediate motions or were in some way mixed. Most of these favored the plaintiff.

**Table 4.2**

**Characteristics of Tying and Related Cases under Section 106, 1972–1992**

| CHARACTERISTIC | NUMBER | PROPORTION OF TOTAL (%) |
|---|:---:|:---:|
| 1. Factors Precipitating Suit | | |
|    Default by Borrower | 27 | 61 |
|    Loan Restructuring or Denial of Credit by Bank | 10 | 23 |
| Other & Insufficient Information | 7 | 16 |
|    Total | 44 | 100% |
| 2. Alleged Tying-Product | | |
|    Business or Mortgage Loan | 41 | 93% |
| Other & Insufficient Information | 3 | 7 |
|    Total | 44 | 100% |
| 3. Alleged Tied-Product or Condition | | |
|    Tied-Product: Traditional Banking Service | 11 | 25% |
|    Tied-Product: "Closely-Related" Activity | 0 | 0 |
|    Reciprocity or Exclusive Dealing | 8 | 18 |
| Conditions Related to Borrowers' Distress | 16 | 36 |
|    Other & Insufficient Information | 9 | 21 |
|    Total | 44 | 100% |
| 4. Factual Indications of Anticompetitive Conditions | | |
|    None | 39 | 89% |
|    Market Power or Likely Anticompetitive Effect | 3 | 7 |
|    Adverse Effect on Competitors in Any Market | 2 | 4 |
|    Total | 44 | 100% |
| 5. Apparent Motivation of Bank | | |
|    Protection/Improvement in Creditor Position | 28 | 64% |
|    Additional Business in Traditional Market | 3 | 7 |
|    Additional Business in "Closely-Related" Market | 0 | 0 |
|    Other & Insufficient Information | 13 | 29 |
|    Total | 44 | 100% |
| 6. Court Decision | | |
|    No Violation | 31 | 71% |
|    Violation | 4 | 9 |
|    Mixed or Indeterminate Decision | 9 | 20 |
|    Total | 44 | 100% |

*Source*: Bernard Shull, "Tying and Other Conditional Agreements under Section 106 of the Bank Holding Company Act: A Reconsideration." *The Antitrust Bulletin* 38: 869–875.

The cases, on the whole, are sufficiently similar to suggest a typical scenario resulting in litigation. A bank and a borrower, frequently a long-term customer, agree on a loan and its terms. The borrower subsequently encounters financial difficulties that is likely to or does result in default. The bank restructures the loan and imposes additional terms and conditions. With further deterioration, the borrower brings suit under Section 106 based either on a condition in the original loan agreement that had not previously created concern and/or a condition imposed in the restructuring which the borrower alleges took advantage of its weakened condition. The circumstances producing litigation have thus been more of a legal recourse for borrowers in distress alleging unfair treatment than a procompetitive restriction on the leveraging of market power and the prevention of injury to competition.

### Economics of Conditional Agreements in Banking

Tying and other conditional agreements have been extensively discussed in the economic literature.[95] Traditionally, tying was considered a form of price discrimination and also a device through which a tying firm could extend its market power to a new market ("tied-market") by foreclosing single product competitors and raising barriers to entry.[96] Modern economic analysis, however, does not accept the view that the effects of tying agreements can be divined merely from their existence, or that tying and other conditional agreements are invariably anticompetitive. It has been persuasively argued that tying lies somewhere between vertical integration and independent pricing for each identifiable product—associated with complex contractual arrangements aimed at minimizing costs.[97] Nevertheless, conditional agreements in banking, most prominently the tying of business loans and other financial services to maintaining a deposit relationship, are widespread. It is necessary to consider whether there is anything unique about the industry that make such agreements likely to be anticompetitive.

In the 1970 congressional debate on amending the Bank Holding Company Act the Justice Department, among others, argued that banks are in a unique position because they enjoy a significant degree of economic power in local markets flowing from legal and regulatory restrictions on entry and from the importance of convenience to retail customers, and ignorance that impedes their mobility.[98] Congress accepted the view that high concentration in local markets and regulatory barriers to entry by branching and new charter invariably provided banks with substantial market power that was likely to be leveraged by tying the availability of traditional banking products like loans to products offered in the new activities banks were entering. It has also been suggested that smaller businesses cannot afford the costs associated with severing their banking relationship and starting another; therefore banks invariably have sufficient power to impose anticompetitive agreements.[99]

Whatever the circumstances in 1970, deregulation has altered the structural conditions contributing to market power. Further, high information and switching costs that provide sellers with favored positions vis-à-vis individual customers are not unique to banking; they can be found, for example, in many durable equipment markets.[100]

There are, moreover, alternative rationales for conditional agreements in banking. Banks offer a number of products that are jointly produced (e.g., various types of loans, deposits, and other services including loan commitments). For the customer, many are complementary. Banks may establish tying agreements for reasons of efficiency and also as a convenience to customers. They are typically explicit or implicit in the long-term customer relationship.

Loan agreements, particularly with long-term customers, typically require relational-specific investment by both parties. Customers invest time, effort, and private information, as well as fees, in particular banks that they expect will provide essential financial services into the indefinite future. Banks invest in particular customers by learning their business, evaluating their needs and capacities, and accommodating specific loans into their portfolios. Relational-specific investments generate transactions costs that can make vertical integration efficient. In banking, however, vertical integration combining banks and commercial firms is, generally, prohibited by law. Conditional agreements may constitute a substitute. Collateral, for example, is an obvious reciprocal condition that would not be necessary in an integrated banking-commercial enterprise. Deposit balances may serve as informal collateral. Payroll, data processing, insurance, underwriting, and so on can provide banks with more timely information on the course of the borrowers' business. They also provide a basis for estimating future customer profitability that could serve both the bank and its customer in periods when profitability diminishes.

The effects on borrowers and on competition of the formal and informal agreements that comprise the bank–customer relationship are not obvious. But there is no reason to believe that they are invariably injurious. The private information banks obtain permit them to develop better default estimates than available to competitors. As a result, they may achieve a competitive advantage that, at least temporarily, permits above normal profits.[101] At the same time, competitive banks have an incentive to attract borrowers by charging prices below their own direct cost in expectation of higher future profits after a relationship has been established. Lower quality borrowers, not readily distinguished by competitive banks, are likely to be benefitted. Bank competition still implies zero expected profits over an infinite time horizon.[102]

Customer defections, for whatever reason, impose losses on the old bank (loss of specific investment and search costs) and additional costs on the new bank (specific investment in the new customer). These costs can be avoided through collusion among banks not only to set uniform prices, but also to constrain customer movement from one bank to another. Interestingly, market-sharing, involving the territorial division of customers among banks in the same local market, in addition to price agreements, were customary in banking during the period of government-sanctioned competitive restrictions, from the 1930s through the 1950s.

Experience under current law, as noted, indicates that litigation has, for the most part, involved firms in or near bankruptcy. It probably reflects the complexity and variety of possible contingencies in bank–customer relationships. The relationship typically involves agreements that are incomplete. For example, lenders' rights and borrowers' obligations when a loan is current may be spelled out in detail, but rights and obligations when default appears likely, are not. The variety of possible circumstances surrounding imminent default generally preclude any specification of the restructuring option in the original contract. Nevertheless, at such times it is often in the interests of both parties to restructure the loan, with a variety of conditional requirements. While not clearly having any impact on competition, Section 106 has intruded on the negotiations between lenders and borrowers in extreme situations.

### Recent Developments

The economic uncertainty concerning the effects of conditional agreements would seem to preclude any per se prohibition of the kind seemingly created by Section 106. The Federal Reserve recognized this reality in 1990 in instituting its first exemption under Section 106. It permitted two holding companies (Norwest Corporation and NCNB) to charge lower interest rates and fees on credit cards issued by subsidiary banks to customers who obtained additional banking services from other affiliates. In its order, the board stated that Congress intended Section 106 restraints to exceed "applicable antitrust standards and imposed a per se prohibition against tie-ins involving credit."[103] But it then proceeded to evaluate the likely competitive effects as they might be evaluated in an antitrust case. It supported its exemption by stating that the banks had little or no market power in the tying product-market (credit cards), and that likely anticompetitive effects were insignificant.

Over the last several years, the Federal Reserve has gone further in liberalizing its regulatory restrictions on tying. It has rescinded its regulation extending the restrictions to bank holding companies and their nonbank affiliates. It has also granted additional exemptions permitting banks to offer discounts on, for example, brokerage services to customers who obtain other services from the affiliated bank. While some industry groups, including insurance and security industry representatives, expressed concerns about tying by banks, a recent GAO report indicates that few cases of tying have been found since 1990.[104]

## CONCLUSIONS

As indicated in the quotation that began this chapter, Congress has always treated banking differently, and the competition policy it devised has been unique. From the pro-monopoly policies of the early days of banking to the anticompetitive restrictions of the 1930s, discussed in the previous chapter, to the introduction of antitrust discussed in this one, special standards have been established—toward mergers, price-fixing agreements, interlocking directorates and tying, and other conditional agreements. Throughout, competition policy has incorporated a tension between the need for competition and concerns stemming from the distinctive role of banking in the economy.

Deregulation in the last twenty years has both augmented and undermined the antitrust-based policy in the 1960s. It produced a more intense competitive environment, which was the underlying aim of antitrust. But it also promoted modifications in policy that made it nonbinding or unreasonable. As discussed in the next two chapters, one result is that large bank mergers and rising aggregate concentration are no longer effectively constrained.

## APPENDIX: HERFINDAHL–HIRSCHMAN INDEX (HHI): ILLUSTRATIVE COMPUTATIONS

The Herfindahl–Hirschman Index is a measure of market concentration. It is defined as the sum of the squares of the market shares of each bank in the market. The index ranges from 10,000 in the case of monopoly (or 1.0 in decimal form) to close to zero when there are large numbers of firms with no one firm having substantial market share. It will vary not only with the proportion of deposits held by an arbitrary number of large banks in the market; for example, the top three, but with the relative distribution of deposits among all banks in the market. A convenient calculation illuminating the significance of any given HHI is its reciprocal which yields a "numbers equivalent"; that is, the number of banks of equal size in the market that would produce it. So, for example, an HHI of 1,000 (0.10) would be produced by ten banks of equal size. An HHI of 1,800 (0.18) would be produced by about six banks of equal size.

The Justice Department's *Horizontal Merger Guidelines* have defined market concentration in terms of the HHI as follows:

Over 1,800—Highly concentrated

Between 1,800 and 1,000—Moderately concentrated

Under 1,000—Unconcentrated

As noted previously, these levels, combined with the size of the increase in the HHI as a result of a merger, provide thresholds on which the Justice Department and the federal banking agencies base the extent of their examination, and the likelihood of denial or challenge. The Justice Department has inflated these thresholds for banking on the rationale that nonbanking firms provide effective competition in some traditional banking markets.

Illustrative calculations of the HHI are provided in Table 4.3.

Table 4.3
Illustrative Calculations of the HHI

| Market Structure | Market Share (%) | Market Share Squared (HHI) |
|---|---|---|
| Monopoly | 100 | (100 x 100) = **10,000** |

| Highly Concentrated | Mkt. Share (%) | Mkt. Share Squared (HHI) |
|---|---|---|
| Largest firm (bank) | 50 | 2500 |
| 2d largest | 20 | 400 |
| 3rd largest | 15 | 225 |
| 4th largest | 10 | 100 |
| 5th largest | 3 | 9 |
| Smallest | 2 | 4 |
| Total = 6 firms | 100 | 3238 |

| Moderately Concentrated Market | | |
|---|---|---|
| Largest firm (bank) | 20 | 400 |
| 2d largest | 15 | 225 |
| 3rd largest | 15 | 225 |
| 4th largest | 10 | 100 |
| ..... | .... | .... |
| 5th to 8th firms | 10 for each of 4 firms | 400 |
| Total = 8 firms | 100 | **1350** |

| Unconcentrated Market | | |
|---|---|---|
| Largest firm (bank) | 10 | 100 |
| 2d largest | 9 | 81 |
| 3rd largest | 8 | 64 |
| 4th largest | 7 | 49 |
| 5th largest | 6 | 36 |
| .... | .... | .... |
| 6th to 17th firm | 5 for each of 12 firms | 300 |
| Total = 17 firms | 100 | **630** |

**Table 4.3** (*continued*)

**Very Unconcentrated (200 firms with equal shares)**

| | | |
|---|---|---|
| Firm 1 | .5 | (.5 x .5) = 00.25 |
| Firm 2 | .5 | (.5 x .5 )= 00.25 |
| ... | ... | ... |
| ... | ... | ... |
| ... | ... | ... |
| ... | ... | ... |
| Firm 200 | .5 | (.5 x .5) = 00.25 |
| Total = 200 firms | 100 | **50.00** |

## NOTES

1. Berle 1949, 590.
2. Ibid., 595. See also Fischer 1968, 251.
3. Through the section called "Early Enforcement and the Evolution of Policy," this chapter draws on Shull 1996.
4. In 1850, in *Nathan v. Louisiana*, the Supreme Court held that "the individual who uses his money and credit in buying and selling bills of exchange . . . is not engaged in commerce, but in supplying an instrument of commerce." See 49 U.S. 73, 81 (1850); see also *Paul v. Virginia*, 8 Wall 168 (1868).
5. Fulbright, 106 *Cong. Rec.* 9711 (1960).
6. U.S. House 1914.
7. *U.S. v Southeastern Underwriters Association*, 322 U.S. 533 (1944).
8. Fischer 1968, 251.
9. As quoted in ibid., 253.
10. U.S. Senate 1965, 329–330.
11. Ibid., 27–28.
12. Ibid., 326.
13. Ibid., 328–329.
14. U.S. Senate 1959, 16, 19.
15. 102 *Cong. Rec.* 6755 (1956).
16. U.S. House 1955, 8.
17. U.S. Senate 1955, 62–63.
18. See "In the Matter of Transamerica," *Federal Reserve Bulletin* 38 (1952): 391–392.
19. *Board of Governors v. Transamerica Corporation*, 206 F. 2d 163, 169 (3rd Cir., 1953).
20. 70 Stat. 133 (1956) (emphasis added).
21. U.S. House 1970, 15–16.
22. 102 *Cong. Rec.* 6761 (1951).
23. Ibid., 6860.

24. *Federal Reserve Bulletin* 507, 579–581 (1962).

25. U.S. House 1960, 28; Horvitz and Shull 1971, 862–876.

26. U.S. Senate 1959, 28.

27. 105 *Cong. Rec.* 8125 (1959).

28. U.S. Senate 1959, 23.

29. U.S. House 1960, 10–12.

30. P.L. 86-463; 74 Stat. 129 (1960).

31. U.S. House 1960, 9, 10; see also U.S. Senate 1959, 3.

32. U.S. House 1960, 9, 10.

33. Office of Comptroller of the Currency 1960, 33.

34. U.S. Senate 1959, 28.

35. *U.S. v. the Philadelphia National Bank et al.*, 201 F. Supp. 348 (E.D. Pa. 1962).

36. *U.S. v. Philadelphia National Bank et al.*, 374 U.S. 321 (1963).

37. Ibid., 373.

38. "Brief for the United States" in 374 U.S. 321 (1963), pp. 74–77.

39. "Brief for Appellees" in 374 U.S. 321 (1963), pp. 29–31.

40. 374 U.S. 321, 337 (1963).

41. Ibid., 342.

42. Ibid., 349–351.

43. U.S. Senate 1965, 327–328.

44. As quoted in Fischer 1968, 299.

45. 374 U.S. 321, 356–359 (1963).

46. Ibid., 363–364.

47. *U.S. v. First National Bank & Trust Company of Lexington*, 376 U.S. 665, 672 (1964).

48. U.S. House 1966, 4.

49. Lifland 1967, 28–29.

50. Bills introduced to extend Section 7 of the Clayton Act to bank combinations, before passage of the Bank Merger Act, are listed in U.S. Senate 1965, 327–328; Senator Fulbright also discusses this approach to the bank combination issue in 105 *Cong. Rec.* 8143 (1959).

51. 80 Stat. 7 (1966).

52. Ibid., 236.

53. These included *U.S. v. First City National Bank of Houston*, 386 U.S. 361 (1967); *U.S. v. Third National Bank in Nashville et al.*, 390 U.S. 171 (1968); *U.S. v. Marine Bancorporation et al.*, 418 U.S. 602 (1974); *U.S. v. Connecticut National Bank et al.*, 418 U.S. 656 (1974); *Mercantile Texas Corporation v. Board of Governors*, 638 F.2d 1255 (5th Cir. 1981); *Washington Mutual Savings Bank v. FDIC*, 482 F.2d 459 (9th Cir. 1973); *County National Bancoporation v. Board of Governors*, 654 F.2d 1253 (8th Cir. 1981). See also Lifland 1967, 28 ff.; Fischer 1968, 301 ff.

54. Horvitz and Shull 1971, 868–875.

55. Heggestad and Mingo 1977, 656.

56. Savage 1993, 1086.

57. U.S. Treasury Department 1991, XVIII–21 ff.

58. Ibid., XVIII–16.

59. 47 *Fed. Reg.* 28493. 1982. Some modifications have been made in subsequent revisions to the *Horizontal Merger Guidelines*, but the essential elements have not changed.

60. For an analysis of the approach for determining the geographic market in a banking case introduced by the revised Justice Department's *Guidelines*, see Shull 1989, 411–428.

61. *U.S. v. Central State Bank*, 621 F. Supp. 1276, 1292 (D. C. Mich. 1985); on appeal *U.S. v. Central State Bank*, 817 Fed.2d 22 (6th Cir., 1987).

62. "Society Corporation," 79 *Federal Reserve Bulletin* 302, 304 (1992). A similar difference of view between the Justice Department and the Federal Reserve can be found in "First Hawaii Inc.," 78 *Federal Reserve Bulletin* 52, 56 (1991).

63. Rule 1985.

64. For example, "First Bank Systems," 79 *Federal Reserve Bulletin* 50, 51 n.10 (1993). For a recent description of the Federal Reserve's approach, see Meyer 1998.

65. Gelder and Budzeika 1970, 258.

66. 78 *Federal Reserve Bulletin* 74, 76 (1992).

67. Holder 1993.

68. "Chemical Banking Corporation," 82 *Federal Reserve Bulletin* 239 (1996).

69. 47 *Federal Reserve Bulletin* 157 (1961).

70. There have been numerous cases of divestitures in recent large bank mergers. For some early examples, see "BankAmerica Corporation," 78 *Federal Reserve Bulletin* 338, 340, n.15 (1992); "Society Corporation," 78 *Federal Reserve Bulletin* 302, 304 (1992).

71. However, see Burke 1998.

72. Holder 1993, 34.

73. "Southern National Corporation," 83 *Federal Reserve Bulletin* 596, 598 and Dissent, 602 (1997).

74. "NationsBank Corp.," 84 *Federal Reserve Bulletin* 130–135 (1998).

75. Full citations for these cases are provided in the list of court decisions.

76. See "First Hawaiian Inc.," 78 *Federal Reserve Bulletin* 52, 56 (1991); "Society Corporation," 79 *Federal Reserve Bulletin* 302, 304 (1992).

77. Link 1956, 220–221.

78. Section 22(g)(h).

79. Willis 1923, 192–193.

80. As noted in Chapter 3, the others are 16, 20, and 21. In general terms, the other restrictions impose these limits: Section 16 limits bank dealing and underwriting to specified types of securities (i.e., obligations of the United States and general obligations of states and political subdivisions), but permits banks to provide brokerage services to customers. Section 20 prohibits banks from having affiliates principally engaged in dealing in securities. Section 21 prohibits any business that deals in securities from being in the business of receiving deposits.

81. Fellows 1977, 1263–1294.

82. Title II of the Financial Institutions Regulatory and Interest Rate Control Act of 1978 (Pub. L. No. 95-630, 12 U.S.C. Sec 3201 et seq.). The act was amended in 1981 (Pub. L. No. 97-110 26 December 1981).

83. Greenspan 1994.

84. This section draws on Shull 1993.

85. As in the case of Section 7, tying agreements were prohibited to the extent they violated Section 1 of the Sherman Act.

86. The statement of President Nixon is reprinted in U.S. House 1970, 11–12.

87. Ibid., 18.

88. See, for example, Clarke 1987, 281–282; Heller 1988, 743.

89. In 1982, the Depository Institutions Act (Title III, Thrift Institutions Restructuring, Sec. 331) made Section 106-type restrictions applicable to federally chartered savings and loan associations by adding Section 5(q) to the Home Owners Loan Act of 1933. See P.L. 97-320; 96 Stat. 1469, 1503, 1504 (1982). In 1987 the Competitive Equality Banking Act (Title I, Financial Institutions Competitive Equality, Sec. 101) amended the Bank Holding Company Act to make Section 106 applicable to trust companies, credit card banks, Edge Act and Agreement corporations, industrial loan companies, savings banks, and companies controlling such institutions. Section 104 amended the National Housing Act to make Section 5(q) applicable to federally insured, state-chartered subsidiaries of savings and loan holding companies, the holding companies themselves, and their other affiliates. See P.L. 100-86, 101 Stat. 552, 561, 574 (1987). In 1989 the Financial Institutions Reform, Recovery and Enforcement Act (Title III, Savings Associations, Sec. 301) made Section 5(q) applicable to savings and loan holding companies and all of their affiliates. See P.L. 107-73, 103 Stat. 183, 335 (1989).

90. "Order Approving Exemption from Anti-tying Provisions in Section 106 of the Bank Holding Company Act Amendments of 1970," 76 *Federal Reserve Bulletin* 702 (1990); "Exemption from Tie-in Prohibitions," 55 *Fed. Reg.* 26453 (1990) (to be codified at 12 C.F.R. 225) (Proposed 28 June 1990); "Exemption Permitting Banks to Offer Reduced-Rate Credit Cards to Customers of Their Affiliates," 55 *Fed. Reg.* 47741 (1990) (codified at 12 C.F.R. 225).

91. Private litigation is reviewed in Shull 1993, 860–886.

92. See, for example, *Mid-State Fertilizer Co. et al. v. Exchange National Bank of Chicago*, 877 F.2d 1222, 1338 (7th Cir. 1989).

93. *Palmero et al. v. First National Bank & Trust Co.*, 894 F.2d 363, 368 (10th Cir. 1990).

94. *Iden v. Adrian Buckhannon Bank*, 661 F. Supp. 234 at 235 (N.D. W. Va. 1987).

95. For reviews of the literature, see Scherer and Ross 1990, 562–569; McGee 1988, 212–222.

96. Kaysen and Turner 1959, 157.

97. Willamson 1975, ch. 14.

98. McLaren 1970, 268 ff.

99. Leonard 1977, 787.

100. See *Eastman Kodak v. Image Technical Services, Inc.*, 62 *Antitrust & Trade Regulation Report* (BNA) 780, 786, and dissent 793 (1992).

101. Fama 1985, 29.

102. See Greenbaum, Kanatas, and Venezia 1989, 222–223.

103. 76 *Federal Reserve Bulletin* 703 (1990).

104. GAO 1997.

## REFERENCES

Berle, Adolph A., Jr. 1949. "Banking Under the Antitrust Laws." *Columbia Law Review* 49, no. 5: 549–606.

Burke, Jim. 1998. "Divestiture as an Antitrust Remedy in Bank Mergers." *Finance and Economic Discussion Series*. No. 1998-14. Washington, D.C.: Federal Reserve Board.

Clarke, Robert L. 1987. *Reform of the Nation's Banking and Financial Systems, Hearings Before the Subcommittee on Financial Institutions, Supervision, Regulation and Insurance of the Senate Committee on Banking, Finance and Urban Affairs.* 100th Cong., 1st Sess., 28 October.

Fama, E. F. 1985. "What's Different About Banks." *Journal of Monetary Economics* 15: 29.

Fellows, Henry D. 1977. "Interlocks in Management between Savings and Loan Associations and Commercial Banks under the Antitrust Laws and the FTC Act." *Georgetown Law Journal* 65, no. 5: 1263–1294.

Fischer, Gerald. 1968. *American Banking Stucture.* New York: Columbia University Press.

Gelder, Ralph, and George Budzeika. 1970. "Banking Market Determination—The Case of Central Nassau County." *Monthly Review* (Federal Reserve Bank of New York) 38, no. 11: 258–266.

General Accounting Office (GAO). 1997. *Bank Oversight: Few Cases of Tying Have Been Detected.* Report no. 97-58. Washington, D.C.: GAO.

Greenbaum, Stuart, Kanatas, and Venezia. 1989. "Equilibrium Loan Pricing under the Bank–Client Relationship. *Journal of Banking and Finance* 13, no. 2: 221–235.

Greenspan, Alan. 1994. Letter to Henry Gonzales, Chairman, House Banking Committee, 20 April.

Heggestad, Arnold, and John Mingo. 1977. "The Competitive Condition of the U.S. Banking Markets and the Impact of Structural Reform." *Journal of Finance* 32, no. 3: 649–661.

Heller, H. Robert. 1989. Committee on Energy & Commerce. Statement before a House Subcommittee on Commerce, Consumer Protection and Competitiveness, 9 Serptember.

Holder, Christopher. 1993. "The Use of Mitigating Factors in Bank Mergers and Acquisitions: A Decade of Antitrust at the Fed." *Economic Review* (Federal Reserve Bank of Atlanta) 78, no. 2: 32–44.

Horvitz, Paul M., and Bernard Shull. 1971. "The Bank Merger Act of 1960: A Decade After." *The Antitrust Bulletin* 16, no. 4: 862–876.

Kaysen, C., and D. F. Turner. 1959. *Antitrust Policy: an Economic and Legal Analysis.* Cambridge: Harvard University Press.

Leonard, D. A. 1977. "Unfair Competition Under Section 106 of the Bank Holding Company Act: An Economic and Legal Overview of Conditional Transactions." *Banking Law Journal* 94, no. 9: 773–775.

Lifland, William T. 1967. "The Supreme Court, Congress and Bank Mergers." *Law and Contemporary Problems* 32, no. 1: 15–39.

Link, A. S. 1956. *Wilson: The New Freedom.* Princeton, N.J.: Princeton University Press.

McGee, J. S. 1988. *Industrial Organization.* Englewood Cliffs, N.J.: Prentice Hall.

McLaren, Richard W. 1970. *One Bank Holding Company Legislation of 1970.* Hearings before the House Committee on Banking and Currency. 91st Cong., 2d Sess., May.

Meyer, Lawrence H. 1998. Statement before the House Committee on Banking and Financial Services, 29 April. Reprinted in 84 *Federal Reserve Bulletin*, 438–451 (1998).

Office of the Comptroller of the Currency. 1960. *Annual Report.* Washington, D.C.: Office of the Comptroller of the Currency.

———. 1995. "Bank Merger Competitive Analysis: Review Screening Process." *Advisory Letter* 95-4, 18 July.

Rill, James. 1992. Letter to Alan Greenspan, Chairman, Board of Governors of the Federal Reserve System, 6 February.

Rule, Charles. 1985. Letter to the Honorable C. Todd Conover, Comptroller of the Currency, 8 February.

Savage, Donald. 1993. "Interstate Banking: A Status Report." 79 *Federal Reserve Bulletin* 1075–1089.

Scherer, F. M., and David Ross. 1990. *Industrial Market Structure and Economic Performance.* Boston: Houghton Mifflin.

Shull, Bernard. 1989. "Provisional Markets, Relevant Markets and Banking Markets: The Justice Department's Merger Guidelines in Wise County, Virginia." *The Antitrust Bulletin* 34: 411–428.

———. 1993. "Tying and Other Conditional Agreements under Section 106 of the Bank Holding Company Act: A Reconsideration." *The Antitrust Bulletin* 38: 869–875.

———. 1996. "The Origins of Antitrust in Banking: An Historical Perspective." *The Antitrust Bulletin* (Summer): 255–288.

U.S. Department of Justice. 1982. *Horizontal Merger Guidelines.* Washington, D.C.: U.S. Department of Justice.

U.S. Department of the Treasury. 1991. *Modernizing the Financial System: Recommendations for Safer, More Competitive Banks.* Washington, D.C.: U.S. Department of the Treasury.

U.S. House. 1914. Committee on the Judiciary, *Report of the Judiciary Committee.* 63rd Cong., 2d Sess., 6 May.

U.S. House. 1955. *Bank Holding Company Act of 1955, Report of the Committee on Banking and Currency.* 84th Cong., 1st Sess., H. Rept. 609.

U.S. House. 1960. *Regulation of Bank Mergers.* 86th Cong., 2d Sess., H. Rept. 1416.

U.S. House. 1966. *House Report.* 89th Cong., 2d sess., H. Rept. 1221.

U.S. House. 1970. *Bank Holding Company Act Amendments, Conference Report to Accompany H.R. 6778.* 91st Cong., 2d Sess., H. Rept. 1747.

U.S. Senate. 1955. *Control of Bank Holding Companies: Hearings before the Subcommittee on Banking of the Senate Committee on Banking and Commerce.* 84th Cong., 1st Sess., July.

U.S. Senate. 1959. *Regulation of Bank Mergers.* 86th Cong., 1st Sess., S. Rept. 1062.

U.S. Senate. 1965. *Amend the Bank Merger Act of 1960, Hearings before a Subcommittee of the Senate Committee on Banking and Currency,* 89th Cong., 1st Sess., May.

Williamson, Oliver. 1975. *Market and Hierarchies: Analysis and Antitrust Implications.* New York: The Free Press.

Willis, Henry Parker. 1923. *The Federal Reserve System.* New York: Ronald Press.

# CHAPTER 5

# Why Banks Merge

The general character of the bank merger movement of the last two decades in the United States was outlined in Chapter 1. As indicated, between 1980 and 1998, 7,400 independent commercial banking organizations merged (Table 1.3). From 1987 through 1998, there were over 200 mergers in which each of the merging partners held over $1 billion in assets.[1] Between 1991 and 1998, there were 29 so-called megamergers in which each of the partners had $10 billion or more in assets; the total volume of assets acquired was over a trillion dollars (Table 5.1).

The consolidation of BankAmerica and NationsBank, approved by the Federal Reserve in August 1998, created a banking organization with about $580 billion in assets, the third largest in the world, holding about 8 percent of the total deposits of all insured depository institutions in the United States.[2] The combination of Deutsche Bank and Bankers Trust created the world's largest banking organization with over $830 billion in assets. More recently, the combination of Sumitomo, Ltd. and Sakura, Ltd., one of three Japanese megamergers announced, will result in a banking institution with over $927 billion in assets.

The bank merger movement in this country is not an isolated phenomenon. Large bank mergers have occurred in Japan and the United Kingdom in re-

Table 5.1
Bank Megamergers, 1991–1998 (Assets in Millions of Dollars)

| YEAR | ACQUIRING FIRM | ASSETS | ACQUIRED FIRM | ASSETS | RESULTING FIRM: ASSETS |
|------|----------------|--------|---------------|--------|------------------------|
| 1991 | NationsBank | $65,285 | C&S/Sovereign | $51,376 | $116,661 |
|      | Chase Manhatten | 98,064 | Manufacturers Hanover | 61,530 | 159,594 |
|      | Fleet Financial Group | 32,507 | Bank of New England | 20,434 | 52,941 |
|      | First Union | 40,781 | Southeast | 13,390 | 54,171 |
| 1992 | Society Corp | 25,599 | Ameritrust | 10,181 | 35,780 |
|      | Comerica Incorporated | 14,530 | Manufacturer National | 13,544 | 28,074 |
|      | BankAmerica | 186,933 | Security Pacific | 76,411 | 263,344 |
| 1993 | NationsBank | 119,805 | MNC | 17,001 | 136,806 |
|      | BancOne | 61,332 | Valley National | 11,497 | 72,819 |
| 1994 | BankAmerica | 186,933 | Continental | 22,601 | 209,534 |
|      | KeyCorp | 32,648 | Society | 59,664 | 92,312 |
| 1995 | Fleet Financial Group | 48,727 | Shawmut | 32,652 | 81,379 |
|      | First Union | 77,314 | First Fidelity | 36,214 | 113,528 |

| Year | Acquirer | Acquirer assets | Acquired | Acquired assets | Combined |
|---|---|---|---|---|---|
| | PNC | 77,551 | Midlantic | 13,305 | 90,856 |
| | First Chicago | 65,900 | NBD | 47,111 | 113,011 |
| 1996 | Bank of Boston | 47,397 | BayBanks | 12,066 | 59,463 |
| | Chemical | 182,296 | Chase Manhattan | 121,173 | 303,469 |
| | Wells Fargo | 50,316 | First Interstate | 58,071 | 108,658 |
| | National City | 50,587 | Integra | 14,391 | 64,978 |
| | CoreStates | 29,729 | Meridian | 14,740 | 44,469 |
| | Fleet Financial Group | 84,973 | National Westminster | 30,094 | 115,067 |
| 1997 | NationsBank | 174,533 | Boatmen's | 41,844 | 216,377 |
| | NationsBank | 240,400 | Barnett | 44,700 | 285,100 |
| 1998 | First Union | 153,700 | Core States | 48,500 | 205,800 |
| | NationsBank | 315,000 | BankAmerica | 265,000 | 589,000 |
| | Bank One | 116,000 | First Chicago | 114,000 | 231,700 |
| | Norwest | 93,100 | Wells Fargo | 93,200 | 188,400 |
| | Deutche Bank | 673,700 | Bankers Trust | 156,267 | 830,000 |
| | Travelers | 420,000 | Citicorp | 331,000 | 751,000 |

*Source:* Stephen Rhoades, "Bank Mergers and Industrywide Structure 1989–94," Staff study no. 169, Board of Governors of the Federal Reserve System; *Federal Reserve Bulletin*, various issues, 1995–1999.

cent years. And it appears that Europe is on the threshold of a merger movement likely to rival that in the United States.

The bank merger movement is, for good or bad, irrevocably reshaping banking structure in the United States and elsewhere in the world. Its causes are only partly understood. In this chapter we consider the questions of why banks merge, what they hope to achieve, and what they actually do achieve, principally based on U.S. experience. Bank mergers in Europe are discussed in the Appendix. Not surprisingly, a general description of plausible motives for merger are relatively easy to provide, but their empirical significance is more difficult to determine.

## ECONOMIC CONDITIONS

It is clear that the bank merger movement in the United States has occurred in at least two stages. The first was during the 1980s, when many banks experienced large loan losses and poor profits associated with a depressed economy and excessive risk taking. Many were severely injured by loan losses associated with crises in the real estate and energy sectors, and debt problems in developing countries. Bank failures rose to high levels (Table 5.2).

So did mergers. At the time, only the better capitalized and profitable banking organizations were in a position to make substantial acquisitions. With the support of the FDIC, they found themselves able to acquire strategically important, though weakened, banks at low cost and risk. FDIC support (disbursements) is also indicated in Table 5.2. Such assistance not only benefited acquiring banks, but met the FDIC's own needs. The deposit insurance fund, particularly in the late 1980s and early 1990s, was diminishing rapidly, as shown in Table 5.3. Such acquisitions reduced the expected cost of closing large banks that were undercapitalized.

Mergers and acquisitions accelerated during the worst of the period from 1986 through 1989 as bank failures peaked at over 200 in the last two years of the period. Failures remained relatively high through 1992 (Figures 5.1 and 5.2). As can be seen, most of the mergers from 1979 to 1992 were the result of failing banks merging with healthier banks.

Beneficial effects with regard to community needs and managerial factors that enter into federal banking agency merger decisions tend to offset most anticompetitive effects in the case of failing or floundering banks. In any event, the increased numbers of mergers, beginning in the early 1980s, were facilitated by a merger policy that had, as discussed in the previous chapter, become relatively permissive.

Commercial bank loan losses and nonperforming loans reached a peak in 1991, and began to subside thereafter (Figure 5.3). Beginning about 1993, bank profitability improved dramatically and remained at historically high levels through the rest of the decade (Figure 5.4). Comparison with the depression years of the 1930s indicate just how low bank profits had sunk in the

1980s, and how much they improved in the 1990s. Large banks, in particular, made substantial improvements in both profitability and capitalization.

With the onset of better times, the numbers of mergers and acquisitions due to failing banks diminished dramatically. Nevertheless, the numbers of mergers continued to increase, and have been at high levels since 1992. Other factors had come into play.

Policy permissiveness was a necessary condition. As noted, merger policy at the federal agencies became less restrictive. Of comparable importance, merger opportunities expanded. In the 1980s, multiple-office banking restrictions with respect to branching and bank holding acquisitions of banks were liberalized at both the state and federal levels, permitting combinations that had not been possible before. This type of deregulation culminated with passage of the Riegle–Neal Act of 1994, effectively repealing the McFadden Act that had created a barrier to interstate branching. Opportunities for banks combining with other types of financial institutions (insurance companies and securities firms), such as the Citicorp–Travelers merger, and the Bankers Trust (Deutsche Bank) acquisition of Alex Brown, were expanded in late 1999 by passage of Financial Modernization legislation. This Act repealed restrictive sections of the Glass–Steagall Act of 1933, and amended the Bank Holding Company Act to facilitate a broad range of nonbank activity expansion.

It might be argued that what has occurred, at least since 1992, reflects a pent-up demand, accumulating over a long period of time, for expansion and diversification, based on one or more factors that managements expect to increase profits. For example, if law and regulation had continuously permitted nationwide branch banking and unrestrained activity expansion from the beginning of the twentieth century, would any "merger wave" now exist? Perhaps not. If that were the case, current banking and financial structure would look different today than it does. But, it does not follow that the structure that would have developed in the absence of restraints would be identical, or even similar, to the structure toward which we are now heading. Given the limited communication and transportation technology of the early twentieth century, it is possible that large numbers of conglomerate financial institutions would have developed in various regions of the country. Whether they would be more resistant to the motives for merger that now exist than the smaller, less complete financial institutions that now populate the banking and financial services industries is, at best, moot.

## ENABLING FACTORS

We now turn to key factors that have permitted the merger movement to develop in the United States. These include the elimination of geographic restrictions on multiple office banking through both holding companies and branching, the relaxation of restrictions on the activities in which banks can engage, and the bank profit and stock market boom of the last decade. The

Table 5.2
Changes in Number of Insured Commercial Banks: United States and Other Areas (Calendar Years 1965–1999)

| | Additions | | Deletions | | | | Total Banks |
| | New Charters | Conversions | Unassisted Mergers | Failures | | | at Year End |
| Year | | | | Mergers | Paid Off | Other | |
|---|---|---|---|---|---|---|---|
| 1999 | 231 | N/A | 417 | 0 | 7 | N/A | 8,580 |
| 1998 | 194 | 24 | 564 | 3 | 0 | 20 | 8,774 |
| 1997 | 188 | 55 | 601 | 1 | 0 | 28 | 9,143 |
| 1996 | 145 | 49 | 554 | 5 | 0 | 47 | 9,530 |
| 1995 | 102 | 37 | 609 | 6 | 0 | 34 | 9,942 |
| 1994 | 50 | 17 | 548 | 11 | 0 | 16 | 10,452 |
| 1993 | 61 | 12 | 481 | 35 | 27 | 36 | 10,960 |
| 1992 | 72 | 11 | 428 | 73 | 25 | 18 | 11,466 |
| 1991 | 106 | 35 | 447 | 85 | 20 | 9 | 11,927 |
| 1990 | 165 | 24 | 393 | 141 | 17 | 6 | 12,347 |
| 1989 | 192 | 9 | 411 | 175 | 31 | 6 | 12,715 |
| 1988 | 229 | 3 | 598 | 173 | 36 | 11 | 13,137 |
| 1987 | 219 | 37 | 543 | 136 | 50 | 14 | 13,723 |
| 1986 | 257 | 31 | 341 | 101 | 40 | 13 | 14,210 |
| 1985 | 331 | 45 | 336 | 87 | 29 | 3 | 14,417 |
| 1984 | 391 | 49 | 330 | 62 | 16 | 5 | 14,496 |
| 1983 | 361 | 22 | 314 | 33 | 12 | 6 | 14,469 |
| 1982 | 317 | 8 | 256 | 25 | 7 | 0 | 14,451 |
| 1981 | 198 | 0 | 210 | 5 | 2 | 1 | 14,414 |
| 1980 | 205 | 1 | 126 | 7 | 3 | 0 | 14,434 |
| 1979 | 204 | 3 | 224 | 7 | 3 | 0 | 14,364 |
| 1978 | 149 | 2 | 165 | 5 | 1 | 0 | 14,391 |
| 1977 | 157 | 3 | 152 | 6 | 0 | 1 | 14,411 |
| 1976 | 161 | 6 | 125 | 13 | 3 | 0 | 14,410 |

| 1975 | 246 | 5 | 84 | 10 | 3 | 0 | 14,384 |
|------|-----|---|-----|----|---|---|--------|
| 1974 | 364 | 6 | 113 | 3 | 0 | 0 | 14,230 |
| 1973 | 332 | 11 | 94 | 3 | 3 | 0 | 13,976 |
| 1972 | 236 | 4 | 118 | 0 | 1 | 0 | 13,733 |
| 1971 | 197 | 5 | 95 | 1 | 5 | 0 | 13,612 |
| 1970 | 178 | 13 | 146 | 2 | 4 | 1 | 13,511 |
| 1969 | 115 | 18 | 138 | 5 | 4 | 0 | 13,473 |
| 1968 | 82 | 19 | 125 | 3 | 0 | 0 | 13,487 |
| 1967 | 94 | 21 | 131 | 0 | 4 | 0 | 13,514 |
| 1966 | 99 | 24 | 121 | 6 | 1 | 4 | 13,538 |
| 1965 | N/A | N/A | N/A | N/A | N/A | N/A | 13,544 |

*Source:* Federal Deposit Insurance Corporation, *1998 and 1999 Annual Reports* (Washington, D.C.: FDIC, 1998–1999).

**Additions:**

*New Charters* represent institutions newly licensed or chartered by the Office of the Comptroller of the Currency (national banks) or by state banking authorities, including banking authorities in the U.S. territories or possessions. Includes de novo institutions as well as charters issued to take over a failing institution.

*Conversions* represent conversions of existing institutions of any type that meet the definition of commercial banks and have applied for and received FDIC insurance. Also includes banks relocating from out of state.

*Unassisted Mergers* represents voluntary mergers, consolidations, or absorptions of two or more institutions.

**Deletions:**

*Failures–Mergers* represents mergers, consolidations, or absorptions entered into as a result of supervisory actions. The transaction may or may not have required FDIC assistance.

*Failures–Paid off* represents institutions that were declared insolvent, the insured deposits of which were paid by the FDIC.

*Other* represents withdrawals from FDIC insurance, voluntary liquidations, or conversions to institutions that are not considered commercial banks. Also includes banks relocating to another state.

**Table 5.3**

**Insured Commercial Banks and FDIC Disbursements (Number and Deposits of BIF-Insured Banks Closed Because of Financial Difficulties, 1960–1999, Dollars in Thousands)**

| Year | Number of Insured Banks — Total | Without disbursements by FDIC | With disbursements by FDIC | Deposits of Insured Banks — Total | Without disbursements by FDIC | With disbursements by FDIC | Assets |
|---|---|---|---|---|---|---|---|
| Total | 2,091 | 19 | 2,072 | $214,333,958 | $4,298,814 | $210,035,144 | $254,381,571 |
| 1999 | 7 | ... | 7 | $1,268,151 | ... | $1,268,151 | $1,423,819 |
| 1998 | 3 | ... | 3 | $335,076 | ... | $335,076 | $370,400 |
| 1997 | 1 | ... | 1 | 26,800 | ... | 26,800 | 25,921 |
| 1996 | 5 | ... | 5 | 168,228 | ... | 168,228 | 182,502 |
| 1995 | 6 | ... | 6 | 632,700 | ... | 632,700 | 753,024 |
| 1994 | 13 | 1 | 12 | 1,236,488 | ... | 1,236,488 | 1,392,140 |
| 1993 | 41 | ... | 41 | 3,132,177 | ... | 3,132,177 | 3,539,373 |
| 1992 | 120 | 10 | 110 | 41,150,898 | 4,257,667 | 36,893,231 | 44,197,009 |
| 1991 | 124 | ... | 124 | 53,751,763 | ... | 53,751,763 | 63,119,870 |
| 1990 | 168 | ... | 168 | 14,473,300 | ... | 14,473,300 | 15,660,800 |
| 1989 | 206 | ... | 206 | 24,090,551 | ... | 24,090,551 | 29,168,596 |
| 1988 | 200 | ... | 200 | 24,931,302 | ... | 24,931,302 | 35,697,789 |
| 1987 | 184 | ... | 184 | 6,281,500 | ... | 6,281,500 | 6,850,700 |
| 1986 | 138 | ... | 138 | 6,471,100 | ... | 6,471,100 | 6,991,600 |
| 1985 | 120 | ... | 120 | 8,059,441 | ... | 8,059,441 | 8,741,268 |
| 1984 | 79 | ... | 79 | 2,883,162 | ... | 2,883,162 | 3,276,411 |
| 1983 | 48 | ... | 48 | 5,441,608 | ... | 5,441,608 | 7,026,923 |
| 1982 | 42 | ... | 42 | 9,908,379 | ... | 9,908,379 | 11,632,415 |
| 1981 | 10 | ... | 10 | 3,826,022 | ... | 3,826,022 | 4,859,060 |
| 1980 | 10 | ... | 10 | 216,300 | ... | 216,300 | 236,164 |
| 1979 | 10 | ... | 10 | 110,696 | ... | 110,696 | 132,988 |
| 1978 | 7 | ... | 7 | 854,154 | ... | 854,154 | 994,035 |
| 1977 | 6 | ... | 6 | 205,208 | ... | 205,208 | 232,612 |
| 1976 | 16 | ... | 16 | 864,859 | ... | 864,859 | 1,039,293 |
| 1975 | 13 | ... | 13 | 339,574 | ... | 339,574 | 419,950 |
| 1974 | 4 | ... | 4 | 1,575,832 | ... | 1,575,832 | 3,822,596 |
| 1973 | 6 | ... | 6 | 971,296 | ... | 971,296 | 1,309,675 |
| 1972 | 1 | ... | 1 | 20,480 | ... | 20,480 | 22,054 |
| 1971 | 6 | ... | 6 | 132,058 | ... | 132,058 | 196,520 |
| 1970 | 7 | ... | 7 | 54,806 | ... | 54,806 | 62,147 |

Source: Federal Deposit Insurance Corporation, *Annual Report*, vasious issues (Washington, D.C.: FDIC).

Note: Does not include institutions insured by the Savings Association Insurance Fund (SAIF), which was established by the Financial Institutions Reform, Recovery, and Enforcement Act of 1989.

**Figure 5.1**
**Bank Acquisitions and Consolidations, 1985–1998**

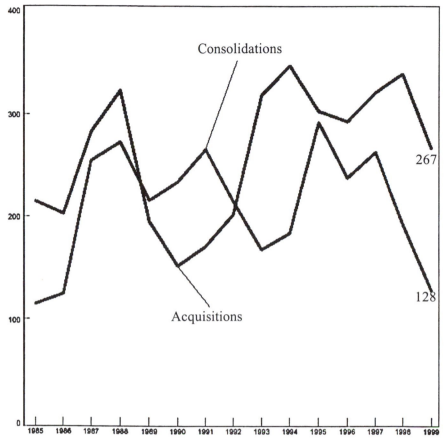

*Note*: See notes to Table 5.2 for definitions of consolidations and acquisitions. Acquisitions include changes in holding company ownership within twelve months of merger, and consolidations have no change in holding company ownership within twelve months of merger. Neither includes commercial banks merged into savings institutions.

liberalization of geographic restrictions culminated with passage of the Riegle–Neal Interstate Banking Act of 1994, and the stock market boom of the past decade has lowered the cost of acquisition. These have been key factors affecting the ability of banks to merge.

### Deregulation: Multiple Office Banking

By the end of the 1980s, most states had liberalized their intrastate restrictions on branching; and, with or without reciprocal agreements and interstate

**Figure 5.2**
**Bank Mergers, Charters, and Failures**

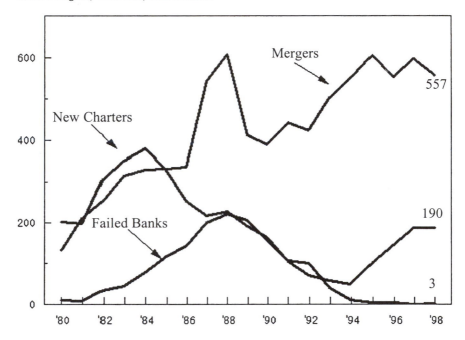

*Note*: See notes for Table 5.2.

compacts, were permitting out-of-state banking organizations to acquire or merge with banking companies in their own states. Passage of the Riegle–Neal Interstate Banking Act of 1994 effectively eliminated most of the McFadden Act constraints on interstate expansion. The Act overrode the reciprocal banking provisions of thirty state laws and permitted bank holding companies to acquire banks in any state, to convert their banks to branches of an interstate bank, and to establish *de novo* or newly chartered interstate branches in accordance with state law. As a result, cross-state mergers that were previously impossible became feasible.

### Deregulation: Activity Restrictions

Geographic deregulation has been paralleled by product deregulation. Product deregulation was initially stimulated by the expansion of savings and loan (S&L) affiliates. In contrast to commercial banks, S&Ls were never subject to the constraints of the Glass–Steagall Act or the McFadden Act. At least since the early 1980s when Congress expanded their powers to provide checkable deposits and make commercial loans, they have served as vehicles to

**Figure 5.3**
**Noncurrent Loans as a Percentage of Loans Outstanding by Loan Type, 1990–1999**

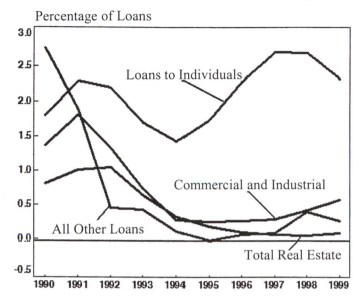

*Source*: Federal Deposit Insurance Corporation, *Quarterly Bank Performance Report, 1999, Fourth Quarter* (Washington, D.C.: FDIC, 1999).

*Note*: Nonaccrual loan rates represent the percentage of loans that are past due ninety days or more in nonaccrual status. All other loans include loans to foreign governments, depository institutions, and lease receivables.

combine traditional banking services with nonbanking businesses. The first S&L holding company (Great Western Financial Corporation) was organized in 1955 by Lehman Brothers, a securities firm. Legislation in 1959 limited such holding companies to no more than one insured S&L. The S&L Holding Company Act of 1968 permitted "unitary S&L holding companies" (holding companies that held only one S&L) that met a "thriftness" test (a minimum percentage of assets in mortgages and other specified securities) to engage through other subsidiaries in any activity. Thus, through a holding company, Sears, Roebuck & Co. could own a retail enterprise and also own insurance, securities, and real estate development companies as well as an S&L.

As discussed earlier, another direct incursion into banking by outside firms was made possible by their acquisition of so-called "nonbank banks." The nonbank bank was a legal construction derived from the definition of the term "bank" which regulated holding companies would control. It emerged after a series of congressional redefinitions aimed at exempting certain types of institutions from regulation. In 1933, when Congress passed its first holding company law, it was only applicable to commercial banks that were mem-

**Figure 5.4**
**ROA and ROE, 1935–1998**

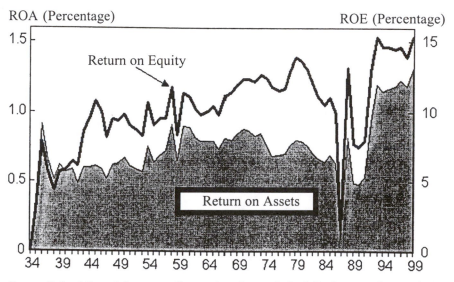

*Source*: Federal Deposit Insurance Corporation, *Quarterly Bank Performance Report, 1999, Fourth Quarter* (Washington, D.C.: FDIC, 1999).

bers of the Federal Reserve System. As pointed out in Chapter 4, in the Bank Holding Company Act of 1956, the term "bank" was broadened to include "any national banking association or any state bank, savings bank or trust company." Congress narrowed the definition in 1966 to include only institutions that accepted demand deposits in order to exempt savings banks, industrial banks and nondeposit trust companies. In 1970, Congress narrowed the definition further to include only institutions that offered *both* demand deposits and commercial loans, to avoid including trust companies, notably Boston Safe Deposit & Trust Company, that accepted demand deposits but did not make commercial loans.

This redefinition opened a loophole that permitted large conglomerates, securities, and insurance firms to acquire banks that refrained either from commercial lending or providing demand deposits. Such banks were duly chartered by the Office of the Comptroller of the Currency or by a state bank supervisory agency, but were not banks under the provisions of the Holding Company Act. By the mid-1980s, General Electric, JCPenney, Gulf + Western, ITT, Prudential Bache, Merrill Lynch, and others owned such nonbank banks.[3]

Congress ultimately closed this loophole in passing the Competitive Equality Banking Act of 1987. In that Act, it again changed the definition of "bank" for bank holding company purposes to include all institutions whose deposits were insured by the FDIC. With over a hundred of these nonbank banks already in existence, Congress grandfathered the existing ones and placed a ceiling on their future growth.

During the course of this unforseen incursion into banking by nonbanking firms, the FDIC established a basis for commercial banks to undertake an incursion of their own into nonbanking activities. It recognized that the Glass–Steagall Act only applied to affiliates of insured commercial banks that were also members of the Federal Reserve System; it did not apply to "state-chartered, non-member insured" banks that the FDIC supervised. By the early 1990s, roughly half the states had authorized affiliates of these typically smaller banks to deal in securities beyond the limits established by federal law and regulation.[4] In a parallel relaxation of restraints on large commercial banking organizations in the late 1980s, the Federal Reserve Board interpreted Section 20 of the Glass–Steagall Act and Section 4(c)(8) of the Bank Holding Company Act to permit bank holding companies to deal in and underwrite, within limits, a wide variety of "ineligible" equity and debt securities in "Section 20 subsidiaries."

The diminishing significance of the legal barriers between commercial banking, investment banking, and other financial businesses culminated in November 1999 with the Gramm–Leach–Bliley Financial Modernization Act that repealed or overrode sections of the Glass–Steagall and Bank Holding Company Acts to permit affiliations among commercial banks, securities firms and insurance companies through newly established financial holding companies.[5]

These end-of-century legislative eliminations of geographic and activity restrictions are, in perspective, momentous. The recent laws did not simply repeal the Depression legislation of the 1930s but removed constraints that were directly or indirectly imposed on commercial banks in the United States at its beginning. Branch banking restrictions, governed by state and federal law, emerged in the early nineteenth century. Narrow definitions of banking powers had been written into the earliest bank charters, beginning in the late eighteenth century.

The effects of the new laws have not, as yet, been fully realized. But it is clear that they have created opportunities for enormous combinations, such as Citicorp–Travelers, that are in process of being exploited.

### Profits and Market Valuation

Since the early 1990s, the profits and market value of large banking companies have increased substantially. After 1991, both returns on assets and equity rose to record levels. By 1996, the top twenty U.S. banking companies had price/earnings ratios of fifteen to thirty-three times, and unprecedented market-to-book value ratios of 1.8 to 3.0. In April 1998, Citicorp stock had a market-to-book value of 3.3. However, by the end of 1999 these multiples had declined for most large banks. For example, Chase Manhattan had a market to book value ratio of 2.7 compared to 3.5 in early 1998 and First Union showed a multiple of 1.9 compare to 3.4 earlier.

The significant improvement in bank profitability and the cash flow generated, revealed in Figures 5.3 and 5.4, encouraged banks to make acquisitions and increased the rewards for acquisition targets. Increased market valuations have provided the fuel for stock swap-based mergers. The subsequent decline in relative stock values substantially reduced the ability of banks to continue a growth-by-acquisitions strategy and has, in turn, lowered their market values relative to other companies. This is demonstrated in Figure 5.5 where the S&P Bank Stock Index is compared with the broader market S&P 500 Index for the period 1988 to August 2000; the recent lack of growth in large bank stock values is also shown.

## MOTIVATIONS

A variety of factors, including a pursuit of larger size and cost reduction, appear to have ratcheted upward the desire to merge. In the following sections, we review the possible impact of competition and its effects on profits, advances in information technology and software development, managerial compensation, and the retention of regulatory protection for the largest banking organizations.

### Competition and Profits

The announcements of bank CEOs, which are generally consistent with statements made by banks in their merger applications, indicate that, as a general matter, the merger wave is a response to increased competition that threatens profits. The increased competition is conventionally traced to deregulation and technological innovation. Deregulation has facilitated competition among banks and other financial firms that previously operated in segmented geographic and product markets. Technological improvements have provided opportunities for cost reduction and new products that must be embraced to compete effectively. In this popular explanation for mergers, deregulation and technology, factors that have enabled the current merger wave have also induced it.

With profits threatened, it is plausible that individual banks will respond by fight or flight; that is, by making acquisitions or being acquired. The benefits of acquisitions (as well as combining with others as more or less equal partners) could be traced to one or more of the following factors: (1) reduced costs through growth to larger size; (2) the provision of additional services that permits more effective competition with larger organizations; (3) the exploitation of new profit opportunities through, for example, restructuring less efficient institutions; (4) protection against unwanted acquisition by larger organizations; (5) protection against one or more kinds of operating risk, for example, by diversifying sources of income; and (6) protection against competition by eliminating actual or potential competitors.

**Figure 5.5**
**Bank Stock Prices Relative to the Broader S&P 500 Index (Weekly, 1988 to August 2000)**

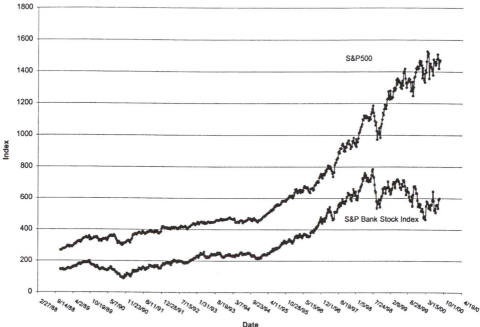

Motivations for banks that wish to be acquired, in this frame of reference, might be traced to an irreparable vulnerability. They find themselves, perhaps because of their size, inadequate management and/or insufficient profitability, unable to make acquisitions or combine to ameliorate their vulnerability. With the stock market boom and increased bank profits, they find the price is right.

As a general matter, in entering new geographic and product markets large banking organizations have sought to achieve a substantial market share rapidly by acquiring leading organizations. Acquisitions are often justified by the argument that they are needed to meet the competition of even larger organizations throughout the world and/or to function profitably in the developing banking environment and/or to avoid becoming an acquisition target themselves.

### Advances in Technology and the Impact on Costs

The role of technological change is potentially of key importance and merits further discussion. Advances in the microcomputer and information technologies may have contributed to the merger wave through both increasing competition and the promise of cost savings. The new technology has driven down the real cost of recording, processing, and distributing information. About a decade ago, it was calculated that between 1964 and 1987 the decline in such costs had been about 95 percent. In other words, what cost $1,000 in 1964, cost $50 in 1987.[6] A more recent calculation in 1998 found that since 1982 the cost of a microprocessor with computing capacity of one million instructions per second had fallen by over 99.8 percent. Computing that cost $1,000 in 1982 had fallen to $1.30. The same study projected that over the next ten years, the cost would likely decline to about one-tenth of one penny.[7]

Reductions in cost have permitted the development of new kinds of financial instruments and modes of transactions, including automated teller machines (ATMs), credit cards, debit cards, money market mutual funds, mortgage-backed securities, and complex derivative instruments. The new technology has facilitated electronic banking and brokerage relationships through desktop computers and high speed networks with growing bandwidth that substantially increases information flow. Innovations in the security of transactions and customer identity will provide broader dissemination of network related transactions among businesses. Providing managements with the ability to monitor and control millions of additional transactions, the new technology has also facilitated the growth of global financial markets.

The result has been a breaking down of entry barriers and the appearance of new competition in traditional bank deposit and loan markets. A wider range of institutional and market options have become available to bank depositors. Many borrowers are able to tap wider lending markets, sometimes directly circumventing banks.

The president of the Federal Reserve Bank of Richmond recently argued that "the extraordinary advances in communications and data processing over the last two decades is the single most important underlying factor" increasing the numbers of mergers.[8] He points to the development of database-management software for mainframe computers that automated record keeping. This made it possible for banks to provide widespread access to their records at branches and ATMs. These advances permitted costs savings in managing information that accrue most fully to very large banking organizations, and lowered cost of maintaining far-flung branches and operating centralized call centers. For example, the 1999 merger announcement by two large Japanese banking institutions, Sumitomo, Ltd. and Sakura, Ltd., to create a new banking company with $927 billion in resources, cited the need to combine resources to upgrade their information systems.

The seeming technological imperative underlying mergers nevertheless raises questions. With the dramatic decline in the cost of computing and network systems, why are massive resources now required to adopt the latest technologies? It would seem that if substantial resources are required to effectively utilize the technological advances available, then economies of scale must be substantial, and banking must be a declining cost industry. If so, such economies should be observable. We discuss this proposition more thoroughly in the next chapter on the economics of the merger movement.

### Diversification and Risk

From a historical perspective in the United States, there would be no better reason for mergers than to expand the geographic reach of banks, and the range of products they sell to permit them to achieve greater stability by offsetting losses in some areas with gains in others. Every major banking crisis in the twentieth century produced proposals to liberalize branching restrictions for the purpose of reducing bank risk.

Reducing exposure to risk through diversification may or may not in actuality result in less risky banks. If banks do not believe a costly episode of financial distress is likely, a value maximizing strategy would be to trade current profitability for reduced risk.[9]

The continuing plausibility of diversification and risk reduction as motives, particularly for large bank mergers, may be questioned in the era of a global economy where large banks have offices throughout the world and have been relatively unrestricted in entering new product markets. This factor is also discussed more fully in the next chapter.

### Managerial Compensation

A motive for mergers might be found in increased managerial compensation. Because banking is not a growth industry, stock appreciation is not likely in the long run to be a major source of compensation for management. Managerial salary, however, is directly related to organizational size. The bank regulatory agencies generally recognize and accept this relationship as consistent with their safety and soundness aims. In examinations, they scrutinize senior officers' compensation for excessive amounts. Greater compensation at larger organizations do not send up warning flags.

There may be a somewhat more complex relationship between mergers, larger size, and managerial compensation. In the current financial environment, high returns on equity and assets not only provide the cash flow needed to support merger offers, but also, when necessary, for stock buybacks aimed at sustaining stock prices after the mergers. A stock price reversal, in the greatest bull market ever, could be viewed by stockholders as a blemish on management performance and lead them to conclude that the merger has simply provided a means to satisfy management demands for higher compensation by diluting the value of existing shares. If the costs of an acquisition, in terms of stock value, turn out to be larger than anticipated, high earnings can provide cover by allowing stock buybacks to placate shareholders and directors.

As can be seen by comparing Figures 5.2, 5.4, and 5.5, the increase in mergers and acquisitions in the 1990s, coincided with the increase in banking profits. The confluence of greater profitability and the stock market boom can be viewed as providing bank management with an incentive to acquire other banks independent of increased competition and its related effects.

It is possible that the best use of free cash flow is to increase or stabilize share value. If this is the case, few mergers will increase value permanently without a fundamental improvement in the way the business of banking is conducted. For example, a study of interstate mergers between 1982 and 1989 found that banks that combined in states that had established regional compacts for interstate banking did have immediate gains; on the other hand, the large money center banks, particularly in states like New York, which were excluded from regional agreements, did not. However, none of the gains proved to be permanent.[10] Bank management can't simply apply more leverage to get increases in value. They need to permanently change bank cost structure, service production methods, and/or product range and mix.

The makeover of many of the money center banks in the 1990s, from traditional commercial banks to hybrid commercial and investment banks, constitutes the kind of change that can improve value. The new financial modernization legislation permitting affiliations among banks, securities firms, and insurance companies is likely to be perceived as providing opportunities for further increases in value and consequently trigger a new merger wave.

### Another Attribute of Size: Too-Big-to-Fail

There is yet another possible motivation to gain larger size by merger. As discussed in Chapter 3, the reforms implemented in the early 1930s were aimed at preventing a recurrence of the massive failures of the Great Depression. In the following three decades, relatively few banks failed each year; and by the 1950s, typically only those that suffered from insider abuse. The restrictions on competition, limitations on activities, and FDIC insurance established all banks as too important to fail.

With the restoration of economic stability in the post–World War II years, the gradual realization that the benefits of competition outweighed the potential costs, the modification or elimination of many of the Depression-borne restrictions in the 1980s, and the costly regulatory support of failing S&Ls, Congress began to view the possible failure of banks as a normal market event that should not require special regulatory intervention. The passage of the FDIC Improvement Act (FDICIA) in 1991 clarified congressional intent that government support for failing banks should be an exceptional event. The exceptional event might be the pending failure of one or more very large banking organizations that could constitute a systemic threat to the financial system and/or the economy; that is, through contagion or in other ways undermine aggregate financial and economic stability.

The federal bank regulatory agencies had long been cognizant of such possibilities. On such grounds, the FDIC announced in 1984 that all the creditors of the failing Continental Illinois banking organization, not simply insured depositors, would be protected from loss. The Federal Reserve organized a consortium of money center banks to support Continental.[11] The agencies supported InterFirst Texas in 1987. They propped up an insolvent Bank of New England from 1989 to 1991 before permitting it to fail and guaranteed all deposits. On the rationale of avoiding a financial disaster, they took extraordinary measures, beginning in November 1990, to keep Citibank afloat.[12]

More recently, in September 1998 the Federal Reserve Bank of New York, with the approval of the Federal Reserve Board, lent its good offices to bring together fourteen of the major creditors of Long Term Capital Management (LTCM) to work out an arrangement to save the company by providing a $3.2 billion capital infusion.[13] Although no U.S. taxpayer funds were used, this was an unprecedented excercise of Federal Reserve authority to organize a private bailout of a nonbanking company whose failure threatened a number of banks and other firms that had loaned it money.

"Too-big-to-fail" may be viewed as a safety net subsidy to large banking organizations. One study by Flannery and Sorescu finds some evidence of increased market discipline that suggests the federal safety net subsidy has become less pronounced.[14] But even if accurate, the extent of the remaining guarantee is likely to be significant.[15]

The idea that banks may be motivated to merge to achieve or solidify too-big-to-fail status was further supported by the recent recognition by the chairman of the Federal Reserve Board that the twenty-five largest banking organizations need to be treated differently, with respect to examination procedures and reporting.[16] Chairman Greenspan suggested that mergers have made large banking companies much less transparent to the investing public and to regulators. It is also supported by a recent FDIC study indicating that the megamergers that took place between 1990 and 1997 increased the risk of Bank Insurance Fund (BIF) insolvency by approximately 50 percent; and that the risk has increased subsequently as the result of megamergers through mid-1999.[17] We note the irony in the willingness of the bank regulatory agencies to approve megamergers without considering the systemic threats that they pose, that they fully understand, and necessarily confront.

The too-big-to-fail policy inevitably provides an incentive for large bank mergers. Because one effect is to reduce the cost of funding for large banking organizations, the policy is likely to distort the competitive relationships between very large banking companies and other banks. These effects are elaborated in Chapter 6.

## EMPIRICAL ANALYSIS OF MERGER MOTIVES

Given the enabling factors outlined, each of the motives described may explain to some extent why banks want to increase their size and scope through acquisition. Their relative importance, if any, is difficult to establish empirically.

The empirical study of merger motives typically begins with a conventional economic assumption; that is, mergers are intended to increase net benefits to the acquiring organization's shareholders and/or management by enhancing profits and/or shareholder value and/or management earnings. As discussed, higher profits, market value, and management compensation may be derived from decreased costs or increased revenues, with the last mentioned also benefitting as a result of growth to larger size.

In searching for significant motives, the typical approach has been to make inferences from the economic and financial condition of merging organizations before they combine (*ex ante*) and from the condition of resulting organizations after combinations have been consumated (*ex post*). Looking at merging banks before they merge, it might be found that they were too small to reach efficient size. It then might be inferred that their mergers were motivated by the aim to realize economies of scale. Alternatively, if merging banks were specialized in different ways with, for example, retail-specialized banks merging with wholesale-specialized banks, it might be inferred that the merger motive was to expand the range of services offered by the resulting organization to achieve better diversification and, perhaps, economies of scope.

Alternatively, postmerger results can be evaluated. If, for example, it is determined that merged banks have experienced reductions in costs, it might be inferred that the intent was to realize economies of scale or scope and/or improved diversification. If, as a result of mergers, revenues of the combined organizations increase, it might be inferred that the intent was to exploit new profit opportunities.

In a recent paper, Stephen Rhoades tested a premerger motivational hypothesis by examining postmerger results. He examined nine mergers that occurred in the early 1990s; each was considered a good candidate for improved efficiency.[18] All involved large banks with substantial market overlap. In each case, premerger projections developed by the merger partners indicated that the combinations would produce substantial reductions in cost. Rhoades found that all of the mergers did result in cost cutting, but that only four of the nine were clearly successful in improving (cost) efficiency. Cost cutting alone is distinguished from cost efficiency which relates costs to assets or revenues. (Efficiency concepts are discussed more fully in Chapter 6.)

Looking at postmerger results in the 1990s, Allen Berger found that mergers have not increased cost efficiency but have increased profit efficiency by waking up inefficient management, by permitting merged banks to shift their outputs mixes from lower rate securities to higher rate loans, and from improved diversification.[19]

Hughes, Lang, Mester, and Moon have also found economic incentives for mergers in postmerger gains, particularly for banks engaged in interstate banking expansion.[20] The source of the improvement they found is in diversification of macroeconomic risk and in the reduced risk of insolvency. Risk reduction increased the merged banks' market value.

Berger, Demsetz, and Strahan have reviewed an extensive literature on merger motives through 1998.[21] They conclude that the acquisition of seemingly inefficient banks in the 1980s and early 1990s suggests efforts to restructure inefficient banks, thus exploiting profit opportunities.

During this period, however, many of the banks in financial distress (more than 2,000 were merged or failed) were in local markets that were experiencing economic recession. Once economic conditions improved, loan losses at the surviving banks in these locations declined, and profitability increased without change in management. Were the banks with low profitability that were acquired during this period really inefficient? Or were they only temporarily impacted by local conditions? Should their acquisition be viewed as efficient banks acquiring less efficient institutions to restructure them, or simply a fire sale motivated by acquiring bank recognition of their long-term franchise value?

Berger, Demsetz, and Strahan also find little to support improved cost efficiency as a rationale for mergers, particularly megamergers. They do find evidence that acquiring banks target banks that can provide a significant competitive advantage by increasing market share substantially.

They conclude

The evidence is consistent with increases in market power from some types of consolidation; improvements in profit efficiency and diversification risks [*sic*, geographic primarily], but little cost efficiency improvement on average; relatively little effect on the availability of services to small customers; potential improvements in payments system efficiency; and, potential costs on the financial system from increasing systemic risk or expanding the financial safety net.[22]

The empirical analysis of motivation throws considerable light on what kinds of banks merge and the effects of mergers on their economic and financial condition, but a number of questions remain as to the relative importance of the several plausible motivations. A key problem lies in making inferences from findings that are consistent with multiple motives. For example, the same premerger conditions that permit an inference that acquiring banks are exploiting profit opportunities by restructuring relatively inefficient banks are consistent with a motive to gain market share, eliminate competitors, and raise management compensation. The same postmerger conditions that permit an inference that the intent of acquiring banks is to reduce costs by reducing risk through diversification and making more efficient use of capital are consistent with an intent to reduce risk by diminishing competition and/or establishing a status as too-big-to-fail. Inferences from postmerger findings also raise the possibility that actual motivation may differ from results; that is, interpretation is confounded by the pervasive affliction of unintended consequences.

The analysis might be rescued from ambiguity if it were viewed as testing independently established motivational hypotheses. For example, the cost reduction projections made by merging banks in the Rhoades study might be taken as such a hypothesis. Unfortunately, the announced cost-reducing projections of merging banks are not independent. They are endogenous in the merger wave–merger policy process as a mitigating factor, offsetting increases in concentration. Eliminating competitors, increasing management compensation, and becoming too-big-to-fail are not mitigating factors. We should never expect them to be mentioned by bank officials in public.

We conclude that the standard economic assumption that mergers aim to increase profit or market value cannot in itself distinguish among the several distinct motivational objectives for reaching this goal or determining their relative importance. The empirical results of recent investigations are consistent with multiple motivations. It is plausible, in fact, that multiple motives for acquisitions are common; that is, simultaneously to reduce costs, eliminate or diminish competitors, achieve higher rewards for management, defend against being acquired, and establish or fortify too-big-to-fail status. While the results of this line of investigation are modest, at bottom, the motivation(s) for merger are less important than the results. These are discussed in more detail in the next chapter.

## SUMMARY AND CONCLUSIONS

Many bank mergers in the less prosperous 1980s constituted a resolution of failed banks through combination with healthy banks. Over the past ten to fifteen years, the underlying factors leading to mergers have changed. The relaxation of regulatory constraints on geographic and product expansion, a less constraining merger policy, increased bank profitability, and a bull market in stocks have established an environment conducive to the merger of sound banks. Motives for mergers can be found in bank managements' efforts to increase profits and shareholder value, as well as to increase their own compensation, through a variety of means including exploiting technological innovations to reduce costs, growing larger, and diminishing competition.

Empirical studies, to this point, have not been definitive in their findings on motivations, but they do shed light on results of mergers. So far, there is no indication that mergers, on average, achieve lower costs as a result of greater scale, permanent increases in value from the combination, lower prices to banking customers, or greater cost efficiencies. There is some evidence that they lead to greater profit efficiencies which may emanate from increased market power and higher prices for retail banking services. Greater bank size tends to enhance compensation for senior management and directors, and to establish or augment a bank's status as too-big-to-fail.

## APPENDIX: BANK CONSOLIDATION IN EUROPE

Even though relatively little bank restructuring has taken place over the last decade in continental Europe, the relatively few studies that have been undertaken reach similar conclusions to those reached in studies of U.S. mergers. European banking, however, now appears on the threshold of a period of intensified competition both from within the Economic Monetary Union (EMU) and from U.S. and U.K. companies, and increased merger activity.[23]

The structure of the financial services industries in Europe varies considerably from country to country. At one extreme, Credit Lyonnaise, one of the largest banking companies in continental Europe, is controlled by the French government. At the other extreme, one of the largest banking companies in the world, the German Deutsche Bank, is privately owned and listed on the New York Stock Exchange. In between, large numbers of financial institutions are partially controlled and/or influenced in their operations by government direction. Regardless of formal ownership, the governments of the several European countries still play major roles in the banking industry, even with the advent of the Euro and an independent European Central Bank (ECB).

European banks have not been as profitable or valuable as U.S. banks over the last decade. In 1996, for example, the return on assets (ROA) for European banks ranged between 0.032 percent and 0.51 percent, compared to an average ROA for U.S. banks of 1.86 percent. Net interest margins in Europe ranged between 1.40 and 2.51 percent compared to an average of 3.83 percent for U.S. banks.[24]

Continental European banks, unlike their U.S. and U.K. counterparts, still have most of their business in relationship banking, in contrast to the emphasis in recent years at U.S. and U.K. banks on fee-based and off-balance sheet activities. The business of lending done in this fashion is reminiscent of banking in the United States in the late 1960s and 1970s. Debt financing is also largely done through traditional banking relationships. In general, European banks have made relatively small investments in current information technology.

Up to now, European bank mergers, with some exceptions, have been within home countries. As markets for private debt develop and/or large European borrowers migrate to the United States for borrowing, there is likely to be the same type of restructuring of large banking companies as is taking place in the United States. In Europe, in contrast to banks, insurance companies have been active in acquisitions. These acquisitions may not have been as profitable as anticipated, but in the coming years insurance companies may find banking acquisitions more satisfying.[25]

Relatively poor profitability and low market values could make European banks acquisition targets by foreign banks. William White of the Bank for International Settlements has suggested that the introduction of the Euro has made it necessary for continental European banks to restructure rapidly to avoid acquisition by foreign companies. Defending against acquisition constitutes an incentive for a new wave of mergers and acquisitions.

The merger wave in Europe has probably begun. Much of the recent acquisition activity has been within countries. Cost reductions have been the announced objective. For example, the new United Bank of Switzerland (UBS) announced plans to cut employment by 13,000 of the 56,000 jobs worldwide, with 7,000 coming in Switzerland. Two private banks in Germany, Bayerische Vereinsbank and Bayerische Hypotheken-und-Wechsel-Bank, have recently merged to form the second largest bank in the country.[26]

So far cross-border mergers have not been prominent. They do not offer the opportunity to eliminate overlapping offices and reduce staff. Increasing market value and profitability becomes a more formidable task.

Cross-border mergers are further confounded by the current institutional framework of the EMU. In practice, responsibility for prudential supervision for financial service firms remains at the national level, while monetary authority has been transferred to the ECB. In times of crisis, the need for coordination will be evident. But conflicts are likely to develop. National supervisors and the national central banks will find it necessary to protect the stability of their own financial systems. Such protection may be inconsistent with the supranational responsibilities of the ECB and the EMU to prevent inflation and restrict bailouts.[27]

A recent study of Italian bank mergers by Focarelli, Panetta, and Salleo utilized a new data base for tracking changes in merging banks that have engaged in combinations, either as active or passive institutions.[28] The authors suggest that those individual banks active in acquiring other banks attempt to exploit profit opportunities or to protect themselves from some kinds of risk; specifically through restructuring less efficient banks, diversifying sources of income, and/or protecting against liquidity-risk exposure. The presumed motives of passive banks are not as clearly specified, but it can be inferred that they accept acquisition because their condition makes them vulnerable, and because the price is right.

"Before" balance sheet-income statement characteristics are interpreted as motives, and "after" comparable accounting statement characteristics are interpreted as results. The authors distinguish between mergers, where independent banks lose their charter and identity, and acquisitions where, without loss of charter or identity, control of a previously independent bank is transferred, through a shift of majority voting rights. They determine the likelihood that a bank will engage in a combination either in an active or passive role through multinomial logit analysis, with independent variables that are subsequently transformed to comparable dependent variables to determine the effects.

The principle findings are that acquiring banks are larger, obtain a larger proportion of their income from services, and have a smaller net interbank balance than banks not involved in any transaction. The primary incentive to merge is interpreted as a desire to acquire bank customers to whom profitable services can be provided, and to reduce liquidity-risk exposure. Acquired banks are less profitable, have higher costs, more bad loans, and appear good candidates for restructuring. Changes following mergers however do not indicate that economies of scale or scope have been exploited. A higher return on equity derives from improvements in profit efficiency; that is, increased profits resulting from a more efficient use of capital, a reduction in the tax burden, and improvements in loan quality. Increased fees are offset by higher labor costs.

While the conclusions reached are similar to those for the U.S. merger studies reviewed, they suffer from the same problems. The assumption of profit and value motivation does not establish specific motivational hypotheses for testing, and premerger characteristics do not in themselves clearly identify specific motives.

## NOTES

1. See Rhoades 1996; Meyer 1998. Large-bank assets acquired by other large banks have risen by a factor of 5 since 1989. See Holland, Inscoe, Waldrop, and Kutta 1996, 12, Table 5.

2. 84 *Federal Reserve Bulletin* 858 (1998).

3. See U.S. Department of the Treasury 1991, XVIII–21 ff.

4. Ibid., XVIII–16.

5. Under the new law, financial holding companies may, through several avenues, also acquire or control any kind of ownership interest in a firm engaged in any kind of trade or business.

6. Huertas 1987, 143.

7. The calculation is reported in "Competition, Competitiveness and the Public Interest" 1998, 13, and is from McKinsey & Company.

8. Broaddus 1998, 5.

9. Hughes, Lang, Mester, and Moon 1999, 299. There is good reason to believe that long expansions tend to reduce the subjective probability of systemic events and financial distress.

10. Goldberg, Hanweck, and Sugrue 1992.

11. FDIC 1997.

12. Fromson and Knight 1993.

13. Raghavan and Pacelle 1998.

14. Flannery and Sorescu 1996, 1347–1377.

15. See Hanweck 1999.

16. Greenspan 1999.

17. Oshinksy 1999.

18. Rhoades 1998.

19. Berger 1998.

20. Hughes, Lang, Mester, and Moon 1999.

21. Berger, Demsetz, and Strahan 1999.

22. Ibid., 135.

23. White 1998.

24. Ibid., 26, Table 2.

25. Ibid., 22.

26. Ibid.

27. Ibid., 25.

28. Focarelli, Panetta, and Salleo 1999. The analysis that follows draws on Shull 1999.

## REFERENCES

Berger, Allen N. 1998. "The Efficiency Effects of Bank Mergers and Acquisitions: A Preliminary Look at the 1990s Data." In *Bank Mergers and Acquisitions.* Ed. Amihud and Miller. Boston: Kluwer Academic Publishers.

Berger, Allen N., Rebecca S. Demsetz, and Philip E. Strahan. 1999. "The Consolidation of the Financial Services Industry: Causes, Consequences, and Implications for the Future." *Journal of Banking and Finance* 23 (February): 135–194.

Broaddus, J. Alfred Jr. "The Bank Merger Wave: Causes and Consequences." *Economic Quarterly* (Federal Reserve Bank of Richmond) 84, no. 3: 5.

"Competition, Competitiveness and the Public Interest. The Changing Landscape for Canadian Financial Services: New Forces, New Competitors, New Choices." 1998. Research paper prepared for the Task Force on the Future of the Canadian Financial Services Center, Ottawa, Canada, September.

Federal Deposit Insurance Corporation (FDIC). 1997. *History of the Eighties.* Washington, D.C.: FDIC.

Flannery, Mark J., and Sorin M. Sorescu. 1996. "Evidence of Market Discipline in Subordinated Debt Issues: 1983–1991." *Journal of Finance* 51: 1347–1377.

Focarelli, Dario, Fabio Panetta, and Carmelo Salleo. 1999. "Why Do Banks Merge?" Paper presented at Meetings of Western Economic Association, San Diego, California, July.

Fromson, Britt, and Jerry Knight. 1993. "The Saving of Citibank." *Washington Post,* 16 June, A1.

Goldberg, Lawrence G., Gerald A. Hanweck, and Timothy F. Sugrue. 1992. "Differential Impact on Bank Valuation of Interstate Banking Law Changes." *Journal of Banking and Finance* 16: 1145–1158.

Greenspan, Alan. 1999. Remarks before the American Bankers Association, Phoenix, Arizona, 11 October.

Hanweck, Gerald A. 1999. "The Issue of the Federal Safety Net Subsidy: Evidence from the Pricing of Banking Company Subordinated Debt." In *Refuting the Federal Safety Net "Subsidy" Argument.* Washington, D.C.: Financial Services Roundtable.

Holland, David, Don Inscoe, Ross Waldrop, and William Kutta. 1996. "Interstate Banking: The Past, Present and Future." *FDIC Banking Review* 9, no. 1: 2–30.

Huertas, Thomas F. 1987. "Redesigning Regulation: The Future of Finance in the United States." In *Restructuring the Financial System.* Kansas City: Federal Reserve Bank of Kansas City.

Hughes, Joseph P., William W. Lang, Loretta J. Mester, and Choon-Geol Moon. 1999. "The Dollar and Sense of Bank Consolidation." *Journal of Banking and Finance* 23: 291–324.

Meyer, Lawrence H. 1998. Statement before the House Committee on Banking and Financial Services. U.S. House of Representatives, 29 April. Reprinted in 84 *Federal Reserve Bulletin* 438–451 (1998).

Oshinsky, Robert. 1999. "Effects of Bank Consolidation on the Bank Insurance Fund." FDIC Working Paper no. 99-3, Washington, D.C.

Raghavan, Anita, and Mitchell Pacelle. 1998. "A Hedge Fund Falters and Big Banks Agree to Ante-Up $3.5 Billion." *Wall Street Journal,* 24 September, A1.

Rhoades, Stephen. 1996. "Bank Mergers and Industrywide Structure, 1980–94." Staff study no. 169. Board of Governors of the Federal Reserve System.

———. 1998. "The Efficiency Effects of Bank Mergers: An Overview of Case Studies of Nine Mergers." *Journal of Banking and Finance* 22: 273–291.

Shull, Bernard. 1999. "Comment." *Research in Financial Services: Private and Public Policy*, 2: 61–65. Stamford, Conn.: JAI Press.

U.S. Department of the Treasury. 1991. Modernizing the Financial System. Washington, D.C.: U.S. Department of the Treasury.

White, William R. 1998. "The Coming Transformation of Continental European Banking." Working Paper no. 54. Bank for International Settlements.

# CHAPTER 6

# The Economics of Structural Reorganization

Every expanding opens frontiers, every conquest exposes flanks.

Erik Eriksen[1]

The evolution of bank merger policy, as reviewed in Chapter 4, coupled with the imperatives for merger considered in Chapter 5, have produced results that could hardly be imagined forty years ago when Congress and the Supreme Court fashioned a merger policy to deal with increasing bank concentration. Today, large bank mergers are never denied; in fact, few bank mergers of any size are denied on competitive grounds. As a result, the numbers of banking organizations in the United States has declined precipitously and a handful of organizations have grown to enormous size. With passage of the Gramm–Leach–Bliley Act in November 1999 that facilitates the affiliation of commercial banks, insurance companies, and securities firms, further conglomerate growth by the largest organizations is in prospect.

The conventional wisdom is that the wave of mergers now underway is leading to improvements in efficiency, diversification and competition; and that bank customers will benefit. In this chapter we undertake an evaluation of the changes now in progress, both through a review of available research findings and through independent analysis. The first three sections provide a review of the impact of the merger movement on banking structure, efficiency, and risk. The remainder of the chapter considers the effects of mergers on the prices of banking services.

In general, we find little evidence that consumers and small businesses have gained from greater efficiency and competition. There is some evidence that mergers, even though carefully scrutinized by the federal banking agencies and the Justice Department for anticompetitive structural effects in local markets, have had anticompetitive consequences; and that the bank consolidation movement is producing new structural configurations that tend to restrain competition.

## MERGERS AND STRUCTURAL CHANGE

As noted, between 1980 and 1998 there were about 7,400 mergers of independent commercial banking organizations. The long-running merger movement has been highlighted by large bank combinations. From 1987 through 1998, there were about 200 mergers in which each of the merging organizations held over $1 billion in assets.[2] And, as shown in Table 5.1, between 1991 and 1998 there have been twenty-nine megamergers involving organizations having $10 billion or more in assets.

Principally as a result of these mergers there has been a substantial decline in the number of commercial banking organizations in the United States, from about 12,300 in 1980 to about 7,000 in 1998. As shown in Table 6.1, national or aggregate concentration among these institutions has increased substantially, with the share of the ten largest organizations rising from 18.6 percent to about 30 percent over this period.

On average, however, as shown in Table 6.2, local market concentration for commercial banks alone has hardly changed at all. In 1980, the three-bank concentration ratio for Metropolitan Statistical Areas (MSAs) averaged 66.8 percent and in 1997, 65.4 percent. In rural (non-MSA) markets, the three-bank ratio averaged 89.6 percent in 1980, and 88.3 percent in 1997. A similar stability is reflected in the Herfindahl–Hirschman Index (HHI) for the period.

Nevertheless, when savings institutions (thrifts) are combined (weighted at 50 percent) with commercial banks, average local market concentration shows a substantial increase, albeit from a lower level (Table 6.3). Including thrifts, the average HHI for MSAs increased between 1985 and 1997 from 1,370 to 1,643, with increases in concentration in more than three times as many MSAs as had decreases.[3]

Linear extrapolations of current numbers and concentration trends indicate various outcomes over the next ten to fifteen years, depending on starting and ending dates, and methodology. One 1992 study made a best-guess estimate of 5,500 independent banking organizations in 2010, with the largest 50 accounting for 70 percent of domestic assets, and the largest 100, 87 percent.[4] This outcome can be compared to the 1989 shares of the top 50 and top 100

**Table 6.1**
**Industrywide Banking Structure, 1980–1997**

| | YEAR | | | | |
|---|---|---|---|---|---|
| | **1980** | **1985** | **1990** | **1997** | **1999** |
| **Structural Characteristic** | | | | | |
| No. of banks | 14,407 | 14,268 | 12,194 | 9,604 | 8,580 |
| No. of banking organizations | 12,342 | 11,021 | 9,221 | 7,122 | 7,120 |
| No. of banking offices | 52,710 | 57,417 | 63,392 | 71,080 | 71,142 |
| Concentration: | | | | | |
| Proportion of deposits held by top 10 | 18.6 | 17.0 | 20.0 | 29.9 | N/A |
| % deposits held by top 25 | 29.1 | 28.5 | 34.9 | 47.0 | N/A |
| %deposits held by top 100 | 46.8 | 52.6 | 61.4 | 69.1 | N/A |

*Source*: This table is adapted from data in Stephen Rhoades, "Bank Mergers and Industrywide Structure, 1980–94," Staff study no. 169, Board of Governors of the Federal Reserve System, 1996. Updated and revised data have been obtained from the *Financial Structure Information Book*, vols. 1 and 2, and from the Financial Structure Section, Board of Governors of the Federal Reserve System, 1997. Data are for all insured commercial banks. Concentration data are consolidated for banking organizations.

**Table 6.2**
**Local Market Concentration, 1980–1997**

| | YEAR | | | |
|---|---|---|---|---|
| **Structural Characteristic** | **1980** | **1985** | **1990** | **1997** |
| Avg. 3-bank concentration for MSAs (%) | 66.8 | 66.7 | 67.5 | 65.4 |
| Avg. 3-bank concentration for non-MSAs (%) | 89.6 | 89.4 | 89.6 | 88.3 |
| Avg. HHI of MSAs | 1973 | 1992 | 1977 | 2010 |
| Avg. HHI of non-MSAs | 4417 | 4357 | 4291 | 4114 |
| No. of markets | 2,736 | 2,693 | 2,681 | 2,582 |

*Source*: This table is adapted from data in Stephen Rhoades, "Bank Mergers and Industrywide Structure, 1980–94," Staff study no. 169, Board of Governors of the Federal Reserve System, 1996. Updated and revised data have been obtained from the *Financial Structure Information Book*, vols. 1 and 2, and from the Financial Structure Section, Board of Governors of the Federal Reserve System, 1997. Data are for all insured commercial banks. Concentration data are consolidated for banking organizations.

*Note*: MSAs are Metropolitan Statistical Areas as defined by the Department of Commerce. Non-MSAs are counties not included within MSAs. HHI is the Herfindahl–Hirschman Index used by the Justice Department and the federal bank regulatory agencies to measure concentration.

**Table 6.3**

**Distribution of Changes in Local Banking Market Concentration (HHI) With and Without S&Ls, 1985–1997**

| | 1985 | 1991 | 1997 | 1985-97 |
|---|---|---|---|---|
| **Commercial Banks** | | | | |
| MSAs, | | | | |
| Average | 1992 | 1977 | 2010 | |
| % with increase | | | | 50 |
| % with decrease | | | | 50 |
| Numbers of MSAs | | | | 319 |
| | | | | |
| NonMSA Counties | | | | |
| Average | 4360 | 4257 | 4081 | |
| % with increase | | | | 39 |
| % with decrease | | | | 61 |
| Numbers of Counties | | | | 2358 |
| | | | | |
| **Commercial Banks + Thrifts @ 50%** | | | | |
| MSAs | | | | |
| Average | 1370 | 1511 | 1643 | |
| % with increase | | | | 76 |
| % with decrease | | | | 24 |
| Numbers of MSAs | | | | 319 |
| | | | | |
| NonMSAs Counties | | | | |
| Average | 3769 | 3831 | 3875 | |
| % with increase | | | | 56 |
| % with decrease | | | | 44 |
| Numbers of Counties | | | | 2220 |

*Source:* Financial Structure Section, Board of Governors of the Federal Reserve System, Washington, D.C.

of 52 percent and 65 percent, respectively. A 1995 study, deriving its estimates from failure and merger models, projected 7,787 by 2000, a reduction that has already been exceeded.[5] However, extrapolating this projection to 2010 yields an estimate of 4,771 banking organizations. Still another study projected 2,390 banking organizations in 2010.[6]

Such extrapolations are impaired because they do not, in any way, specify the process generating structural change. A more sophisticated methodology, discussed in the Appendix, suggests that the number of banks (in contrast to banking organizations) will fall to about 8,000 (with the numbers of banking organizations being considerably less) in the year 2002, and then begin to increase. A number of factors are likely to slow the decline and subsequently produce an increase. These include a decrease in the number of consolidations and mergers as the best deals are consummated (see Figure 5.1); and an increase in de novo entry by new banks filling niche markets abandoned by the larger, consolidating banks (see Table 5.2).

The impact of mergers on future levels of national, regional, and local concentration, then, remains uncertain within a relatively wide range. There is nevertheless a general consensus on important elements of the emerging financial structure. Given the size of the acquisitions now possible under current policy standards, it is reasonable to believe that by 2010 there will exist a small number, perhaps five to ten very large multinational organizations that are present in most urban areas, along with a large number of relatively small, local community or regional institutions. Contributing to the size of these large organizations will not only have been domestic mergers, but international combinations such as the recent acquisition of Bankers Trust by Deutsche Bank. By 2010, they are also likely to have combined with large insurance and/or securities firms under the terms of the Gramm–Leech–Bliley Act, with the 1998 Citicorp–Travelers merger as a model. They almost certainly will have a dominant share of the local banking and related financial business in many of the local areas in which they operate. As a result of their widespread operations, the numbers of separate geographic and product markets in which these large organizations meet as rivals will have increased substantially.

The numbers of smaller fringe banks in local and regional markets will depend on the size of the niche markets that they occupy; and the relative cost structure of large and small banking organizations, and the strategic pricing arrangements that develop.

## MERGERS AND BANK EFFICIENCY

In Chapter 5 we reviewed improvement in efficiency as a motive for merger. By increasing bank size and varying product mix, mergers and expansion into new activities may reduce bank costs of production. As noted, there have been numerous empirical studies of economies of scale and scope in banking over the past four decades.[7] By and large it has been difficult to find efficiency to be a strong motivating factor.

Here we turn to a more detailed consideration of the effects of mergers on efficiency by reviewing the current understanding of how size and efficiency are related. Key studies of economies of scale and scope in the late 1980s, using the Federal Reserve's functional cost data, found that banks experienced significant economies of scale along the ray for the mean bank product mix up to about $100 million in total assets. Banks with assets greater than $300 million at that time exhibited significant diseconomies of scale. There is some evidence that large banks have diseconomies of scope, suggesting that they could reduce costs by realigning their output mix.

Studies using functional cost data and providing numbers of accounts have been termed the "production approach." They permitted estimates of the average account size for each banking function for each bank in the sample. Scale economy estimates were made using the number of accounts adjusted for activity rates at each bank. With a method that became known as the "intermediation approach," estimates of the change in cost with respect to dollar amount of outstanding value could be computed for each product along an output ray. Typically using the translog functional form, estimates of scale and scope economies could then be made in terms of dollar values of outputs. A well-known study found little difference between the two approaches.[8] The same study found that large banks in branching states had lower costs for the same output mix than large banks in unit banking states; and that banks in states where branching was permitted exhibited significantly lesser diseconomies of scale than banks in unit banking states. While significant cost complementarities existed among several of the products (e.g., real estate loans and consumer loans), overall economies of scope were not significant.

In recent years, there has been a shift toward analyzing efficiency in a multiproduct context.[9] These studies use call report data. An important deficiency of the functional cost data has been that relatively few banks are included in the Federal Reserve data set. Further, the numbers have fallen from about 1,300 in the early 1980s to about 200 in 1996. The several types of efficiency identified and measured by the newer approach include allocative efficiency, technological efficiency, and product mix efficiency.

Allocative efficiency refers to the choice of inputs by banks, with the least cost choice indicating greatest efficiency. Technological efficiency refers to the choice of technology to produce bank products and services (e.g., use of antiquated computing and telecommunications technology is inefficient). Product mix efficiency refers to the bank's choice of products and services and their respective amounts given output and input prices. A profit function can be used to measure product mix efficiency and allocative efficiency can be measured from estimates of cost or profit efficiency.

Efficiency, in terms of costs or profits, can be estimated with reference to a frontier function; that is, in terms of how well a bank is performing relative to the best performing (best practices) institutions. Measurement is made given the choice of output mix and input and output prices. Which of these factors is held constant depends on whether cost or profits efficiency is being estimated. Cost efficiency is usually measured in terms of the ratio of the estimated cost of the bank's output mix, if it were as efficient as the best-practices bank facing the same set of input prices and other factors, divided by the bank's actual cost (after adjusting for the random error term). Profit efficiency is the ratio of estimated profits of the bank to the estimated maximum profits under the same conditions as if the bank were the most profit efficient bank. In both cases, efficiency lies between zero and one with a measure of 1.0 being the most efficient or best-practices bank given what is held constant.

Several estimating methods have been used. These include the thick frontier approach (TFA), stochastic frontier approach (SFA), and the distribution free approach (DFA). These methods have been adopted because of the shortcomings of the nonparametric approaches to frontier estimation.[10] However, a cost or profits function must first be estimated using the same methodology as has been used in the economies of scale and scope studies. A conceptual difficulty lies in the assumption that the bank is either minimizing cost or maximizing profit. If banks are performing inefficiently, these forms do not apply, and make sense only as approximations. While it can be argued that efficient banks behave in an optimal manner, and the function fits them best, the assumption(s) generating the efficiency terms are ad hoc, with neither economic nor econometric foundation. One innovation has been to enhance the standard translog form with a set of terms in trigonometric functions of outputs and input prices; that is, a Fourier-flexible function form. This is a curve-fitting methodology, attempting to account for higher order approximations than the quadratic of the standard translog. Studies using this approach claim to fit cost or profits functions better than the translog form, with $R^2$ of nearly 99 percent. But a recent paper reports that results are unchanged by the use of the Fourier-flexible form.[11]

Efficiency estimates typically find a substantial proportion of banks highly inefficient. Profit efficiency estimates range from 24 percent to 67 percent of potential profits for the average bank and cost efficiencies from 21 to 30 percent. Although the average bank differs from study to study, a key finding has been that by reallocating inputs and outputs and improving practices banks can save upward of 30 percent on costs and 50 percent on profits. Such findings are remarkable. While there is some recent evidence that mergers creating large organizations have increased profit efficiency, this result could be attributable to pricing policies available only to larger, dominant firms.[12]

If banks can improve profits by 50 percent by becoming more efficient, why haven't they? There is no simple answer. One study, using three distinct profit functions, finds most of the variation in estimated efficiency remains unexplained.[13] The authors speculate that unmeasured factors, such as differences in managerial ability, have been inadvertently excluded, or there is an error in the measurement of efficiency. The efficiency measures themselves may be defective.

In fact, there is no reason why management factors should not be included in the cost or profits functions directly since these are input resources and management's opportunity cost is generally neglected. If included, it may be possible to identify overpayments to management arising from entrenchment and incompetence. The current approach seems to say more about markets for bank management than markets for bank products and services.[14]

To summarize the still developing research: (1) based on extrapolation, banks up to about $1 billion in assets are likely to have scale economies; (2) banks may suffer from some scale diseconomies when approaching very large sizes; (3) there is little evidence of economies of scope; (4) the high estimate of bank inefficiency is not fully explainable; but (5) if, to the extent it is accurate, banks have substantial incentives for improvement.

The findings imply that mergers of small banks are likely to lower costs and improve efficiency at combined output levels, but mergers of large banks are not. Rhoades reports on nine merger case studies regarding efficiency. The mergers studied were selected as most likely, a priori, to yield efficiency gains. Although all nine resulted in significant cost cutting, only four yielded clear improvement in cost efficiency. No systemic factor(s) producing efficiency gains could be identified, not even the condition where one merger partner was more efficient than the other.[15]

Exceptions can exist for large banks where one of the merger partners is considerably more efficient than the other. It could then be argued, assuming competition remained effective, that such a merger would improve efficiency and yield meaningful gains to consumers. But there is no evidence that the acquisition of relatively inefficient large banks by relatively efficient ones has characterized recent megamergers.[16] While there appears to be considerable scope for greater efficiency independent of mergers, effective competition remains an essential determinant of consumer gains.

## MERGERS, DIVERSIFICATION, AND RISK

Diversification can be distinguished from efficiency as an operational characteristic of banking whose benefits might be achieved through merger and passed on to local bank customers. From a historical perspective in the United States, there has been no better argument for mergers that expand the size and geographic reach of banks than that they produce geographic and product diversification, permitting banks to achieve greater stability by offsetting losses in some areas with gains in others. Prior to passage of the Riegle–Neal Act in 1994, every major banking crisis in the twentieth century produced proposals to liberalize branching restrictions to reduce bank risk.

Today, however, there exists a question as to the marginal contribution of the current merger movement to risk reduction through diversification. Over the last several decades, banks have been able to diversify extensively through loan production offices, bank networks for loan sales and syndication, through correspondent banking arrangements, deposit brokers, and secondary securities markets in asset-backed, municipal and U.S. government securities.

Secondary markets are important sources of geographic diversification for home mortgage financing and credit card and automobile loan and lease receivables. While actual geographic diversification in loan originations has been largely confined to larger banks that have established offices nationally, smaller banks have taken advantage of regional diversification by others. An example is the secondary markets for home mortgages where pools of mortgages have been securitized into a wide variety of mortgage-backed securities (MBS). These securities usually contain thousands of individual mortgages representing a wide spectrum of regions, economic conditions and prepayment behavior. Such marketable securities are better diversified geographically and in terms of prepayment risk than any single mortgage lender could afford through geographically-dispersed origination offices and direct investment. Innovations in other asset-backed securities, such as commercial loans, automobile loans, credit card receivables, and home equity loans, have provided similar benefits. Loan sales and syndications also provide geographic diversification without a network of widely dispersed offices.

Further, continued developments in capital markets not only provide banks with expanded opportunities for diversification but with substitutes for diversification in reducing risk exposure; these permit banks to take advantage of closer approximations to a Modigliani–Miller world of efficient financial markets.

While diversification could conceivably benefit stockholders and help meet regulatory objectives by reducing bank risk, the potential advantages are dubious. Banks can and do shift a substantial portion of their portfolios at low cost to take advantage of opportunities.[17]

Further, the well-known Modigliani–Miller propositions suggest that diversification is of little value to shareholders since they can, on their own, efficiently diversify using securities available in competitive financial markets. Firms need only produce efficiently and choose an optimum capital structure to achieve the lowest cost for their risk class, and to maximize the value of their stock. In considering regulatory objectives, it is worth noting that the FDIC insurance fund is already diversified by premiums paid by banks nationwide. In any event, the likelihood of a bank's insolvency depends not only on the volatility of its returns, but also on its expected rate of return and capitalization.[18] There remains a tradeoff between expected profitability and diversification. Perhaps smaller banks may still benefit from the diversification potential provided by some mergers, but there is no compelling evidence that the same is true for large banks.

## PRICE EFFECTS OF MERGERS

As mentioned, one of the principal expectations of the deregulation movement in banking that has helped generate the ongoing merger wave, is that customers would benefit through an intensification of competition. An evaluation of competitive effects requires consideration of the impact that mergers have on the prices of bank services. We consider these effects here.

### Price Expectations

The high levels of concentration in local banking markets and restrictions on competition that existed through the 1970s are generally believed to have resulted in relatively high prices for retail banking services. Subsequent procompetitive structural improvements were widely expected to result in significant price reductions. In other industries, where deregulation and/or rapid technological change have occurred, price reductions have been perceptible and dramatic; for example, in the case of long-distance telephone rates, computer prices, and in some airline fares.

Before and after price comparisons in banking are not easily made. Other factors, such as differential Federal Reserve policy and inflationary expectations, can swamp competitive and efficiency effects. In addition, structural change in banking has been gradual over a number of years, so there is no simple identifiable event that marks before and after. Further, the same institutional changes that have improved structure have also altered the character of prices by encouraging an unbundling of services and new or higher explicit fees for services on which there may be no "before" equivalent.

There have, however, been few indications that the prices of retail banking services have declined, as one might have expected with more intense competition and technological advances. To the contrary, there is some evidence that they have increased.

First, with respect to rates paid on savings deposits relative to money market rates, as measured by the three-month Treasury bill rate, it can be observed that the differential has widened significantly since the early 1990s. Beginning in October 1993, a historically wide Treasury bill--passbook savings rate differential of over 200 basis points has continued through April 1998 (Figure 6.1). Such differentials, in the face of reasonably strong demands for credit, and bank demands for deposits to meet customer funding needs, are reminiscent of the pre-deregulation environment in which competition for deposit funds in local retail markets were severely restrained.

Income reports and surveys of bank fees, summarized in Table 6.4, also indicate that important elements of bank prices have increased. Bank revenues from service charges on all deposits (consumer and business) rose substantially between 1989 and 1993, with the increase being more pronounced at larger banks.[19] Fees associated with the maintenance and use of retail deposit accounts have risen substantially; and fees associated with specialized services, such as money orders, stop payment orders, and overdrawn accounts have risen faster than the rate of inflation.[20] Fees for a variety of retail accounts and services have been consistently higher at banks with multistate operations than at banks that operate within one state. Even with some evidence that these

**Figure 6.1**
**Savings Deposit Rates Compared to Three-Month T-Bill Rates**

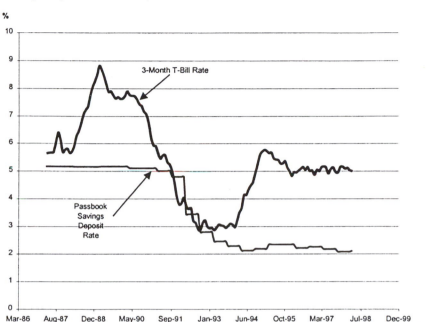

*Source*: Board of Governors of the Federal Reserve System, *Federal Reserve Bulletin* (1996–1998).

differences in fees reflect the disproportionate presence of larger banks in urban areas where costs tend to be higher, they have not been satisfactorily explained by either location or size characteristics; no relationship has been found between local market concentration and the level of bank fees.[21]

In its most recent survey, the Federal Reserve has continued to find that the average fees charged by multistate organizations are higher than those charged by single-state organizations and that the difference is statistically significant.[22]

Changes in the structure of bank pricing itself is also consistent with less rather than more competition. While new fees are explainable as an unbundling of services resulting from deregulation, a complexity in pricing has developed that has tended to make comparative shopping costly, thereby raising switching costs and discouraging consumer movement.[23] Under the pressure of competition, individual banks should be anxious to differentiate themselves from high-price institutions by enlightening consumers about their actual and potential costs. The failure of banking organizations to promote aggressive simplification implies market imperfections that sustain higher prices. This failure has apparently been recognized by consumers who do not rely very much on their banks for relevant information. A recent study based

**Table 6.4**
**Reports on Bank Fees and Rates, 1989–1998**

| Period | Rates and Fees | Sources |
|---|---|---|
| 1989-93 | Federal Reserve surveys of banking services and fees between 1989 and 1993, indicated that certain kinds of fees, associated with special actions, such as bounced checks, overdrafts and stop-payments orders have risen faster than the rate of inflation. Increase more pronounced for large banks. | Hannan, 80 FED. RES. BULL. 771 (1994). |
| 1994 | In a report based on 1994 data, the Federal Reserve found that average fees did not increase very much from 1993, but that "out-of-state banks, typically the larger banks," had higher fees than "in-state banks" | ANNUAL REPORT OF FED. RES. BOARD TO THE CONGRESS ON RETAIL FEES AND SERVICES OF DEPOSITORY INSTITUTIONS, (June 1995) |
| 1995 | Yearly costs for a NOW interest bearing account rose 11 percent from 1993 to 1995 during a period when inflation increased only 5 percent | U.S. Public Interest Research Group, "Banks Think Fees, Not Free: The 1995 PIRG Bank Fee Survey" INTERNET DOCUMENT (August, 1995). |
| 1996 | Fees highest at largest institutions. Multi-state banks charged higher fees than banks serving only one state. | ANNUAL REPORT OF FED. RES. BOARD TO THE CONGRESS ON RETAIL FEES AND SERVICES OF DEPOSITORY INSTITUTIONS, (June 1997); and U.S. Public Interest Research Group, "National Survey Documents Widening Fee Gap between Large and Small Banks," INTERNET DOCUMENT (July 31, 1997). |
| 1997 | Fees highest at largest institutions. Multi-state banks charged *significantly* higher fees than banks that operate in a single state | ANNUAL REPORT OF FED. RES. BOARD TO THE CONGRESS ON RETAIL FEES AND SERVICES OF DEPOSITORY INSTITUTIONS, (June 1998). |

on the Federal Reserve's Survey of Consumer Finances, reported that only about 2.5 percent of households use a banker as a source of information for either saving or borrowing decisions, preferring "calling around for information," newspapers, magazines, TV and radio, and friends and relatives.[24]

Recent research further suggests less competition and higher prices. Bank concentration has increased in a substantial number of MSAs since 1985, particularly when concentration is defined to include thrift institutions. Because analysis continues to produce a significant positive relationship between concentration and prices, it can be inferred that many local areas have experienced changes in banking structure conducive to higher retail prices. Repeated studies at widely separated points in time, using vastly different samples, a variety of independent variables, and increasingly sophisticated techniques, have reported surprisingly comparable results. A large scale 1989 study by Berger and Hannan, using 1985 data, found interest rates paid on money market deposit accounts (MMDA) by banks in the most concentrated markets to be 25 to 100 basis points below those in the least concentrated markets.[25] One of the earliest studies in 1964 found interest rates on time deposits in isolated one-bank towns to be 17 basis points lower than in isolated two-bank towns.[26] More recently, using data for 1989 and 1990, Hannan found a significant relationship between local market concentration and business loan rates, but could no longer find one for deposit prices.[27] The importance of this finding, however, is moot in light of subsequent studies, discussed below, that have found mergers that increase local market concentration also lower deposit rates of interest.

Such tendencies toward higher prices could, of course, be offset by structural improvements, including easier entry for nonlocal banks and thrifts, and the emergence of new nonbank competitors. But two recent studies have found direct evidence of higher prices following mergers that result in higher concentration in local markets. In one, a reduction in rates on local deposit accounts was found resulting from horizontal mergers that raised concentration substantially; that is, mergers that produced a pro forma increase in the market HHI of at least 200 points to a level of at least 1,800.[28] The other, using data for the period 1986 to 1994, found that a 1.0 percent higher HHI was associated with a 1.2 percent lower rate on MMDA and a 0.3 percent lower rate on CDs.[29] It also found that deposit rates of interest dropped after a bank's participation in a merger, for any level of market concentration, at least for sometime thereafter. Further, following the merger, other banks in the same local market first increase their rates, but then lower them in the following year. The authors hypothesize that service quality, a substitute for prices, deteriorates at the merged banks, thus preventing them from lowering their rates, and inducing the reduction by local rivals.[30]

These last mentioned findings are in conflict with the recent findings that the effect of local market concentration on deposit rates of interest has evaporated. They are also in conflict with the expectation that local markets would erode as regulatory restrictions disappeared and technology undermined the separation between banks and other financial firms. Had such been the case, significant positive relationships between concentration and prices in local areas would also disappear and mergers that increased local market concentration would have no effect on prices.

The implication that local markets remain relevant has been supported for many years by survey results.[31] One recent study, however, has found that branch banking organizations ignore differences in demand in local market areas by setting uniform prices for retail deposit services over relatively broad geographic areas; that is, states or regions.[32] The seeming disappearance of geographic discrimination requires further investigation. However, even if it has developed over the last decade or so, it does not necessarily mean geographic markets have expanded, competition in expanded markets has intensified, or that prices of banking services have fallen as a result.

### The Price-Effect Anomaly

Given the apparently procompetitive changes of the last two decades, the evidence that prices for retail banking services have not declined, and probably have increased, constitutes an anomaly. Higher prices imply that competition has diminished in the post-deregulation years, not intensified. Mergers that increase concentration in local areas and create large, multistate banks are the most likely source of higher prices. Direct evidence that mergers are at the root of the disconnect is indicated by both statistical analysis and by survey reports that multistate institutions, typically the product of mergers, have relatively high fees.

The difficulty of imagining mergers leading to price increases without competition diminishing is illustrated by Figure 6.2 that summarizes the possible combined effects of the two principal merger effects causing prices to change; that is, effects on efficiency and competition. Lower prices would result from gains in both efficiency and increases in competition, as indicated in cells (1), (2), and (4). Higher prices would result from losses in efficiency and decreases in competition, as indicated in cells (6), (8), and (9). In those cases where mergers result in efficiency gains and decreases in competition, cell (7) prices would only rise if competitive effects dominated. Other combinations would result in no change in prices, or in prices declining because competition increased. In cell (5), mergers do not result in either changes in efficiency or competition. In cell (3), increased competition is accompanied by losses in efficiency; price changes would reflect whichever effect is dominant, but are more likely to fall than rise because mergers are unlikely to diminish efficiency in any significant way.

The underlying reasons for any diminution of competition, however, are not obvious. One researcher has recently suggested that economic barriers to entry in local retail banking markets have remained high, principally due to switching costs and to the strategic behavior of established banks.[33] High entry barriers, coupled with stable or rising concentration in local markets, depending on how concentration is defined, could produce stable or rising prices. The question remains, however, as to why the effects of these structural factors wouldn't deteriorate under the pressure of entry by large, multimarket banks, new computer technology that fosters nonbank competitors, and telecommunication advances that tend to expand geographic markets. Further, there re-

**Figure 6.2**
**Potential Effects of Mergers on Prices**

|  | Efficiency Gains | No Change in Efficiency | Efficiency Loss |
|---|---|---|---|
| Increase in Competition | (1) – | (2) – | (3) 0 or - |
| No Change in Competition | (4) – | (5) 0 | (6) + |
| Decrease in Competition | (7) 0 or + | (8) + | (9) + |

mains the question of why fees for retail banking services are higher at multistate banks, independent of local market concentration.

We suggest in the following section that the effects of procompetitive technological and institutional change have been offset by anticompetitive effects emanating from changes in both local markets and multimarket structures.

## ANALYSIS OF THE ANOMALY

Our explanation builds on several observations. First, an increasing number of local markets, particularly those with MSAs as their core, are characterized by one or a few very large multimarket banking organizations and a larger group of smaller fringe institutions.

Second, very large multimarket banking organizations remain likely to be protected by the policy of too-big-to-fail (TBTF), while smaller banks are not. FDICIA made clear that the managers, owners, and uninsured creditors of most banks will not be protected from failure, as they previously were. The FDIC is now required to resolve failed banks by the method least costly to the insurance fund, precluding the kind of purchase and assumption deals that had protected all depositors in the past.[34] On the other hand, special provisions remain that are likely to benefit large organizations. We find, as discussed below, that these large organizations have substantially lower funding costs than other banks, though it is admittedly difficult to disentangle the cost-lowering effects of TBTF and other factors.

Finally, the number of markets in which large, multimarket organizations confront one another; that is, the number of linkages has increased, and is likely to continue to do so as large banking organizations expand nationally and internationally and affiliate with other large financial firms.[35] This increase in linkages is likely to promote mutual forbearance.

Markets characterized by one or a few large firms, and a group of fringe firms, suggests the applicability of the dominant-firm price leadership model.[36] If dominant firms in local markets are very large banking organizations, they are likely to be beneficiaries of a TBTF policy with a funding cost advantage over smaller fringe firms. We reserve judgment on lower operating costs due to greater efficiency. Finally, the increasing numbers of multimarket linkages among a small group of very large organizations, individually dominant in one or more local markets, suggests that any dominant-firm price leadership model needs to be modified by the possibility of mutual forbearance as a value maximizing interaction.

We now consider in more detail the significance of TBTF, multimarket structures, and mutual forbearance. We then develop a model of dynamic limit pricing that explains many of the empirical findings we have reviewed.

### Too-Big-to-Fail

The competitive importance of any level of concentration in local banking markets should diminish as procompetitive structural changes, such as lower barriers to entry and/or the emergence of new nonbank competitors, are realized; but only as long as the competitive significance of any given level of concentration does not change. There is, however, reason to believe that the concentration measuring rod for market power in local banking markets has changed, ratcheting upward the significance of any given level. We suggest this ratcheting effect would make the competitive significance of, for example, an HHI of 1,600 today comparable to a much higher HHI fifteen years ago.

A change in the measuring rod can be traced to deregulation in the 1980s that altered effective regulatory policy from one that considered all banks to be too important to fail to one that established only the largest as too-big-to-fail. The change in policy provided the largest organizations with competitive advantages that they formerly did not have. Passage of FDICIA in 1991 codified the policy, even though it limited federal banking agency discretion in supporting large, floundering banking organizations, in part, by making their decisions subject to approval by the executive branch. Nevertheless, it provided the banking agencies with authority to protect all creditors and stockholders of a failing bank when the failure is perceived as giving rise to a systemic event.

The policy has been important. Regulators have, over the last two decades, sustained a number of the largest banks, at or near insolvency, by forbearing with respect to capital requirements, through financial aid, and simply by disregarding asset losses. As noted earlier, these include Continental Illinois in 1984, Interfirst Texas in 1987, Bank of New England in 1989–1991, Sovran, C&S, and Citibank in 1991. In the late 1980s and early 1990s, the regulators did not close Citibank or Bank of New England in a timely fashion despite substantial losses in real estate loans and derivatives that reduced their book and market value capital below acceptable levels. Extraordinary measures were taken by the federal bank regulatory agencies, beginning in November 1990, to assist Citibank, at or near insolvency, on the rationale of avoiding a financial disaster.[37] The most recent evidence that this policy remains in effect, and of the underlying logic of large size that compels it, can be found in the organization of a loan syndicate for Long-Term Capital Management by the Federal Reserve, presumably to protect not only financial markets but also large banking organizations exposed to its possible default.[38]

It is generally acknowledged that the TBTF policy creates an incentive for protected banks to take excessive risk because of their ability to acquire funds at lower yields from investors and depositors who perceive them as safer repositories than nonprotected institutions.[39] The competitive implication of the policy shift is that it provides a cost-of-funding advantage to the largest banking organizations.[40] Such cost advantages are indicated in Table 6.5.

Using effective rates paid on domestic deposits, the 10 largest banks in 1997 paid much less for funds than the smallest banks; that is, those not in the largest 1,000. They paid 49 basis points (bp) less for interest bearing checkable deposits, 36bp less for large denomination CDs, 22bp less for small denomination CDs, and 20bp less for Gross Fed Funds Purchased and RPs. The largest difference was for savings accounts and money market deposit accounts where the top ten banks paid 68bp less than the smallest banks.

The data in Table 6.5 also indicate a substantial cost advantage for the largest 10 banks over those ranked in size from 101 to 1,000. Further, inspection of the data for years back to 1988 suggest that 1997 is not an anomaly; the differentials have persisted for at least a decade.[41]

The data also indicate that the largest banks can operate with lower capitalization rates and, therefore enjoy lower equity costs of capital. For example, as shown in Table 6.5, the largest ten banks had ratios of book value equity-to-average assets of 7.39 percent compared to 10.30 percent for the smallest banks. Because the latter also have relatively restricted access to equity capital markets, their cost-per-dollar of equity is also likely to be higher. Debt and equity capital are the principal inputs of banking firms; the cost advantage provided by TBTF is likely to be great. As indicated, some researchers have found economies of scale for large banks through the more efficient use of capital. Their findings, however, are consistent with the analysis presented here. TBTF status reduces observable bank costs but increases the unobservable, contingent costs borne by the FDIC and taxpayers; that is, the costs related to the moral hazard created by TBTF. Large banks, too-big-to-fail, are thereby able to economize in their use of capital. Such economies of scale need not reflect actual improvements in bank operating efficiency, but only the public policy that favors larger banks.

Table 6.5
Cost of Funds by Bank Size Classes, 1997

| | 10 Largest Banks | 11 to 100 Largest Banks | 101 to 1000 Largest Banks | Smaller than 1000 |
|---|---|---|---|---|
| Other Checkable Deposits (%) | 1.97 | 2.00 | 2.17 | 2.46 |
| Savings (including MMDAs) (%) | 2.68 | 2.84 | 3.07 | 3.36 |
| Large - Denomination Time (%) | 5.17 | 5.46 | 5.54 | 5.53 |
| Small Denomination Time (%) | 5.45 | 5.43 | 5.57 | 5.67 |
| Gross Fed Funds and RPs Purchased (%) | 5.02 | 5.30 | 5.20 | 5.22 |

| Difference From Top 10 Banks | | Basis Point | | |
|---|---|---|---|---|
| Other Checkable | - | +3.0 | +20.0 | +49.0 |
| Savings (including MMDAs) | - | +16.0 | +39.0 | +68.0 |
| Large - Denomination | - | +29.0 | +37.0 | +36.0 |
| Small Denomination | - | -2.0 | +12.0 | +22.0 |
| Gross Fed Funds Purchased and RPs | - | +28.0 | +18.0 | +20.0 |

| | | | | |
|---|---|---|---|---|
| Equity to Average Assets % | 7.39 | 8.16 | 9.21 | 10.30 |
| ROA % | 0.98 | 1.42 | 1.37 | 1.31 |
| ROE % | 13.21 | 17.37 | 14.91 | 12.70 |
| | | | | |

*Source*: William B. English and William R. Nelson, "Profits and Balance Sheet Developments at U.S. Commercial Banks in 1997." 84 *Federal Reserve Bulletin* 391–419 (1998), Tables A.2.B. through A.2.E.

If only the largest banking organizations are protected, they achieve a cost advantage over local and regional banks that did not exist in the pre-deregulation period. This change in relative costs would make it more difficult for smaller banks in local markets to compete effectively with large banking organizations, a number of which have long been the largest banks in local markets.

## Multimarket Structure and Mutual Forbearance

The dominant-firm effect in local markets may be supported by a changed relationship among the largest banking organizations that meet in many markets. Large bank combinations have expanded the geographic scope of the largest organizations that now operate in many states and offer a wide variety of services. Multimarket linkages among the largest banking organizations have increased in recent years.[42]

It has been hypothesized that multimarket contacts among large firms result in mutual recognition of each other's interests and in mutual concern about retaliatory actions. A cooperative spirit of mutual forbearance, a golden rule, is thereby cultivated; and an opportunity is provided for firms to learn to cooperate.[43] If each firm believes its strategic behavior will be matched by rivals, it will conclude that it has nothing to gain by cheating. Without such contact, coordination is likely to break down because diversified firms are likely to have different costs and demands and therefore different preferred terms and prices.[44]

For similar reasons, the likelihood of collusion is higher if the large firms expect little turnover in their group, and if the appropriate punishment strategy for cheating is adopted. For example, a tit-for-tat policy that punishes cheating by one rival in any one market by inflicting punishment in more than one market.

The anticompetitive effects of a growing number of market linkages, however, remains an empirical question. There has been empirical support for the mutual forbearance hypothesis in nonbanking industries. For example, multimarket contacts in manufacturing industries in the United States have been found to be associated with lower profits in markets where there is low concentration, and higher profits in markets where there is higher concentration.[45] Multimarket contact may be a necessary condition for agreement among diversified oligopolists.[46] Empirical support has also been found in manufacturing industries in the United Kingdom and in the airline industry in the United States.[47]

Empirical support in banking has, however, been spotty.[48] Recent work nevertheless has indicated that the number of multimarket contacts are positively associated with higher profits. One recent paper found that, in combination, statewide concentration and numbers of contacts are associated with higher levels of profits.[49] Another also found that the numbers of multimarket contact are positively related to profitability. Meaningful increases in profits resulted for the small group of banks most heavily exposed to contact.[50] The newer findings are plausible in light of recent increases in the number of linkages and the establishment of a small set of large banking organizations with a multistate presence.

Mutual forbearance tends to reinforce the effects of the TBTF policy by constraining competition in local markets in which two or more prominent organizations are already established; and also where one or more nationally prominent organization is a potential competitor. In this sense, it would exacerbate the existence of high economic barriers to entry. It also tends to alter for the worse the significance of any given level of local market concentration.

Mutual forbearance coupled with dominant-firm pricing also provides an explanation for relatively high fees at multistate banks. These are, generally, the largest banking organizations that have regulatory cost advantages permitting them to out-compete smaller rivals. They can thus sustain higher fees without substantial threat of losing market share, as long as they do not compete with each other.

## A Model of Dynamic Limit Pricing

Dynamic limit pricing analyzes the pricing strategy of a dominant firm that must consider the effects of entry and expansion of fringe firms on its profits. Models of dynamic limit pricing and price leadership indicate that dominant firms with cost advantages and lower rates of discount can retain, and even gain market share, while setting prices to limit entry and/or to drive out smaller rivals with higher funding/capital costs.[51] They also indicate a tradeoff between market share of the dominant firms and their discounted future profits, with a determinant optimal maximum market share of less than 100 percent. In banking, TBTF status constitutes a strategic advantage comparable to a technological advantage that augments a dominant market position.

Concentration has increased, as noted, in many local markets; but even in those in which it has not increased, or even decreased, alteration in the strategic advantage of the largest firms would have raised the significance of any given level. As a result, the prices of retail services might increase even if local market concentration does not.

The Gaskins's model of dynamic price leadership under threat of entry is well suited for the initial analysis. It takes a dynamic approach with future market share and profits of the dominant firm dependent on the pricing strategy chosen in the current period.[52] The model's assumptions include the following: (1) a single product with one price depending on time, a defined market demand depending on time, a constant average total cost, c, a discount rate or cost of capital, r, the presence of a competitive fringe of rival firms, potential entrants, and a constant limit price $\bar{p}$; (2) dominant firms will choose an optimal pricing strategy that will maximize the present value of expected future profits over the life of the firm (e.g., infinity); (3) an entry response function that is proportional to the difference between the current market price and the entry limiting price:

$$\dot{x}(t) = k(p(t) - \bar{p}) \tag{1}$$

where x(0) is the initial output of the competitive fringe, $\dot{x}(t)$ is the change in output due to entry, $p(t)$ is the current market price and k is the response coefficient for new entrants, assumed to be positive or zero, that indicates how fast new entrants respond to a change in the market price differential from the entry limiting price. The limit price is defined as the price that will limit net entry to zero.

Gaskins uses a control theoretic approach to maximize the functional of the present value of the dominant firm's profits with respect to a trajectory of market price over time:

$$V = \int_0^\infty [p(t) - c][f(p) - x(t)]\exp(-rt)dt \tag{2}$$

subject to the entry response function of equation (1), where $f(p)$ is the market demand function and $f(p)-x(t)$ is the output of the dominant firm. The solution to this problem is a market price that will move toward the limit price and a dominant-firm market share, s, that has the following form in long-run equilibrium:

$$\hat{s} = \frac{k(\bar{p}-c)/r - f'(\bar{p})(\bar{p}-c)}{f(\bar{p})} \tag{3}$$

The last term in the numerator of this expression is the equilibrium output of the fringe firms. The rate at which this equilibrium will be achieved depends on the entry response coefficient and is symmetrical if the market price is below the entry limiting price, resulting in exit, or above, resulting in net entry.

The static and dynamic implications of this model are as follows: (1) the market share of the dominant firm will be larger: (a) the greater its cost advantage, $\bar{p} - c$, (b) the lower its cost of capital, r, and (c) the greater the response rate, k, of new entrants (a lower cost of capital for the dominant firm may be interpreted as a cost advantage over smaller fringe firms tending to raise its market share); (2) the optimal price trajectory for the dominant firm will be higher: (a) the greater the cost of capital, (because future profits are worth less), (b) the greater its average cost, c, (c) the lesser the initial period fringe output, $x(0)$, and (d) the lower the entry limiting price, $\bar{p}$. This last result may seem contradictory. However, with a cost advantage, a lower limit price implies a lower short-run optimal price that will drive out relatively inefficient fringe firms and increase the long-run market share of the dominant firm.

These results hold in a growing market as well as in a no-growth market. The principal distinction is that growing markets are the more profitable for dominant firms, permitting them to maintain a constant market share without a significant cost advantage, and with a higher long-run price above the entry limiting price.

### An Extension to Incorporate Mutual Forbearance

The Gaskins's model is confined to a single market. In this extension, we assume that dominant firms engage in many separate markets, facing a small group of similarly positioned firms (global rivals), as well as a competitive fringe (local rivals). To structure the analysis, we assume that all global rivals set their prices to maximize the value of their firms in all local markets in which they are present. If all global rivals have similar operating and capital costs, a "follow the leader" strategy in markets in which they do not dominate will maximize their value in the same way it maximizes the locally dominant firm's value. It follows that global rivals in markets in which they are not dominant will follow the dominant firm's price leadership.

The final part of the extension requires specification of the entry response of large firms not in a local market. In banking, experience indicates that large organizations do not enter new local markets de novo or by small acquisition. Rather, they enter by large acquisition. Whatever the reason for this behavior, we infer a value-maximizing basis for large organizations to have a large-scale presence. If such firms do not face significant cost disadvantages compared to a dominant firm in a local market, then, through entry de novo at large scale, prices would be driven below the limit price and possibly close to marginal cost. Mutual forbearance would involve recognition of this likelihood by global rivals and compel entry into new markets by large acquisition. In terms of Gaskins's model, entry by acquisition can be interpreted as a low response rate, k, resulting in a higher limit price in each market.

As shown in equation (3), a lower response rate will tend to decrease the market share of the dominant firm while a higher limit price will tend to increase market share. To some extent these factors will offset each other, such that the market share of the dominant firm tends to remain constant over time, even where it has little or no cost advantage or disadvantage relative to global rivals that make large acquisitions. The entry of global rivals into local markets by large acquisition and the prospect of mutual forbearance will tend to keep the dominant firms' market share from eroding over time.

More formally, the extension that we are proposing makes the response rate in the Gaskins's model for each market a function of the extent of contact (number of linkages) among dominant firms in separate markets. The greater the extent of contact, the greater will be the extent of mutual forbearance, and the lower will be the entry response rate, $k$, in each market. This implies that mutual forbearance will tend to lower each dominant firm's market share.

If we assume that the extent of multimarket contact and mutual forbearance are independent of the pricing policies of the dominant firm in each local market, the results of dynamic limit pricing can be extended directly to the multimarket contact model. However, if the degree of mutual forbearance depends on the pricing policies of dominant firms in each market, the solution for dynamic limit pricing must be simultaneous in all markets. This solution is achieved by adding an additional response so that large firms operating in multiple markets can apply resources to those markets that earn the greatest profits. The solution is in the form of a differential equation which sets the output of each large firm in each market according to the pricing policy in that market. The result is a value of $k$ in each market that is inversely related to the degree of mutual forbearance which, for the no-growth model, is the difference between the entry limiting price, $\bar{p}$, and average cost, c; and for the growth model, the difference between the long-run optimal price, $p^*$, and average cost.

### Predictions

The extended model predicts certain price characteristics of retail banking markets with dominant firms that are also very large multimarket organizations confronting similar rivals in other markets: (1) Dominant firms with a funding cost advantage will be able to sustain a substantial market share. (2) With the dominant-firm optimal strategy resulting in prices above the limit price, de novo entry by small firms will occur. (3) Because the optimal strategy for small firms below efficient size is to attract customers and grow, their prices are likely to be lower than that of the dominant firm. (4) In the course of the structural transition now occurring, the negative relationship between local market concentration and prices, often found in earlier cross section studies, will tend to diminish in significance because of omitted structural variables. Some markets will be characterized by dominant-firm pricing while others are not. Among the markets characterized by dominant-firm pricing, some will be characterized by mutual forbearance, while others are not.

A number of these predictions are consistent with recent research findings: (1) On average, local market concentration has been relatively stable in the face of rapidly rising aggregate concentration. Further, a recent study by Pilloff and Rhoades of market share changes in about 940 MSA and non-MSA counties for the period 1990–1996 found that large, geographically diversified banking organizations did not, in general, increase their market share. The authors interpret this finding as indicating that smaller banks can compete effectively with larger organizations. However, the finding is also consistent with our analysis that implies dominant firms can establish relatively high prices without substantial loss of market share.[53] (2) There has been a substantial increase in de novo entry in recent years; and an indication that mergers and acquisitions increase the likelihood of de novo entry.[54] (3) While survey reports indicate that large banks have posted uniform prices across local areas for a number of retail banking services, pricing by smaller banks in local areas have not converged to these uniform levels.[55] Relatively high fees and low deposit rates at large, multistate banking organizations is consistent with the expectation of higher prices for dominant firms and mutual forbearance. (4) The cross-section statistical analyses that indicate a disappearing relationship between local-area concentration and deposit prices are consistent with the models' implications. However, when price changes are directly observed in those local areas where mergers have resulted in increased concentration, the expected relationship has been observed. In this latter type of study, the omitted variables need not be critical. If the mergers have created a dominant firm, a price increase (above the limit price) would be expected. If they have augmented a dominant firm, the elimination of an important rival might make a price increase optimal. If the mergers have not created or augmented a dominant firm, the traditional relationship between concentration and prices would still hold.

Finally, the model also throws light on the puzzle of relatively high fees at multistate banks and suggests one possible explanation for uniform pricing across many local areas. Large banks, as noted, are now posting uniform deposit and consumer loan rates statewide, and have apparently reduced the discretion provided local managers in altering them. Their posted uniform prices are public knowledge.[56] For purposes of optimal pricing in the dominant firm-mutual forbearance model, such uniformly set prices would have to exceed the limit prices in the markets in which they apply. The high fees repeatedly reported at multistate banks are consistent with this condition. One characteristic of such centralized decision making is to make "secret" price cuts by any one large bank, in one or more local areas, a relatively conspicuous departure from mutual forbearance. Centralized price setting also evokes a threat of a massive retaliation through a reduction in the uniform posted prices by other banks.

### *Hypotheses*

The model provides testable hypotheses. First, we expect large dominant multimarket firms to maintain their local market shares, even in markets where their prices are high. Secondly, we expect markets dominated by such firms to be characterized by lower deposit rates and higher loan rates than markets without such firms, given the same level of concentration and holding constant other relevant market factors. Finally, we expect structure performance studies that regress prices of banking services with significant local, nonarbitragible characteristics, such as small business loans and retail deposits, on concentration to find a significant relationship when the measure of concentration is properly scaled for the presence of such firms.

### PRELIMINARY IMPLICATIONS FOR MERGER POLICY

Specific suggestions for a new merger policy to meet the problems presented here are provided in the next chapter, but some preliminary implications for policy may now be presented.

The federal agencies adapted merger policy standards to the more competitive environment produced by deregulation in the 1980s, but they have yet to adapt to the competitive implications of the bank merger movement that their modified standards have facilitated. Current policy standards, on which the federal agencies evaluate mergers, are blind to declines in total numbers of banks, the establishment of a small set of very large organizations that are too-big-to-fail, and multimarket linkages; and to the possibility that the concentration measure of market power in banking needs to be recalibrated.

The recent survey and research findings on bank fees and interest rates should be considered seriously in light of the irreversible structural changes that are now occurring. Even if it were uncertain that large bank mergers are impairing competition, it is difficult to show that such mergers have improved efficiency. Modifications in policy to slow down large bank mergers are thereby unlikely to inflict any significant cost while achieving potentially substantial benefits.

It should not be beyond the capacity of the federal agencies to further adapt bank merger policy to the cumulative structural developments to which individual merger decisions contribute. They need to expand their analysis to consider the effects of their decisions on competition and efficiency, on creating and augmenting banking organizations that are too-big-to-fail, and on the likelihood of mutual forbearance among organizations that engage one another in numerous markets. New structural screens need to be developed that take into consideration accumulating evidence on strategic pricing in local markets. Put simply, the federal agencies need to consider aggravating as well as mitigating factors in evaluating merger proposals. If necessary, new legislation may be needed to bring policy in line with developing structural changes.

The issues raised in the United States are also relevant globally. The bank consolidation movement has not been confined to one country. In Europe, cross-country mergers of large banking organizations are expected with the introduction of the euro. The recent acquisition of Bankers Trust by Deutsche Bank is the most recent of a number of large U.S.–foreign bank combinations. In Canada, two proposed mergers by four of the top five banks, reducing the number of large organizations to three and raising aggregate concentration in the top two organizations to about 70 percent, have recently been blocked, at least temporarily, by the Federal Finance Minister.

The competitive consequences of too-big-to-fail and multimarket contacts may well materialize globally, and particularly in those countries without a strong antitrust tradition. It is incumbent on bank regulators and antitrust authorities to evaluate such developments on an international basis, as well as in the United States, somewhat in the way that bank regulators throughout the world have collectively addressed the issues of safety, soundness, and capital requirements.

## CONCLUSIONS

The bank merger movement of the last two decades has held promise for more efficient and better diversified banks, and more intense competition in local markets. However, there is accumulating evidence in surveys and empirical research that the promise has not been fulfilled for retail customers in local banking markets. Neither greater efficiency nor substantial improvements in diversification appear to have been realized. There is evidence of less, rather than more, competition. A plausible explanation of anticompetitive developments can be found in changes in both local and intermarket structures in the deregulated environment. These developments emerge from large bank combinations and the substitution of a too-big-to-fail regulatory policy for one in which all banks were protected. They are beyond consideration in merger evaluation by the federal agencies under current policy standards. There is, therefore, a need to reconsider existing policy standards, with a view toward slowing down large bank combinations and constraining their regulatory cost advantages.

## APPENDIX: BANK STRUCTURE PROJECTIONS

Several recent studies noted in the text have made projections based on methodologies which can best be described as judgmentally extrapolative. The wide variation in linear extrapolations of recent trends reflects the inadequacy of the methodology. Populations of banks (as well as other populations) are better represented by steady state or dynamic equilibrium analysis. This alternative approach considers the process generating the population as nonlinear and dynamic. Changes are generated by establishing a stable dynamic population of banks under an existing state, and then subjecting that state to a shock. After a particular shock, a new steady state equilibrium population will be approached that will be determined by endogenous factors driving the system.

Consider a population resulting from a process tending toward equilibrium, and that substantial changes result from the impact of exogenous shocks. In the 1980s, an equilibrium in the number of banks that had been established in the aftermath of the Great Depression was disturbed by economic, institutional, and technological changes, including the liberalization of legal restrictions on interstate banking and the sharp decrease in the cost of processing, analyzing, and transmitting information. Subsequent changes can be viewed as a transitional movement toward a new dynamic equilibrium.

The transition can be observed in Figure 6.3, a phase diagram, with the rate of change in numbers of banks plotted against actual numbers of banks.[57] The diagram indicates a limit cycle that can be interpreted as a dynamic equilibrium under conditions existing before the 1980s, at about 13,600 banks (the right-hand side of the figure). It shows at least two points in time (two bank populations) prior to 1985 when the rate of change in the number of banks was effectively at zero.

Since 1985, the population has first declined at an increasing rate, and then at a decreasing rate. As of year-end 1999, a new dynamic equilibrium appears to be approached (where the rate of change in the number of banks is zero) at about 8,000 banks. This can be determined by extrapolating, using the curvature of the data plotted, to the zero rate of change line. With the deceleration in the decline in numbers of banks, a new equilibrium might be even greater than the 8,000 banks. This analysis suggests that the number of banks will continue to decline, at least to about the year 2002, and then begin to increase. A simple extrapolation of the growth cycle may require at least ten more data points (to 2010) to provide an adequate level of confidence regarding a dynamic equilibrium. As noted in the text, factors likely to slow the decline include a decrease in the number of potential multibank holding com-

**Figure 6.3**
**Phase Diagram of Numbers of Banks, 1934–1999**

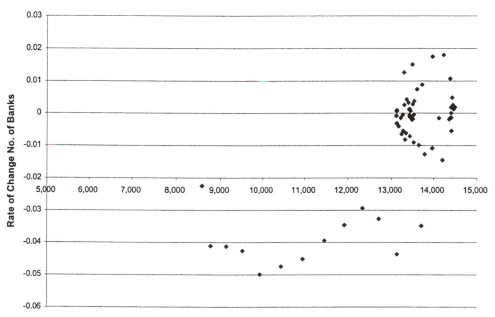

pany consolidations and entry by independent de novo banks filling niche markets abandoned by the larger banks, particularly after consolidation. Moreover, increases in the number of banking institutions beginning in the early twenty-first century are unlikely to disturb the dominance achieved by a relatively small group of very large organizations.

## NOTES

1. Eriksen 1962, 76. Material in this chapter is drawn from Hanweck and Shull 1999 and Shull and Hanweck 2000.

2. See Rhoades 1996; Meyer 1998. Large-bank assets acquired by other large banks have risen by a factor of 5 since 1989. Holland, Inscoe, Waldrop, and Kutta 1996, 12, Table 5.

3. Rhoades 1996, n. 1; Meyer 1998, n. 1; unpublished 1999 data provided by Financial Structure Section, Board of Governors of the Federal Reserve System.

4. Hannan and Rhoades 1992, 737.

5. Nolle 1995.

6. Holland, Inscoe, Waldrop, and Kutta 1996.

7. Berger, Demsetz, and Strahan 1999 have reviewed extensive literature on merger motives through 1998. Bartholomew, Benston, and Mote 1997 also provide a recent review of the literature. For an earlier review, see Gilbert 1984.

8. Berger, Hanweck, and Humphrey 1987.

9. See Berger and Humphrey 1997 for a review of 130 separate studies of efficiency in financial institutions.

10. Berger 1993. Also see Mester 1994 for a description of nonparametric applications in banking.

11. Berger and Mester 1997.

12. Berger 1998.

13. Ibid.

14. Two recent studies attempt to evaluate management incentive structures in banking as sources of efficiency using the stochastic frontier and DFA approaches. See DeYoung, Spong, and Sullivan 1997; Brewer and Evanoff 1997.

15. Rhoades 1998.

16. For example, Rose 1992.

17. Boyd, Hanweck, and Pithyarchariyakul 1980; Boyd and Graham 1988.

18. A discussion of these three factors as they relate to risk premiums on CDs can be found in Hannan and Hanweck 1988.

19. Hannan 1994.

20. Ibid.

21. Hannan 1996. See also Board of Governors of the Federal Reserve System 1998a, 10–11.

22. Board of Governors of the Federal Reserve System 2000, 2.

23. Rhoades 1997.

24. Kinnichal and Kwast 1997; Rhoades 1997, 1005–1006, n. 30.

25. Berger and Hannan 1989, 24.

26. Horvitz and Shull 1964.

27. Hannan 1992.

28. Prager and Hannan 1998.

29. Simons and Stavins 1998, 24.

30. Ibid., n. 32.

31. Elliehausen and Wolken 1990, 1992; Kwast, Starr-McCluer, and Wolken 1997.

32. Radecki 1998.

33. Rhoades 1997.

34. Shull 1995, 597–560. The continued existence of the too-big-to-fail policy has been addressed by Feldman and Rolnick 1998.

35. Shull 1999; Pilloff 1999.

36. The development of the dominant-firm dynamic price leadership model is reviewed in Gilbert 1989.

37. Fromson and Knight 1993.

38. See, for example, Raghavan and Pacelle 1998.

39. For example, Hetzel 1991; Feldman and Rolnick 1998, n. 38.

40. A recent empirical study of the wealth and risk effects of the relevant provisions of FDICIA found large banks benefitted as expected. See Angbazo and Saunders 1996.

41. English and Nelson 1998, 413 ff.

42. Data on the growing numbers of linkages among large banking organizations can be found in Shull 1999.

43. Hughes and Oughton 1993, 211.

44. Scott 1989, 1991.

45. Scott 1982.

46. Scott 1991.

47. See Hughes and Oughton 1993; Evans and Kessides 1994.

48. For early applications in banking, see Solomon 1970; Heggestad and Rhoades 1978; Whitehead 1978; Hanweck and Rhoades 1984; Rhoades and Heggestad 1985.

49. Whalen 1996.

50. Pilloff 1999.

51. Gaskins 1971; Gilbert 1989, 475; Scherer and Ross 1990, ch. 10.

52. See Gaskins 1971.

53. Pilloff and Rhoades 2000.

54. See Berger, Bonime, Goldberg, and White 1999; Nisenson 1999. For a contrary view, see Seelig and Critchfield 1999.

55. Heitfield 1999; Radecki forthcoming.

56. For a recent review of these phenomena and recent data on deposit and loan rates at multimarket banks, see Radecki forthcoming. The data indicate small differences in rates by large banks in the same cities. For some banking services, at least, rate data are an incomplete measure of price.

57. Tabor 1989. In Figure 6.3, which plots the rate of change in numbers of banks against actual number of banks from 1934 to 1999, year-end 1999 is the last data point.

## REFERENCES

Angbazo, Lazarus, and Anthony Saunders. 1996. "The Effect of TBTF Deregulation on Bank Cost of Funds." Working Paper, Graduate School of Business, New York University, September.

Bartholomew, Philip, George J. Benston, and Larry L. Mote. 1997. "Defining and Measuring Bank Output." Paper presented to WEA International Conference, Seattle, Washington, July.

Berger, Allen N. 1993. "'Distribution-Free' Estimates of Efficiency in the U.S. Banking System and Tests of the Standard Distributional Assumptions." *Journal of Productivity Analysis* 4: 261–292.

———. 1998. "The Efficiency of Bank Mergers and Acquisitions: A Preliminary Look at the 1990s Data." In *Bank Mergers and Acquisitions*. Ed. Amihud and Miller. Boston: Kluwer Academic Publishers.

Berger, Allen N., Seth D. Bonime, Lawrence J. Goldberg, and Lawrence J. White. 1999. "The Dynamics of Market Entry: The Effects of Mergers and Acquisitions on De Novo Entry and Small Business Lending in the Banking Industry." Board of Governors of the Federal Reserve System, Finanace and Economics Discussion Series 1991-41.

Berger, Allen N., Rebecca Demsetz, and Philip E. Strahan. 1999. "The Consolidation of the Financial Services Industry: Causes, Consequences, and Implications for the Future." *Journal of Banking and Finance* 23, no. 2–4: 135–194.

Berger, Allen N., and Timothy M. Hannan. 1989. "Deposit Interest Rates and Local Market Concentration." In *Concentration and Price*. Ed. Leonard Weiss. Cambridge: MIT Press.

Berger, Allen N., Gerald A. Hanweck, and David B. Humphrey. 1987. "Competitive Viability in Banking: Scale, Scope and Product Mix Economies." *Journal of Monetary Economics* 20: 501–520.

Berger, Allen N., and David B. Humphrey, 1997. "Efficiency of Financial Institutions: International Survey and Directions for Future Research." *European Journal of Operations Research* 175–212.

Berger, Allen N., and Loretta J. Mester. 1997. "Inside the Black Box: What Explains Differences in the Efficiencies of Financial Institutions." *Journal of Banking and Finance* 21: 895–947.

Board of Governors of the Federal Reserve System. 1997, 1998a, 2000. *Annual Reports to the Congress on Retail Fees and Services of Depository Institutions.* Washington, D.C.: Board of Governors of the Federal Reserve System.

———. 1998b. "Order Approving Formation of a Bank Holding Company: Travelers Group and Citicorp." 84 *Federal Reserve Bulletin* 985.

———. 1998c. "Order Approving Merger of Bank Holding Companies: Banc One Corporation and First Chicago NBD Corporation." 84 *Federal Reserve Bulletin* 961.

———. 1998d. "Order Approving Merger of Bank Holding Companies: NationsBank Corporation and BankAmerica Corporation." 84 *Federal Reserve Bulletin* 858.

Boyd, John, and Stanley L. Graham. 1988. "The Profitability and Risk Effects of Allowing Bank Holding Companies to Merge With Other Financial Firms: A Simulation Study." *Quarterly Review* (Federal Reserve Bank of Minneapolis), Spring, 3–20.

Boyd, John, Gerald A. Hanweck, and P. Pithyarchariyakul. 1980. "Optimal Bank Holding Company Diversification into Nonbank Activities." *Bank Structure and Competition* (Federal Reserve Bank of Chicago), May, 105–111.

Brewer, Elijah, III, and Douglas D. Evanoff. 1997. "Small Business Investment Companies: Market Distortions and Firm Behavior." Draft, *Federal Reserve Bank of Chicago*, 7 July.

DeYoung, Robert, Kenneth Spong, and Richard Sullivan. 1997. *Ownership, Control, and Performance at Small Commercial Banks.* Kansas City: Office of Comptroller of the Currency and Federal Reserve Bank of Kansas City.

Edwards, Corwin. 1955. "Conglomerate Bigness as a Source of Power." In *Business Concentration and Price Policy.* Princeton, N.J.: Princeton University Press.

Elliehausen, Gregory E., and John D. Wolken. 1990. "Banking Markets and the Use of Financial Services by Small and Medium-Sized Businesses." 76 *Federal Reserve Bulletin* 801–817.

———. 1992. "Banking Markets and the Use of Financial Services by Households." 78 *Federal Reserve Bulletin* 169–181.

English, William B., and William R. Nelson. 1998. "Profits and Balance Sheet Developments at U.S. Commercial Banks in 1997." 84 *Federal Reserve Bulletin* 391–419.

Eriksen, Erik. 1962. *Young Man Luther.* New York: W. W. Norton.

Evans, W. N., and I. N. Kessides. 1994. "Living by the 'Golden Rule': Multimarket Contact in the U.S. Airline Industry." *Quarterly Journal of Economics* 109: 341–366.

Feldman, Ron J., and Arthur J. Rolnick. 1998. "Fixing FDICIA: A Plan to Address the Too-Big-to-Fail Problem." In *1997 Annual Report.* Minneapolis: Federal Reserve Bank of Minneapolis.

Fromson, Brett D., and Jerry Knight. 1993. "The Saving of Citibank." *Washington Post*, 16 June, A1.

Gaskins, Darius W. 1971. "Dynamic Limit Pricing: Optimal Pricing Under Threat of Entry." *Journal of Economic Theory* 3: 306–322.

Gilbert, Alton R. 1984. "Bank Market Structure and Competition." *Journal of Money, Credit and Banking* 16, no. 4: 617–661.

Gilbert, Richard J. 1989. "Mobility Barriers and the Value of Incumbency." *Handbook of Industrial Organization*. Ed. Richard Schmalensee and Robert D. Willig. Amsterdam: Elsevier Science Publishers.

Hannan, Timothy H. 1992. "The Functional Relationship between Prices and Market Concentration: The Case of the Banking Industry." *Empirical Studies in Industrial Organization: Essays in Honor of Leonard W. Weiss*. Amsterdam: Kluwer Academic Publishers.

———. 1994. "Recent Trends in Retail Fees and Services of Depository Institutions." 80 *Federal Reserve Bulletin* 771–781.

———. 1996. "Bank Fees and Their Variation Across Banks and Locations." Unpublished paper, December.

Hannan, Timothy H., and Gerald A. Hanweck. 1988. "Bank Insolvency Risk and the Market for Large Certificates of Deposit." *Journal of Money, Credit and Banking* 20: 203–211.

Hannan, Timothy H., and Stephen A. Rhoades. 1992. "Future U.S. Banking Structure: 1990–2010." *The Antitrust Bulletin* 37, no. 3: 737–798.

Hanweck, Gerald A., and Stephen A. Rhoades. 1984. "Dominant Firms, Deep Pockets, and Local Market Competition in Banking." *Journal of Economics and Business* 36: 391–402.

Hanweck, Gerald A., and Bernard Shull. 1996. *Interest Rate Volatility*. Chicago: Irwin Professional Publishing.

———. 1999. "The Bank Merger Movement: Efficiency, Stability and Comptetitive Policy Concerns." *The Antitrust Bulletin* 44, no. 2: 251–284.

Heggestad, Arnold, and Stephen A. Rhoades. 1978. "Multimarket Interdependence and Local Market Competition in Banking." *The Review of Economics and Statistics* 60, no. 4: 523–532.

Heitfield, Eric A. 1999. "What Do Interest Rates Say about the Geography of Retail Banking Markets?" *The Antitrust Bulletin* 44, no. 2: 333–347.

Hetzel, Robert L. 1991. "Too-big-to-fail: Origins, Consequences and Outlook." *Economic Review* (Federal Reserve Bank of Richmond) 77, no. 6: 3–15.

Holland, David, Don Inscoe, Ross Waldrop, and William Kutta. 1996. "Interstate Banking: The Past, Present and Future." *FDIC Banking Review* 9, no. 1: 2–30.

Horvitz, Paul M., and Bernard Shull. 1964. "The Impact of Branch Banking on Bank Performance." *The National Banking Review* 2, no. 2: 143–188.

Hughes, Joseph P., and Loretta J. Mester. 1998. "Bank Capitalization and Cost: Evidence of Scale Economies in Risk Management and Signaling." *Review of Economics and Statistics* 80: 314–325.

Hughes, Kirsty, and Christine Oughton. 1993. "Diversification, Multi-Market Contact and Profitability." *Economica* 60: 203–224.

Jackson, William. 1992. "The Price Concentration Relationship in Banking: A Comment." *Review of Economics and Statistics* 74: 373–376.

Kinnichal, Arthur B., and Myron L. Kwast. 1997. "Who Uses Electronic Banking: Results from the 1995 Survey of Consumer Finances." Paper presented to the Annual Conference on Bank Structure and Competition, Federal Reserve Bank of Chicago, May.

Kwast, Myron, Martha Starr-McCluer, and John D. Wolken. 1997. "Market Definition and the Analysis of Antitrust in Banking." *The Antitrust Bulletin* 42, no. 4: 973–995.

Mester, Loretta J. 1994."How Efficient are Third District Banks?" *Business Review* (Federal Reserve Bank of Philadelphia), January–February, 3–18.

Meyer, Lawrence H. 1998. Statement before Committee on Banking and Financial Services. 29 April. 84 *Federal Reserve Bulletin* 438–451 (1998).

Nisenson, Richard. 1999. "The Recent Resurgence of De Novo Banks." Unpublished paper, Office of the Comptroller of the Currency.

Nolle, Daniel, E. 1995. "Banking Industry Consolidation: Past Changes and Implications for the Future." Economic & Policy Working Paper no. 95-1. Office of the Comptroller of the Currency, April.

Pilloff, Steven. 1999. "Multimarket Contact in Banking." *Review of Industrial Organization* 14, no. 2: 163–182.

Pilloff, Steven, and Stephen A. Rhoades. 2000. "Do Large Diversified Banking Organizations Have Competitive Advantages?" *Review of Industrial Organization* 16, no. 3: 287–302.

Prager, Robin A., and Timothy H. Hannan. 1999. "Do Substantial Horizontal Mergers Generate Significant Price Effects? Evidence from the Banking Industry." *Review of Industrial Economics* 46: 433–452.

Radecki, Lawrence J. 1998. "The Expanding Geographic Reach of Retail Banking Markets." *Economic Policy Review* (Federal Reserve Bank of New York) 4, no. 2: 15–34.

———. forthcoming. "Competition in Shifting Product and Geographic Markets. *The Antitrust Bulletin*.

Raghavan, Anita, and Mitchell Pacelle. 1998. "To the Rescue: A Hedge Fund Falters, and Big Banks Agree to Ante Up $3.5 Billion." *Wall Street Journal*, 24 September, A1.

Rhoades, Stephen. 1996. "Bank Mergers and Industrywide Structure, 1980–94." Staff study no. 169. Board of Governors of the Federal Reserve System, January.

———. 1997. "Have Barriers to Entry in Retail Commercial Banking Disappeared?" *The Antitrust Bulletin* 42, no. 4: 997–1014.

———. 1998. "The Efficiency Effects of Bank Mergers: An Overview of Case Studies in Nine Mergers." *Journal of Banking and Finance* 22: 273–291.

Rhoades, Stephen, and Arnold Heggestad. 1985. "Multimarket Interdependence and Performance in Banking: Two Tests." *The Antitrust Bulletin* 30, no. 4: 975–995.

Rose, Peter S. 1992. "Interstate Banking: Performance, Market Share and Market Concentration Issues." *The Antitrust Bulletin* 37, no. 3: 601–630.

Scherer, F. M. 1970. *Industrial Market Structure and Market Performance*. Chicago: Rand McNally.

Scherer, F. M., and David Ross. 1990. *Industrial Market Structure and Economic Performance*. Boston: Houghton Mifflin.

Scott, John T. 1982. "Multimarket Contact and Economic Performance." *Review of Economics and Statistics* 64, no. 3: 368–374.

———. 1989. "Purposive Diversification as a Motive for Merger." *International Journal of Industrial Organization* 7, no. 2: 35–47.

———. 1991. "Multimarket Contact Among Diversified Oligopolists." *International Journal of Industrial Organization* 9, no. 2: 225–238.

Seelig, Stephen A., and Timothy Critchfield. 1999. "Determinants of De Novo Entry in Banking." Working Paper no. 99-1. Washington, D.C.: Federal Deposit Insurance Corporation.

Shull, Bernard. 1995. "The Limits of Prudential Supervision: Experience in the United States." *Economic Notes* 26, no. 3: 585–612.

———. 1996. "The Origins of Antitrust in Banking: An Historical Perspective." *The Antitrust Bulletin* 41, no. 2: 255–288.

———. 1999. "Merger Policy in the United States: Is There a Need for a Change." In *Modernizing the Global Financial System.* Ed. Dimitri Papadimitriou. New York: St. Martin's Press.

Shull, Bernard, and Gerald A. Hanweck. 2000. "A New Merger Policy for Banks." *The Antitrust Bulletin* 45, no. 3: 679–711.

Simons, Katerina, and Joanna Stavins. 1998. "Has Antitrust Policy in Banking Become Obsolete?" *New England Economic Review*, March–April, 13–26.

Solomon, Eleanor. 1970. "A Linkage Theory of Oligopoly." *Journal of Money, Credit and Banking* 2: 323–336.

Tabor, Michael. 1989. *Chaos and Integrability In Nonlinear Dynamics.* New York: John Wiley & Sons.

U.S. Department of Justice. 1982. *Horizontal Merger Guidelines.* Washington, D.C.: U.S. Department of Justice.

U.S. Public Interest Research Group. 1997. "National Survey Documents Widening Fee Gap between Large and Small Banks." 31 July. Available <http://www.pirg.org>.

Whalen, Gary W. 1996. "Nonlocal Concentration, Multimarket Linkages, and Interstate Banking." *The Antitrust Bulletin* 41, no. 2: 365–398.

Whitehead, David. 1978. "An Empirical Test of the Linked Oligopoly Theory: An Analysis of Floridan Holding Companies." In *Proceedings of a Conference on Bank Structure and Competition.* Chicago: Federal Reserve Bank of Chicago.

# CHAPTER 7

# Toward a New Competition Policy for Banking

We are to look for intelligible reasons for which one state should give way to another.

John R. Hicks[1]

The deregulation movement in banking which slowly started in the early 1960s, accelerated in the 1980s, and culminated with the elimination of restrictions on branching and financial activities in the 1990s has been a momentous victory for the competitive ideal over centuries-old government restraints aimed at protecting banks against failure. Communication and computer advances have augmented the procompetitive policy changes, facilitating the emergence of new competitors in local banking markets, increasing the numbers of financial firms in competition with one another, promoting an expansion of geographic markets, intensifying potential competition, enabling the elimination of inefficient banks, and permitting the realization of whatever economies of scale and/or scope might exist. Such changes should themselves produce a revolution in competition for financial services and generate innovations in their scope and delivery.

On the other hand, deregulation has also launched an unprecedented wave of bank mergers, the causes for which were discussed in Chapter 5. The merger wave has already gone a long way toward reshaping the banking system and market structures. Passage of the Gramm–Leach–Bliley Act in November 1999, facilitating the combination of banks, insurance companies, and securities firms, is likely to further increase the size and scope of the largest organizations and reshape the entire financial system. The competitive impact in local markets is moot.

The dynamic processes of structural reorganization thus generate conflicting developments, some of which are pro- and others which are anticompetitive. The more intense competition promised by deregulation and technological advance is threatened by the merger movement.

Bank merger policy would seem to protect against the anticompetitive effects of mergers. As reviewed in Chapter 4, each merger must be approved by a federal banking agency after an evaluation of its competitive effects in local markets. Approvals are subject to antitrust challenges by the Justice Department. However, our review in Chapter 6 found little evidence that consumers and small businesses that purchase banking services in local markets have benefitted from improved efficiency and more intense competition. Relying on a model that combined dynamic price leadership with mutual forbearance and the regulatory policy of protecting large banking organizations near failure, we concluded that merger policy, as currently implemented, is blind to some of the long-term, cumulative, cross-market effects of the merger movement.

In this chapter we consider the deficiencies of current merger policy and make a number of proposals for change. The issues we address are affected with a deep-rooted government interest that has permeated banking policy from its origins, but whose significance we believe has in recent years been underestimated. Despite the radical institutional and technological changes of the last several decades, an effective revision of current policy must take into consideration enduring factors that continue to be operative. Our proposals are developed within the context of the history lessons of Chapters 2 and 3.

In the next section, we briefly recapitulate current merger policy and the economic issues that it has raised. Thereafter, we elaborate the deficiencies of current policy, and establish a framework for our proposals. The proposals themselves are then presented.

## A RECAPITULATION OF CURRENT BANK MERGER POLICY

Current bank merger policy developed in the 1960s through passage of the Bank Merger Act, the Supreme Court's decision in the *Philadelphia–Girard Trust* merger case and amendments to both the Bank Merger Act and Bank Holding Company Act in 1966. These developments made antitrust standards applicable, gave each banking agency prior approval authority, in accordance with the regulatory status of the resulting institution, and required them to deny mergers that violated Section 2 of the Sherman Act, and also Section 7 of the Clayton Act unless "the anticompetitive effects of the proposed transaction are clearly outweighed in the public interest on the probable effect . . . in meeting the convenience and needs of the community." As a result, the agencies could continue to take into consideration the "financial and managerial resources and future prospects of the existing and proposed institutions." The Justice Department could challenge any federal banking agency approval by obtaining an automatic injunction to stay an approved merger by entering suit within thirty days.

The Supreme Court's decision in the *Philadelphia* case in 1963 established a geographic market ("the area in which the seller operates and the purchase can practicably turn for supplies"), a product market ("the cluster of products . . . and services . . . denoted by the term commercial banking"), and a method for measuring a "substantial lessening of competition" in terms of levels and changes in market concentration resulting from a merger.

From the mid-1960s through the 1970s, federal banking agency evaluations resulted in periodic denials of merger applications and some approvals which were challenged by the Justice Department in court. Subsequent court decisions did not modify the economic analysis prescribed by the Supreme Court in its *Philadelphia* decision; that is, the geographic, product market, and concentration determinations, but they did elaborate the scope and limits of the law. They established how a merger's contribution to "convenience and needs" might offset its anticompetitive effects, standards for evaluating potential competition as a basis for denial, and whether or not a banking agency could deny a merger if the anticompetitive effects were not so serious as to violate Section 7. Of particular importance, the courts established a high enough barrier for denying a merger on the basis of its effect on potential competition, as to effectively preclude such denials after the 1970s. These decisions deterred the Federal Reserve, in particular, from requiring that new entry by established banks be de novo or by "foothold" acquisition, thereby preserving large banking organizations in local areas for future competition. The courts also determined that it was not within the power of the federal banking agencies to deny a merger whose anticompetitive effects did not reach Section 7 standards.

The established policy effectively precluded horizontal bank mergers among large banks in metropolitan areas and where there were few banks in rural areas. The new understanding among bankers that the antitrust laws were applicable to banking effectively eliminated price fixing and market sharing that had been common in banking for many years.

By the early 1980s, nonbank depository institutions, such as savings and loan associations and savings banks, and nondepository financial institutions, like the money market mutual fund found new opportunities to compete in traditional banking markets. Congress undertook substantial deregulation, eliminating important competitive restrictions on the pricing of deposits and liberalizing the restrictions that separated commercial banks from other depository institutions. Both the Comptroller of the Currency and state bank supervisors liberalized restrictions on new charters. States began to liberalize restrictions on both intrastate and interstate branching, as well.

Revision of the Justice Department's *Horizontal Merger Guidelines* in 1982 provided the federal agencies with an opportunity to consider the new competitive developments in evaluating merger proposals. The revised *Guidelines* outlined a geographic and product market analysis that permitted banking markets to be larger than the service area definition established by the *Philadelphia* decision. They also adopted the Hirfindahl–Hirschman Index as a more refined measure of market power and established thresholds that were roughly consistent with court decisions.

Further, the *Guidelines* made clear that levels and changes in the HHI were a screen for scrutinizing proposed mergers, not the only relevant factors. The size distribution of firms, potential competition, and efficiency effects, among others, might also be considered. They thereby introduced a set of mitigating factors that would permit mergers that exceeded the department's HHI thresholds. However, they did not introduce any new adverse factors. Further, the introduction of negotiated divestitures, first by the Federal Reserve and subsequently by the Justice Department made it possible for the federal agencies to eliminate rejections of large bank mergers entirely.

## THE DEFICIENCIES OF BANK MERGER POLICY

In the financial environment that existed in the 1960s, the bank merger policy that was instituted, with its focus on local markets, was an important procompetitive measure. In the evolving financial environment, each of the modifications of the 1980s might well be warranted. In combination, however, they have facilitated large bank mergers that have changed the financial environment, and whose competitive effects may well extend beyond local market conditions. The result is that current merger analysis by the federal agencies is, at best, incomplete. It does not deal with the developing issues that were beyond the scope of concern when the policy was originally established. We have found, based on our analysis in Chapters 4 and 6, the deficiencies reflected in two areas, one economic and the other legal/regulatory.

### Economic Issues

It has been difficult to find gains resulting from large bank mergers due to greater efficiency or diversification. On the other hand, there has been evidence that mergers have adversely impacted competition in local markets. Prices of retail banking services have not declined, as one might have expected, with more intense competition and cost-saving technological advance.

There is good reason to believe that large bank mergers have changed the competitive relationship between large banking organizations and their smaller competitors. Increasing numbers of local MSA markets are characterized by one or a few very large banking organizations and a group of smaller fringe institutions. The large organizations confront one another in increasing numbers of product and geographic markets. It is generally understood, at least since the passage of FDICIA in 1991, that the owners and uninsured creditors of most banks will not be protected from failure, as was previously the case, while very large banking organizations remain beneficiaries of the seemingly indestructible policy of too-big-to-fail. Admittedly, it is difficult to disentangle the benefits of too-big-to-fail from other risk and efficiency factors that also affect bank funding costs, but as might be expected, these large organizations have substantially lower costs than other banks.

The recently passed Gramm–Leach–Bliley Act nods at the problem of creating still larger banking organizations that are too-big-to-fail. It does so in several ways. First, it makes an effort to restrict whatever moral hazzard problem exists at larger banking organizations due to market recognition that the federal government is not likely to permit the largest banks to fail in any conventional sense. Thus the FDIC is prohibited from assisting nonbanking affiliates and subsidiaries of banks. Further, it requires, as a condition for engaging in expanded activities through financial subsidiaries, that the largest 100 banks issue subordinated debentures so as to create a class of creditors with a strong incentive to monitor and constrain excessively risky activities which such safety net–protected banks might otherwise find profitable. However, in apparent uncertainty as to effectiveness of the subordinated debt requirement, the Act also mandates a Treasury–Federal Reserve study on the use of subordinated debt for this purpose and, ultimately, to protect the financial system and the federal deposit insurance funds. Finally, in support of smaller banks in lending to small businesses, small farms, and small agribusinesses, the Act also provides for long-term advances from Federal Home Loan Banks (FHLB) for institutions with less than $500 million in assets.

The quantitative significance of these measures in offsetting the competitive cost-of-funds advantage of the largest banks, discussed in Chapter 6, is uncertain. However, neither higher costs associated with subordinated debentures for the largest organizations, nor lower costs associated with FHLB advances for smaller banks are likely to be sufficient to level the playing field. At this point, there is no good reason to believe that investors owning subordinated debentures in a large bank will view themselves at risk if the bank, whatever its problems, cannot be closed. Further, low cost, long-term advances from FHLBs would impose collateral damage that increases with their effectiveness. The advances are likely to be made on terms that encourage smaller banks to take on higher risk in lending and investing. Unless the advances fully substitute for federally insured deposits, which seems unlikely, they would intensify a moral hazzard problem at smaller banks that would tend to raise the cost to the FDIC of resolving any that failed. Further, the requirement that such advances be fully collateralized would give the FHLBs first claim on good assets of failed banks, and again increase costs to the deposit insurance funds. Thus, any new federal support for small banks, tending to offset the inequalities produced by federal support for large banks, would shift costs from consumers impacted by insufficient competition to the FDIC and taxpayers.

We do not expect, then, that the changes introduced by the new Gramm–Leach–Bliley legislation will alter the relevance of the modified dominant-firm price leadership model we developed in Chapter 6 to explain the disappointing price effects of deregulation and technological advance. Large, national banking organizations that are also locally-dominant firms will have a funding cost advantage over their small local competitors. Because they confront one another in many markets, mutual forbearance will constitute a value maximizing interaction. Our analysis, based on the model, indicates that dominant firms will be in a position to charge prices above competitive levels while neutralizing potential competition and sustaining their market share. The model coherently explains both the failure of deregulation and technological advance to generate substantial price reductions for banking services, as well as a number of puzzling research findings.

### The Regulatory Process and the Courts

In eliminating rejections of large bank mergers, the policy modifications implemented by the federal banking agencies and the Justice Department over the last two decades have effectively eliminated litigation. As observed in Chapter 4, the result has been that the judiciary no longer participates in either the decision-making process in specific mergers, nor in the conventions on which these decisions are based.

Valuable as some of the changes made by the federal agencies have been, they have not been legitimized by the courts. In the last decision in a banking case in the mid-1980s, the court rejected the Justice Department's new approach to product market definition; but without apparent effect on the Department's practices. There have been no subsequent decisions because there has been no subsequent litigation. The courts have not had an opportunity to review the new decision-making approaches, the continuing differences in standards among the agencies, or the new economic problems raised by the merger movement.

In effect, the federal agencies have immunized themselves from court review by adopting policies that have precluded almost all denials. From the point of view of the federal agencies, such immunization may in itself be a valuable byproduct; it provides an autonomy that previously did not exist.

### THE PRESENCE OF THE PAST: A FRAMEWORK FOR ANALYSIS

The issues we have raised suggest the need for change in bank merger policy, but the precise changes must be considered within the context of enduring institutional arrangements. A historical perspective on these arrangements was provided in Chapters 2 and 3.

### Historical Perspective on the Modern Paradigm

It is certainly legitimate to ask why competition policy in banking, including policies affecting mergers, can't be identical to competition policies for other private sector firms such as automobile manufacturers, computer companies, and food producers. Given the scope of deregulation of the last two decades, shouldn't banking now be fully incorporated into the universe of private business where the antitrust laws alone govern competition?[2]

It is patently clear, however, that notwithstanding extensive deregulation, banking continues to be a highly regulated business. Banking firms are still organized on the basis of limited-purpose charters that intentionally restrict their activities; unlike most corporations, they are not permitted to engage in any lawful business. They are thus established as unique institutions by government, identified by their charter as a separate group of institutions that operate under special laws and regulations. A 1997 newspaper story described the continuing regulatory vigilance against unchartered financial firms that used the term "bank" in their title. It indicated that state regulators had issued a cease and desist order against a bank and its three top officials ordering them "to stop using the words 'bank,' 'banking,' or 'banker' in its name or promotional materials or otherwise implying that it is a bank." The story concluded by saying that an official of the Office of the Comptroller of the Currency indicated that it typically issued forty to fifty warnings against such entities each year.[3] Those institutions that have bank charters continue to be subject to extensive regulation and supervision implemented by an extensive network of federal and state regulatory agencies. It is unlikely that these fundamentals of bank regulation will change in the foreseeable future.

The modern paradigm on which banks are regulated locates their special status in the contribution they make to the general objectives of economic stability and welfare. The government has taken responsibility to achieve these goals and to protect against bank failures that could undermine them.

Edward Kelley, a member of the Federal Reserve Board, recently reiterated the standard argument. He indicates that even in the light of recent competitive and technological developments that have diminished the importance of banks as providers of credit and safe repositories for savings, they remain the institutional mechanism through which monetary policy is transmitted and, through wire transfer and check, a principal component of the payments system. Banks are therefore retained as a separate group of firms subject to regulation and supervision because their successful performance in these functions is immensely important to economic welfare, and because they remain susceptible to failure as a result of runs and large-scale banking crises.[4]

Governor Kelley might have included the services banks provide in meeting other governmental objectives. One of the most debated in recent years has been the requirements imposed on banks by the Community Reinvestment Act (CRA) of 1978 that they reserve resources for their local communities. In 1999, Congress reaffirmed its seriousness about CRA in passing the Gramm–Leach–Bliley Act. Under the new Act, a banking organization can engage in previously prohibited financial activities only if all of its depository institutions have satisfactory CRA ratings.

The merger movement itself has provided governments with an opportunity to extract bank resources for public purposes. The 1995 testimony of Richard Blumenthal, Attorney General for the State of Connecticut, before the Federal Reserve Board on the proposed merger of Fleet Financial Group and Shawmut National Corporation is illuminating:

> Economic development is a critical piece of this proposed merger, and a condition that I will not compromise. Since Fleet, post-merger, would be Connecticut's largest bank, surely it recognizes that its own success is largely linked to the success of Connecticut's economy. There is a natural opportunity for Fleet to forge with the state a public/private partnership in economic development. As a condition of allowing the merger, the new Fleet must accept a leadership role in Connecticut's economic development initiatives. . . . Before we allow Fleet to gain the vast benefits of its merger with Shawmut, we must insist on more than promises or platitudes. Hard commitments to programs that will result in real, measurable benefits to Connecticut's communities should be in place before approving this merger.[5]

Mr. Blumenthal announced on September 11, 1995 that he had reached an economic development agreement with Fleet and Shawmut whereby the resulting bank would invest $207.5 million in several government programs for loans to small business, housing, and community development.[6] Connecticut's success in extracting development funds from merging banks has not been unique.[7]

Governor Kelley's views, those of Congress, and Mr. Blumenthal's are hardly new. Banks have been special to governments since their early development in the Mediterranean city states in the thirteenth and fourteenth centuries. Tommaso Contarini, the sixteenth-century Venetian senator quoted in Chapter 2, made clear that the commerce of his city depended on banks, even though they typically failed, leaving serious wreckage behind. This specialness continued through the period of public banking in Europe in the sixteenth and seventeenth centuries, in the Bank of England, in the first bank charters in the United States, and through subsequent legal and regulatory reorganizations, including free banking laws, the National Banking Act, the Federal Reserve Act and the Banking Acts of 1933 and 1935. It has continued through the deregulation of the 1980s and 1990s.

While CRA and Blumenthal's interventions are viewed by some as extortion, they are not much different than the interventions by governments beginning with the first banks in the United States. It can be recalled that the Bank of North America was chartered by the Continental Congress to help finance the Revolutionary War. From that time until the Civil War, banks accommodated the financial deficiencies of state governments through investment earnings and tax revenues. A number of states also chartered banks with the express purpose of financing internal improvements. Those seeking a bank charter knew they had to provide reciprocal benefits, often determined in negotiation with state legislatures. When Congress passed the National Banking Act during the Civil War in 1863–1864, its intentions were to create banks that would purchase federal government securities and contribute to financing the Civil War. Congress found new ways to obtain financial assistance from banks during World War I and II. In the 1970s, Congress's encouragement to banks to help in the "recycling of petro-dollars," to invest in Mexico, and for community reinvestment fall in the same category of using these institutions to do the work of the state.

Whether for the general purpose of economic welfare, or special purposes involving specific projects or sectors of the economy, the government continues to make banks special. And specialness continues to evoke special government regulation and support. Such policies invariably result in a quid pro quo, whether it be in approving a merger, permitting expanded financial activities, or in some other way. The contribution of banks invariably leads to regulation and supervision because bank failure has an impact on the services banks provide. Finally, the disruption created by their failure has often led to policies of support and assistance, like too-big-to-fail. At bottom, government continues to have a keen and persistent interest in the success of banking firms. CRA and Blumenthal's intervention are traditional. A better word than extortion is symbiosis.

It is this continuing government interest in the success of banking firms that has always required special competition policies for banking. From the first banks in the United States through the 1950s, these policies were, on the whole, anticompetitve, with restrictions on new entry into local markets and acceptance of price fixing and market sharing. More recently, partial deregulation combined with continuing regulation has set in motion a structural reorganization that requires the continuation of special procompetitive policies.

Of particular importance in this reorganization has been the emergence of the policy of too-big-to-fail. We have observed that from the early 1930s to the 1960s, the government treated all banks as if they were too important to fail. But during the subsequent period of deregulation large banks, whose failure might create systemic problems, were separated out as too-big-to-fail.

With a sharp decline in bank failures since FDICIA was passed in 1991, the new approach to too-big-to-fail has yet to be tested, but recent experience in other countries, including France and Japan, where governments continue to protect their largest banks from insolvency, is indicative of the hold they have on government resources. There is no reason to believe, despite the as yet untested contraints of FDICIA, that too-big-to-fail, in a world where big is becoming a lot bigger, will be abandoned.

## Outlook

Given the deficiencies in current merger policy our policy proposals emerge from several expectations and presumptions.

### High Concentration and Large Bank Dominance Will Prevail

All indications show that in the future there will be much larger and fewer banks. Concentration among the largest banking organizations at the national level and within regions of the country will be higher. Concentration in local markets will continue to be high, though we recognize that the competitive significance of local markets may, over time, change. Local markets may well grow into regional markets, but even these are likely to be dominated by a small number of very large banking organizations.

In these circumstances, an apparent evolutionary intensification of competition, with banks providing services to households and small business over the Internet, and via business-to-business or auction Web sites, may be less than it seems. Competition through these new methods of distribution would be stunted if the largest banking companies come to dominate them. Given their funding advantages, it is difficult to see why this would not happen. If the new methods of distribution grow significantly, local market concentration, as currently measured, will prove to be less significant; but high levels of national concentration and anticompetitive multimarket relationships would be significant in the pricing of local financial services.

### Banks Will Remain Special

We expect large banking organizations to remain special in the sense indicated earlier. Government will retain an intense interest in their safety and soundness, and a continued concern as to the effects of possible failure. Government support for floundering organizations, as characterized by the policy of too-big-to-fail, will persist.

### A Procompetition Policy Will Endure

The procompetition policies that were initiated in the 1960s in the United States were sufficiently unique to warrant an explicit statement that we expect their objectives to be sustained into the foreseeable future. The goals of the proposals outlined below build on the view that competition in banking is desirable, achievable, and sustainable through appropriate policy.

## PROPOSALS FOR CHANGE

The proposed policy modifications presented in this section address competitive and related issues raised.[8] They are outlined on the likelihood that the analysis developed previously is correct, and a belief that it is necessary to consider policy changes before the structural transition now underway results in the irreversible establishment of a small set of very large organizations, variously dominant in numerous markets and too-big-to-fail.

### Change in Authority:
### The Federal Banking Agencies and the Justice Department

The current overlapping arrangement for competitive evaluations at the federal banking agencies and the Justice Department was necessary in 1966 to reconcile banking and antitrust laws. It appears to have outlived the imperatives that required the banking agency involvement in most mergers.

The original basis for banking agency prior approval authority derived from their supervisory responsibilities. Authority gave the agencies leverage in securing supervisory objectives. It also provided a method for working out ownership and managerial problems that could not at the time be easily dealt with in other ways. Over the last several decades, the agencies have obtained an arsenal of new weapons to compel compliance to existing law and regulation, including written agreements and cease-and-desist orders, with the power to impose substantial fines and penalties. With the passage of FDICIA in 1991, they have been authorized to promptly escalate their intervention in cases where banks do not meet capital requirements. FDICIA has also made clear that prompt closure of weak banks is in most cases required; and precludes the agencies from providing financial assistance to floundering institutions or to bail-out uninsured depositors except where failure poses the risk of a systemic event. These changes make it questionable as to whether, in most cases, the federal banking agencies need to retain merger authority for supervisory reasons. We recognize that the provisions of the Community Reinvestment Act are currently enforced in the merger process, but it would seem that they could be just as well enforced through the prompt corrective action measures now used to assure compliance with capital requirements.

If the banking agencies need not evaluate most mergers for supervisory reasons, and there is no obvious reason for a dual antitrust evaluation, there seems to be little basis for continuing banking agency involvement. The dual evaluation of competitive effects is costly in terms of expenditures of public funds; and to banks that must accommodate at least two independent evaluators with the power to increase the costs of their proposals.[9] Such overlap is also potentially corrosive. Differential criteria and actual and potential conflicts tend to undermine the legitimacy of the evaluation process. The elimination of prior approval authority, where possible, would be consistent with the spirit of legislative deregulation.While prior approval authority for small bank mergers might be safely relinquished by the federal banking agencies, retention of authority for large bank mergers seems necessary. The continuing bank regulatory concern for large bank safety is reflected in the wide latitude the agencies have exercised in preserving them through forbearance;

and, as mentioned, in the systemic risk provisions of FDICIA. As discussed, the large organizations that are, or may become through merger, too-big-to-fail, raises unique competitive issues. The Federal Reserve and the FDIC, on the basis of their monetary and insurance responsibilities, are in a unique position to determine if a failure of one or more large banks poses the risk of a systemic event. Data availability and experience place all the banking agencies in a favored position for evaluating the competitive advantages of bank size provided by current supervisory arrangements. Arguments, nevertheless, can be made both for maintaining current arrangements and for eliminating competitive review authority in the federal banking agencies. With respect to the former, it is possible that the few denials in recent years, all involving small banks in rural markets, would not have occurred had the banking agencies relinquished prior approval authority; they would not have attracted the attention and limited resources of the Justice Department. Because small banks in rural areas still play an important role in their communities, it would not be wise to permit anticompetitive mergers. Further, there are practical difficulties in drawing a line in terms of asset or deposit size for banks whose mergers would not be subject to prior approval by the banking agencies. The definition of asset limits below, under which there would be an exemption, may be viewed as preliminary. The asset limits are, however, intentionally substantial such that federal banking agency authority would apply only to the very largest organizations. Alternatively, if it were possible to eliminate the unique support provided large banks, they should be no more subjected to special merger evaluation than any other business. The middle ground, as discussed earlier, can be summarized as follows:

1. *Eliminate federal bank regulatory authority over mergers for banks under a specified size; for example, where both banks have less than $10 billion in assets; and also where the acquirer has less than $30 billion and the acquired bank less than $5 billion. Mergers of smaller institutions would be left to antitrust evaluation alone, as are mergers in other industries. These cutoff values can be adjusted as inflation increases size of banks.*

2. *Retain federal banking agency authority for mergers involving large banks; that is, those with assets above the exemption indicated above. As is the case today, retention of banking agency authority would not preclude the applicability of the antitrust laws.*

### Modification of Competitive Analysis

The current procedure for evaluating the competitive effects of bank mergers is derived from the Supreme Court's analysis in the *Philadelphia* case, as modified by the Justice Department's *Guidelines*. In 1966, the Court focused on the shares of the largest banks in *Philadelphia* as a uniquely important structural element. The dominance of a declining number of large banks would worsen an already unfavorable competitive environment. On the other hand, the experience of several decades influenced by depression legislation indicated that vigorous competition could not necessarily be expected from the remaining banks, whatever the number. Potential competition was not relevant because restrictive branching and chartering law effectively immunized the four-county Philadelphia area from new entry.

In the early 1980s, the *Guidelines* provided an efficient method for merger evaluation by substituting the HHI, a concentration measure inclusive of all banks, for the market shares of the largest banks, establishing presumptive thresholds for likely competitive effects and taking into consideration other factors that might enhance or diminish the exercise of market power. These modifications, as applied to banking, were attractive. Intensified competitive behavior among smaller banks required consideration, as did a revival of new potential rivals as restrictions on multiple-office banking and new charters were relaxed. The introduction of efficiency effects was also reasonable, as earlier restrictions disappeared and inefficient banks could now exit through merger.

The Federal Reserve's application of the *Guidelines* included use of HHI threshold levels which permit approval in most cases. Mitigating factors and divestitures are only considered if levels are exceeded. The system has an advantage of simplifying the evaluation process and making the outcome reasonably certain to merger partners who know the effects of their proposals on concentration.

As has always been the case with respect to the antitrust laws, certainty as to outcome is purchased at the price of accuracy in predicting competitive effects. Under current procedures, it is unlikely that mergers that should be approved will be denied if only because the Federal Reserve has only invoked mitigating, not aggravating, factors in its decisions. It is more likely that mergers that should be denied will be approved. For example, the early *Guidelines* explicitly included a "leading firm proviso" that indicated a likely challenge by the Justice Department of a horizontal merger of a small firm into a leading firm (market share of at least 35 percent; approximately twice as large as the second largest firm) regardless of effects on the HHI. The Federal Reserve, in its 1997 decision in the *Southern National Corporation* case referred to in Chapter 4, permitted a bank with about 61 percent of market deposits to acquire the second largest bank in the market with about 19 percent. It did indicate a concern with augmenting the leading bank's dominant position but approved the merger, principally on the basis of divestitures that only raised the leading bank's market share to about 64 percent.

As discussed, it is doubtful that sufficient consideration is given to the dominant-firm model in a deregulated environment of structural transformation. A more complete competitive analysis in each large bank merger, regardless of whether HHI thresholds are exceeded, might yield better predictions of likely competitive effects.

The Justice Department's *Guidelines*, as currently written, appear to accommodate this more complete approach, at least for mergers in markets with an HHI above 1,000 that increase the HHI by at least 100 points. In such cases, potential adverse effects, including the likelihood of effective tacit collusion and anticompetitive unilateral behavior, as specified, should be evaluated. In any event, the current balance between the costs of a more complex analysis and less certainty for merging banks, on the one hand, and the costs of better estimates of competitive effects, on the other, merits a reconsideration. There are alternative approaches for implementing a new balance. First, the federal banking agencies, focused on large bank mergers, could reduce the presumptive significance of the HHI, at least for mergers that increase concentration significantly to levels above 1,000, and adopt a more complete competitive analysis. Alternatively, a net benefits test might be established.

1. *In all large bank mergers where the effect is to increase market concentration to levels above 1,000 by a significant amount, the federal banking agencies will consider all competitive factors, including the effects of the merger on concentration, market dominance of the resulting banking organization, effectiveness of competition among the remaining banks, intermarket cooperation, and the establishment or augmentation of a banking organization to too-big-to-fail.*

The federal banking agencies are uniquely positioned to undertake such analyses because the information they either collect now, or could collect, in meeting their supervisory responsibilities can illuminate relevant competitive factors, including the effectiveness of competition among other banks in the market, and the cost effects of banking agency support.

2. *The regulatory authorities will evaluate large bank mergers on the basis of net public benefits. In this test, gains in efficiency, stability through diversification, and so on would be balanced against potentially adverse effects, including increases in concentration, other competitive factors, and the extent of local market dominance, growth to a size too-big-to-fail, and so forth.*

Each factor would play a role in the analysis, and competitive effects would be evaluated as a net result. In a net public benefits test, aggravating as well as mitigating factors would have to be considered. Potentially adverse effects, including the likelihood of tacit collusion, dominant-firm pricing, and too-big-to-fail considerations would be included. We are not particularly sanguine about the application of a net public benefits test such as applied to the nonbank acquisitions by bank holding companies under Section 4(c)(8) of the Bank Holding Company Act. Without particular factors having specific weights, almost any result is possible, but the test does establish an appropriate framework for dealing with the issues raised here.

### Restriction on Negotiated Divestitures

Divestitures, regardless of their immediate effects on market concentration, are not necessarily a satisfactory method for dealing with the adverse structural effects of large bank mergers. The sale of branches may not affect local market loan concentration because loans are booked at central locations. The net effect of such branch sales need to be considered in light of the likely movement of some borrowers and depositors to other banks after a merger has eliminated their first choice. Further, the reduction of higher levels of concentration through divestiture permits mergers that produce, or augment the size of, large banks that are too-big-to-fail.[10]

In effectively eliminating merger rejections, divestitures have saved substantial litigation costs. A side effect has been the disappearance of the federal courts as active participants in the reorientation of bank merger policy. We do not necessarily believe that the courts would be more restrictive than the banking agencies in approving large bank combinations; only that it is important that there be ongoing oversight with regard to the methodologies adopted by the federal agencies in evaluating mergers, and some intervention to promote uniformity among the agencies. In 1966, in the case of a merger approved by the Comptroller of the Currency, the Supreme Court stated the following:

The 1966 Act provides that the court in an antitrust action "shall review *de novo* the issues presented." . . . The courts may find the Comptroller's reasons . . . well nigh conclusive. But it is the court's judgement, not the Comptroller's, that finally determines whether the merger is legal. . . . A determination of the effect on competition . . . is a familiar judicial task.[11]

It has not been a familiar judicial task in banking for sometime now.[12]

To facilitate a broader competitive analysis that includes organizational size and scope as a factor and to reintroduce the courts to bank merger policy, restrictions could be placed on divestitures in merger cases that establish or augment a bank that is too-big-to-fail.

*The federal banking agencies and the Justice Department will no longer negotiate divestitures, for purpose of approving a merger, where the resulting bank will become, as the result of the merger, too-big-to-fail, or where one or both have already achieved that status.*

### A Structured Response to Increasing Aggregate Concentration

In passing the Riegle–Neal Interstate Banking and Branching Efficiency Act of 1994, Congress was aware, in general, of the issues raised by the growth of a small group of large banking organizations through interstate expansion by merger.[13] It imposed concentration limits for merging institutions: 10 percent of nationwide deposits and 30 percent of deposits in each state.[14]

Congress's approach to limiting aggregate concentration is moot. There is a deficiency of empirical evidence on the economic effects of aggregate concentration. Among other things, the use of deposits to measure the business activity of banks has become less accurate as banks have diversified and increasingly raised funds from other sources. As a result, defining concentration in terms of deposits for purposes of establishing limits may invite regulatory arbitrage involving the substitution of nondeposit for deposit sources. Banking concentration in a state or the nation may be better measured in terms of total assets or the revenue generated within the particular geographic area. At best it might serve as a proxy for other effects. Further, it remains to be seen whether the legislatively determined concentration limits will be adhered to when they becomes binding.

If national or statewide banking concentration has any anticompetitive significance as a proxy for other effects, including market dominance and multimarket contacts, they are not likely to occur suddenly above a particular limit. Rather they would develop in a progressive manner as the limit was approached. The modification suggested below imposes progressively increasing negative weights as the limit is approached. In this respect, it mimics prompt corrective action procedures under FDICIA that require an escalating regulatory response to diminishing capital ratios. It also finesses the political questions that inevitably arise in precipitously confronting the applicability of an absolute, and therefore seemingly arbitrary, barrier.

*In the course of evaluating competitive effects, the federal bank regulatory agencies will develop a structured analysis for large bank proposals such that increasing negative weights are imposed as the congressionally determined absolute aggregate concentration limits are approached. For example, other things equal, an acquisition that would give the merged banks an 8-percent share of national deposits should be evaluated as raising more significant competitive issue than an acquisition that would result in a 2-percent share.*

### Adjustment to Capital Requirements of Large Banks

A regulatory policy modification might be considered to address the competitive issues raised by the financial market stabilization imperative to support large, troubled banking organizations. As noted, the likelihood of regulatory support for large banks tends to reduce capital costs and expand borrowing capacity, providing large banks with a competitive advantage. Through regulation, capital costs might be adjusted in order to level the playing field and dissipate the dominant-firm advantage. Although the Gramm–Leach–Bliley Act requires large banks that wish to engage in a broader range of activities through financial holding companies and financial subsidiaries to issue subordinated debt, it does not increase their capital requirements.

Higher capital requirements would also tend to discourage megamergers by eliminating the incentive to grow larger to achieve regulatory support. They would also address the need for additional capital by large, global banking organizations to meet the credit risk exposures, not well measured, in bilateral swap relationships with large clients that are not hedged in capital markets.

To implement such a modification, the value of the federal guarantee, implicit in supervisory forbearance and too-big-to-fail policies, would have to be measured. Difficulties exist in disentangling lower funding costs, due to the guarantee and due to extensive diversification. The calculation would be innovative, but not impossible. It would aim to make large bank capital requirements consistent with the cost of capital of unregulated firms in the same risk class.[15]

The value could be derived by comparing the volatility of returns on assets and earnings of large banks with market-based measures of asset-value volatility from an options pricing analysis. The performance of the subordinated debt of large, complex banking organizations provide ample opportunity to determine default risk premiums. These premiums can be related to market-based measures of asset-value volatility to estimate the additional capital needed to reduce banks' risk of default to levels resulting from the federal guarantee.

Others, including the Shadow Regulatory Committee, have suggested higher capital requirements for large, complex, internationally active banks that pose systemic risks in failure. Before the establishment of federal deposit insurance, banks commonly had capital-asset ratios in excess of 10 percent. The committee recommended that minimum risk-adjusted capital ratios, under the Basle Agreement, be raised from the present 8 percent for Tier I and Tier II capital.[16]

*To offset the too-big-to-fail subsidy and level the cost of funds (equity, subordinated debt, and deposits costs) for smaller banks, the very large, complex banking organizations who, in failure, pose a systemic threat, should be required to have higher ratios of capital-to-assets. On a regulatory determination that the insolvency of a large banking organization would require special assistance; that is, that the bank is too-big-to-fail, its capital requirements would be raised to approximate the capital cost of smaller, otherwise comparable banks that are clearly not too-big-to-fail. The higher capital cost would need to include an amount equal to the reduction achieved as the result of the supported status of the large organization.*

## CONCLUSIONS

There is little question that in evaluating current bank merger policy, we are in an area of some uncertainty, in which conflicting factors are operative. The elimination of anticompetitive regulations and advances in computer and telecommunication technologies has, without question, tended to intensify competition. The merger wave that has been generated is, in some important respects, a counterweight. It remains an open question as to which effects will dominate in the long run. The existence of prudential supervision for banking and, in particular, the policy of too-big-to-fail, provides very large banks with special advantages, and represents a credible threat to maintaining competition.

The issues that should confront current merger policy in banking involve not only the immediate competitive effects of each proposed merger, but also the long-term competitive effects of the structural reorganization now being shaped by the merger movement itself. Merger policy has not addressed the latter issue, even with the distinct possibility that mergers approved on the basis of existing competitive standards could contribute to cross-market anticompetitive structural results.

This blindness is partially understandable in that current policy was formulated in an environment where the issue did not exist, but adaptations by the federal agencies have been possible, and it is a moot question as to why they have not as yet focused on the developing threat. The result is that each decision they make may be right within the existing merger policy framework, but the end result could be wrong. Such apparent contradictions are not foreign to economic analysis, and have been considered at the macro level, with respect to individual savings, as a "fallacy of composition," and, at the micro level under the rubric of the "tyranny of small decisions."[17]

It is reasonable, then, to further adapt bank merger policy to meet its original and continuing aim of preventing anticompetitive structural developments. To this end, a number of revisions to policy, including restraints on large bank mergers, have been proposed.

## NOTES

1. Hicks 1969, 6.
2. For an argument in favor of doing so, see Eisenbeis 1996.
3. The name of the unchartered firm was Access Bank International Ltd. See "In Brief" 1997.
4. Kelley 1997, 4, 7–9.
5. Blumenthal 1995.
6. "Blumenthal Announces" 1995.
7. On challenges to bank mergers under state antitrust laws, see Roach 1994.
8. These proposals are developed somewhat differently in Shull and Hanweck 2000.
9. On the high costs of the current arrangement, see Eisenbeis 1996, 65–66.
10. However, see Burke 1998 for recent evidence that divestiture policy has been procompetitive. As noted, questions about the focus of divestitures and their long-run competitive impact remain.
11. *U.S. v. First City National Bank of Houston et al.*, 386 U.S. 361, 368 (1967). The provision for court review of the issues de novo was established by the 1966 amendments to the Bank Merger Act. See 12 USC Sec. 1828(c)(7)(A). In financial modernization legislation passed by the House of Representatives in 1998 but not enacted, this provision was repealed.
12. For an "interest-group" analysis of the role of an independent judiciary in making wealth-transferring contracts durable, see Landes and Posner 1975, 875; Shugart 1990, ch. 6.
13. 108 Stat. 2338, P.L. 103-328.

14. U.S. House 1994, 22. The 10-percent or 30-percent limit did not create any presumption of nonviolation under the antitrust laws (Sections 101 and 102).

15. An estimating approach for the guarantee is discussed in Merton and Perold 1993, 16; Hanweck 1997.

16. U.S. Shadow Regulatory Committee 2000.

17. With regard to the latter, see Kahn 1966.

## REFERENCES

"Blumenthal Announces Economic Development Agreement with Fleet and Shawmut to Pump $207.5 Million in New Money into Connecticut's Economy." 1995. *News from Attorney General Blumenthal.* 11 September.

Blumenthal, Richard. 1995. *Testimony before Federal Reserve Board on Fleet–Shawmut Merger.* 28 August.

Burke, Jim. 1998. *Divestitures as an Antitrust Remedy in Bank Mergers.* Finance and Economic Discussion Series, 1998–14. Washington, D.C.: Federal Reserve Board.

Eisenbeis, Robert A. 1996. "Regulation: Eliminating Special Antitrust Treatment for Banking." *Journal of Retail Banking Services* 18, no. 1: 65–66.

Hanweck, Gerald A. 1997. "Financial Regulators as Risk Managers: A New Paradigm for Capital Adequacy." Paper presented at the Financial Management Association Annual Meetings, Honolulu, Hawaii, October.

Hicks, John R. 1969. *A Theory of History.* London: Oxford University Press.

"In Brief." 1997. *The American Banker,* 14 August.

Kahn, Alfred E. 1966. "The Tyranny of Small Decisions: Market Failures, Imperfections, and the Limits of Economics." *Kyklos* 19, no. 1: 23–47.

Kelley, Edward W. Jr. 1997. "Are Banks Still Special?" International Monetary Fund, Seminar on Banking Soundness and Monetary Policy in a World of Global Capital Markets, Washington, D.C., 29 January.

Landes, William M., and Richard A. Posner. 1975. "The Independent Judiciary in an Interest Group Perspective." *Journal of Law and Economics* 18: 875–901.

Merton, Robert C., and A. F. Perold. 1993. "Theory of Risk Capital in Financial Firms." *Journal of Applied Corporate Finance* 6 (Fall): 16–32.

Roach, Robert F. 1994. "Bank Mergers and the Antitrust Laws." *William and Mary Law Review* 95 (October): 95–145.

Shugart, William F., II. 1990. *Antitrust Policy and Interest-Group Politics.* New York: Quorum Books.

Shull, Bernard, and Gerald A. Hanweck. 2000. "A New Merger Policy for Banks." *The Antitrust Bulletin* 45, no. 3: 679–711.

U.S. House. 1994. *Report, No. 103-448, to Accompany H.R. 3841.* 103rd Cong., 2d Sess., 22 March.

U.S. Shadow Regulatory Committee. 2000. *Reforming Bank Capital Regulation: A Proposal by the U.S. Shadow Regulatory Committee.* Washington, D.C.: AEI Press.

# CHAPTER 8

# Summary and Conclusions

At the beginning of this book, we asked whether the promise of deregulation and the structural reorganization it has generated would be fulfilled as the changes now underway have vast implications for bank performance and the welfare of bank customers. The answer we have reached is that there is a reasonable likelihood that it will not unless changes are made in merger policy, and particularly with respect to large bank mergers and acquisitions. While the growth of individual banks can be beneficial, large bank expansion through mergers and affiliation is the progenitor of an emerging structural configuration that, while suspect, is not addressed by current policy. It should be. The previous chapters, which have ranged from a historical review of competition policies to an economic analysis of the impact of the current merger movement on competition, and include proposals for modifying existing policy, constitute our passage to this answer.

The second half of the twentieth century has been a unique period with respect to bank competition and merger policy in the United States. For the first time, competition standards long considered appropriate for other private sector firms became applicable in banking. Before then banks, as private firms with unique public purposes, were treated differently and immunized from the antitrust laws.

Separating out banks from other commercial firms was not originated in the United States. Modern banking in Europe developed four to five hundred years before the first banks came into existence in the United States. From the beginnings of modern banking in the Mediterranean city-states in the twelfth and thirteenth centuries, banks served not only the interests of commerce, but also the interests of governments, frequently at war and typically short of money; they provided credit directly and, by contributing to commercial growth, augmented the tax-paying and lending capacities of commercial firms. Governments, understanding the vital importance of banks, adopted regulations and anticompetitive policies to promote their safety and soundness. In extremis, they provided financial assistance and established public and quasi-public banks. An enduring, mutually beneficial relationship—a symbiosis—developed among governments, banks, and bank customers in which competition was perceived as a dangerous luxury.

Early banking in the United States derived from English experience, where the Bank of England, through the eighteenth century, was the dominant commercial bank, as well as a lynchpin of government finance. Alexander Hamilton and others who contemplated the establishment of banks in the United States were knowledgeable of English banking practices and, more generally, European experience. As noted in Chapter 2, Hamilton understood banks to be "the happiest engines that ever were invented for advancing trade"; and, he might have added, for advancing government as well. The attractiveness of free markets and competition notwithstanding, he and other founders of American banking opted for monopoly.

Monopoly was the first competition policy for banking in the United States. The policy emerged out of a need to finance the revolution and followed the example of the Bank of England. The chartering of additional banks after the Revolution followed the English model. Banking was to be a regulated industry, with limited purpose charters, monopoly characteristics, supported by government and, in turn, supporting government. Even after "free banking" spread to many states prior to the Civil War, banking continued to be a regulated industry, with limited purpose charters, restrictions on branch office location, and supporting the public purposes for which they had been brought into existence. Restrictions to a limited set of financial activities, first embedded in banking charters and then in banking law, were aimed not simply at restricting risk taking but at constraining increases in concentration in other areas of the economy.

Through the nineteenth century and into the twentieth century, the unique banking arrangements raised issues that were periodically addressed through legislation. The initial decision to establish the first banks as monopolies was modified by both market developments and legislation, but banking continued to be treated differently than other commercial firms. Restrictions on branch banking were periodically endorsed by Congress as a method for preserving opportunities for small banks, and keeping national and statewide concentration in banking low.

In the depths of the Great Depression of the 1930s, with thousands of banks failing, Congress returned to a monopoly policy. The case for government regulation and support, including extensive restrictions on competition, over-whelmed all procompetitive arguments, but the Depression-borne policies were not entirely to blame for anticompetitive practices in banking. Prior to the 1930s, price fixing agreements among banks, through clearinghouse associations and other banking groups, were an established way of doing business. Neither the Sherman Antitrust Act of 1890 nor the Clayton Act of 1914 affected banking in any material way.

The suppression of competition that was sanctioned by the federal government in the 1930s appeared, for a time, to be permanent. It was credited by many as contributing to a more stable banking and financial system. Long-existing anxieties about the dangers of competition in banking seemed to have been confirmed. Bank regulatory agencies and legislatures, with responsibilities for maintaining commercial bank safety and soundness, preferred cooperation among banks to competition.

The development of procompetitive banking policies in the 1950s and 1960s came, then, as something of a shock. In retrospect, it is understandable that, over time, the operations of free markets in a period of prosperity would tend to limit and disrupt the anticompetitive restrictions and practices of the 1930s; and that the dissipation of concern about financial stability would lead legislators and courts to reconsider the cartel-like arrangements that had been established.

A growing worry about bank mergers and rising concentration resulted in the Bank Holding Company Act of 1956 and the Bank Merger Act of 1960. Both instructed the federal banking agencies, for the first time, to evaluate the competitive effects of mergers and acquisitions. Thereafter in 1963 and 1964, to the astonishment of many, the Supreme Court found that both Section 7 of the Clayton Act and the Sherman Act were applicable to bank mergers.

There followed an integration of antitrust and banking law that established the foundation for current competition policy in banking. Among other things, it lead to the virtual disappearance of overt price fixing, and also horizontal mergers of large banks that had substantially increased local market concentration.

It was another two decades before deregulation, also initiated by market developments and institutionalized by regulation and legislation, began the process of dismantling the government-imposed anticompetitive restrictions of the 1930s, including maximum deposit rates of interest, restrictions on easy entry by new charter, and limits on powers of thrift institutions. Ultimately, deregulation went further, eliminating restrictions on branching and product expansion that had characterized banking in the United States for two centuries.

In going further, deregulation has initiated a bank merger wave of unprecedented proportions. Mergers are largely responsible for a dramatic reduction in the numbers of independent banks. Further, hundreds of mergers of large banks have raised concentration at the national level and created a relatively small group of very large, multimarket banking organizations with national and global reach. Under the 1999 Gramm–Leach–Bliley Act, affiliations among banks, insurance companies and securities firms are almost certain to result in new combinations like Citicorp–Travelers that established Citigroup. While large bank mergers have produced enormous organizations, mergers of enormous organizations with large insurance companies and securities firms are primed to produce even more enormous universal banks along the lines of those that have long existed in Germany and other continental European countries. Given the merchant banking and "complementary activities" provisions of Gramm–Leach–Bliley, it is by no means certain that the influence of the newly created universal banks will not extend to commercial and industrial sectors of the economy. For good or bad, the merger movement is irrevocably reshaping the banking and financial structure of the United States.

The bank merger movement of the last two decades in the United States is not an isolated phenomena. Large bank mergers have occurred in Japan, the United Kingdom, and elsewhere in Europe in recent years. It appears that Europe is on the threshold of a merger movement likely to rival that in the United States.

The motives for these mergers are moot. A number of plausible motives are relatively easy to suggest, but their empirical significance is difficult to determine. Many mergers in the 1980s can be traced to the resolution of failures that transferred the good assets and liabilities of failed banks to healthy banks. By the mid-1990s, however, failures diminished to very small numbers and other factors became important. The relaxation of regulatory constraints on geographic and product expansion, increased bank profitability, the longest expansion in U.S. history, an unparalleled bull market in stocks, along with a less constraining merger policy, have established an environment conducive to mergers. In this environment, possible motives can be found in the efforts of bank managements to increase shareholder value through exploiting technological innovations that reduce costs, reducing competition, growing in size to obtain the advantages of being too-big-to-fail, and simultaneously increasing their own compensation as well.

The quest for greater efficiency through growth has often been identified as a principal motive for merger. Whatever the expectations of merger partners, empirical studies have cast doubt on the achievement. Mergers, on average, appear not to have reduced bank costs as a result of greater scale or scope. There is some evidence that mergers have permitted very large banks to economize on capital, and resulted in greater profit efficiency. It is not possible to differentiate among the several possible causes for a market perception of reduced bank risk, including more diversification, more market power, and/or achieving or augmenting a too-big-to-fail status.

A relaxation of policy restraints on mergers began in the 1980s, in part as a response to deregulation. With the phasing-out of anticompetitive restrictions on the pricing of deposits, the gradual liberalization by states of restrictions on branching and holding company expansion, and the introduction of new competition from thrifts, the bank merger policy that had been established in the 1960s and 1970s went through a metamorphosis. New analytic techniques for determining relevant markets, along with newly developed concentration-screening standards, provided a new way of evaluating mergers. But in what appeared to have been an overly enthusiastic response to the more competitive environment created by deregulation, the Federal Reserve established a set of mitigating factors, while ignoring factors that might aggravate merger outcomes. As a result, mergers that produced very high levels of concentration could be approved. In those cases where mitigating factors proved inadequate, a new policy of negotiated divestitures was implemented to lower concentration to a level where an approval could be justified.

The original antitrust-based merger policy had successfully reduced the number of large bank mergers. The deregulation-induced modifications successfully eliminated denials of large bank mergers. In the process, they also eliminated litigation that had involved the courts in the 1960s and 1970s in the formulation of merger policy. Today, only the mergers of small banks in small towns are denied, and only on those rare occasions where concentration is so high that it cannot be offset by mitigating factors. These modifications to merger policy have facilitated the irreversible change in banking structure now under way.

As a result, deregulation has mixed implications. The immediate effect is without question procompetitive. The elimination of restrictions has permitted bank customers to find substitutes for traditional banking services at credit unions, savings associations, at money market mutual funds, and other types of financial institutions. Nationwide branch banking tends to intensify potential competition in local markets. And today, many customers can find some financial services offered by distant banks on the Internet. In the future, financial subsidiaries and financial holding companies that combine commercial banking, investment banking, insurance, merchant banking, and other financial and complementary nonfinancial activities, should provide still greater convenience.

The "worm in the bud" is that over the longer run, a relaxed merger policy does not simply permit a substantial reduction in the number of banking firms, but advances the development of a small group of very large organizations. It is the way in which these large organizations behave that will determine the long-run competitive effects of deregulation.

Bank behavior, to this point, has not been encouraging. At the least, the pricing of retail banking services in local markets has not been reflective of the kinds of improvement that one should expect from deregulation coupled with rapid technological change. We believe there exists evidence of anti-competitive pricing. We have suggested that a plausible explanation for these disappointing results can be found in changes in both local market and intermarket banking structures in the deregulated environment.

Behavior is the residue of structure and government policy. The structure and government policy we have modeled to explain observed pricing behavior and to reconcile otherwise discordant research findings involves a dominant firm and dynamic price leadership, coupled with cost advantages emanating, if from no other source, from a too-big-to-fail status. Very large banks have, through rapid growth, fortified their positions as too-big-to-fail, a status that did not differentiate large banks from small in the 1960s when current merger policy was developed. We add to this model the likelihood of mutual forbearance as a profit-enhancing strategy for the small set of dominant firms that confront one another in increasing numbers of geographic and product markets.

The assumptions on which this model are based are plausible. Further, the model has considerable explanatory value. Empirical testing of the hypotheses it provides is, of course, necessary.

We do not believe, however, that a careful consideration of merger policy can wait for definitive research findings. The problem in postponing policy considerations is that definitive results are unlikely to exist in the foreseeable future. Waiting will, of course, make the problem go away in that beyond some point there will be little that can be done about it. The structural reorganization will have been completed, and the results will be impervious to all but draconian measures.

The policy proposals we make are relatively moderate, reflecting the uncertainties that continue to exist, but recognizing that little is likely to be lost by slowing down the continuing expansion of the relatively few very large banking organizations that now exist. They are based on the reasonable assumption that a procompetition policy will remain a permanent characteristic of the financial market landscape. They are also based on the historical reality that, deregulation notwithstanding, banking will remain an extensively regulated industry, and very large banking organizations will be supported in distress by government. Too-big-to-fail has deep historical roots that are nurtured by an intractable political–economic logic. It is naïve to believe that government support for large banking organizations in distress can be simply eradicated by pointing out its faults. When problems occur in the new structural setting, the imperatives for government intervention will be patent. Future problems will be of far greater magnitude than those faced in the failure of Continental Illinois in the 1980s, or the near failure of Citibank in the early 1990s, or in the systemic threat arising from the meltdown of Long Term Capital Management in 1998. The government of the United States has never had to deal with a potential failure of a conglomerate organization as important to the financial system and the economy as the Credit Lyonnais of France, the big banks of Germany, or the *kieratsu* banks of Japan.

The proposals aim at both simplification of existing merger policy organization and reducing the numbers of large bank mergers. They are designed to limit federal banking agency jurisdiction to those mergers in which they have a direct interest and special expertise; and to require that the agencies take into consideration the new structural factors that were not relevant when merger policy was originally formulated in the 1960s, or when it was reformulated in the 1980s. We view current policy as plagued by a "tyranny of small decisions" with each decision plausibly right in its own frame of reference, but wrong in the aggregate. The proposals include (1) changes in the allocation of authority between the federal banking agencies and the Justice Department to eliminate duplication and conflicting merger evaluations; (2) a modification of competitive analysis to take into consideration aggravating factors suggested by our model; (3) restrictions on negotiated divestitures to preclude at least some approvals and reintroduce the courts to the further development of merger policy; (4) a structured response to increasing aggregate concentration, in recognition of a need to prevent a small group of very large financial organizations from dominating the financial system; and (5) an adjustment to the capital requirements of large, complex banks to modify their cost advantages over smaller rivals emanating from too-big-to-fail.

As we noted at the outset, there has always existed in the United States a political tension between a perceived public need to regulate and support commercial banks and the generally accepted presumption that unrestricted competition among private firms is a necessary condition for economic welfare. The centuries-old tension has emanated from banking instability, the impact of instability on other sectors of the economy, and the reliance of governments on the unique capacity of banks to assist them in meeting public objectives. The compromises that have been forged to alleviate this tension have necessitated unique competition policy. It should come as no surprise that, even after deregulation, banking remains a highly regulated industry requiring specially designed policies.

It should also come as no surprise that successful achievements, such as the extent to which banking, through antitrust-based policy and deregulation, has been brought into the mainstream of private enterprise, can be expected to create a whole range of new problems. This has certainly been the case with breakthroughs in technology, business, geographic exploration, politics, and religion. We believe we have shed light on the competitive aspects of these new success-generating problems in banking, and proposed remedies that will help fulfill the promise of deregulation.

# Selected Bibliography

Berger, Allen N., Rebecca S. Demsetz, and Philip E. Strahan, eds. 1999. Special Issue on the Consolidation of the Financial Services Industry. *Journal of Banking and Finance* 23, nos. 2–4.

Berger, Allen N., and Timothy M. Hannan. 1989. "Deposit Interest Rates and Local Market Concentration." In *Concentration and Price*. Ed. Leonard Weiss. Cambridge: MIT Press.

Berger, Allen N., Gerald A. Hanweck, and David B. Humphrey. 1987. "Competitive Viability in Banking: Scale, Scope and Product Mix Economies." *Journal of Monetary Economics* 20: 501–520.

Federal Deposit Insurance Corporation. 1997. *History of the Eighties*. Washington, D.C.: FDIC.

Finel-Honigman, Irene. 1999. *European Monetary Union Banking Issues: Historical and Contemporary Perspectives*. Stamford, Conn.: JAI Press.

Hannan, Timothy, and Stephen Rhoades. 1992. "Future U.S. Banking Structure: 1990–2010." *The Antitrust Bulletin* 37, no. 3: 737–798.

Rhoades, Stephen A. "Bank Mergers and Industrywide Structure, 1980–94." Staff study no. 169. Board of Governors of the Federal Reserve System.

———. 1998. "The Efficiency Effects of Bank Mergers: An Overview of Case Studies of Nine Mergers." *Journal of Banking and Finance* 22: 273–291.

Savage, Donald. 1993. "Interstate Banking: A Status Report." 79 *Federal Reserve Bulletin* 1075–1089.

Scott, John T. 1991. "Multimarket Contact Among Diversified Oligopolists." *International Journal of Industrial Organization* 9, no. 2: 35–47.

Shull, Bernard, ed. 1996. Special Issue on Antitrust and Banking. *The Antitrust Bulletin* 41, no. 2.

Shull, Bernard, and Gerald A. Hanweck, eds. 1998. "Competition and Competition Policy in the Banking Industry." *The Journal of Reprints for Antitrust Law and Economics* 27, no. 1: 5–15.

U.S. Department of the Treasury. 1991. *Modernizing the Financial System: Recommendations for Safer, More Competitive Banks*. Washington, D.C.: U.S. Department of the Treasury.

White, William R. 1998. "The Coming Transformation of Continental European Banking." Working Paper no. 54, *Bank for International Settlements*, Basle, Switzerland.

# Index

## ABOUT THE AUTHORS

**Bernard Shull** is a professor in the department of economics at Hunter College, a member of the graduate faculty at City University of New York, and a special consultant for National Economic Research Associates. He has held various positions with the Federal Reserve Board, served as senior economist in the Office of the Comptroller of the Currency and as an economist at the Federal Reserve Bank of Philadelphia, and has testified before the Banking Committees of the U.S. Senate and House of Representatives. Widely published in the professional and academic journals of his field, he is coauthor, with Gerald A. Hanweck, of one previous book.

**Gerald A. Hanweck** is professor of finance in the School of Management, George Mason University. Dr. Hanweck has held positions with the Federal Reserve Board and the Federal Reserve Bank of St. Louis and has been a consultant to government agencies, an expert witness in litigation involving financial institutions and government agencies, and a visiting scholar with the Division of Insurance at the FDIC. He has published extensively in professional and academic journals and is the coauthor, with Bernard Shull, of a book on interest rate volatility and interest rate risk.